Teaching Composition: 10 Bibliographical Essays

EDITED BY GARY TATE

Texas Christian University

TEXAS CHRISTIAN UNIVERSITY PRESS
Fort Worth, Texas 76129

Library of Congress Catalog Card No. 76-629
Manufactured in the United States of America

CONTENTS

PREFACE

At the 1973 meeting of the Conference on College Composition and Communication in New Orleans, Paul T. Bryant of Colorado State University chastised teachers of college composition for not learning from the past and for not systematically accumulating a body of knowledge to undergird their practice:

> Too often we behave as if there is no continuity in the teaching of composition, as if the subject has just been invented and every idea for teaching it is new at the moment. We fail to draw on the experience of colleagues. We learn neither from past successes, of which there have been a few, nor from past failures, of which there have been all too many. As a group, we are the living proof of the adage that those who do not know history are condemned to repeat it.

In his speech, later printed in the February 1974 issue of *College Composition and Communication (CCC)*, Bryant argued that the teaching of composition is both a science and an art. Because it is partially a science, we can "move ahead in the accumulation of . . . knowledge in a clearly linear fashion."

> Once a principle is established, it can be stated and used, and need not be reestablished for every new generation. Every generation of composition teachers not only can, but is obligated to, stand upon the intellectual shoulders of the generations that have gone before. An historical, know-nothing approach to this type of knowledge is wasteful and stupid, to say the least.

Bryant concluded his speech by calling for annual bibliographies on teaching composition that would serve, as do such works in other fields, as a means for learning what has already been discovered and published, bibliographies that "would help us to avoid meaningless repetition."

"Meaningless repetition" was also one of the topics touched upon in the spring of 1973 by William F. Irmscher in an article published in *Freshman English News*. In looking back over his nine-year editorship of *CCC*, Irmscher wrote:

> One observation I can make from my own editorial experience is that there are people who constantly write articles about well-established principles and procedures — what one could call the clichés of the profession — and write them as if they were discoveries, being thought of for the first time. To these people, their findings are new. But they have not learned a fundamental tenet of good scholarship; it is hardly possible to discover new ground if one does not even know what is established territory.

The words of Bryant and Irmscher have not gone unheeded. Annual bibliographies concerned with the teaching of composition have begun to appear, most notably in the May issues (1975 and 1976) of *CCC*. In these two issues, Richard L. Larson has listed and described the contents of well over one hundred articles, monographs, and books on the teaching of composition that appeared between 1973 and 1975. Another bibliography well worth consulting, although the works listed are followed by no commentary, appears in the *Rhetoric Society Quarterly* (formerly the *Newsletter: Rhetoric Society of America*). This bibliography is published more often than once a year. One hopes that these listings will continue to appear because they are excellent guides for anyone interested in more than the "clichés of the profession."

But what of the work published before 1973? It is to this question that the ten essays which follow address themselves, although the authors have not used 1973 as a *terminus ad quem*. They have, rather, ranged widely, listing and commenting on important works from Aristotle to the present. The topics discussed are those that seem to me central to the teaching of composition today, but I am aware that another editor might well have chosen other topics, different authors, etc. My approach was to find the best people I knew and turn them loose, asking only that they write bibliographical *essays* rather than mere listings of important works. The essay form has allowed the authors an opportunity to give shapes and emphases to their citations and commentaries in a way that would not have been possible without the essay structure. And I take comfort in my belief (and hope) that this will not be the final book of its kind, that other, better books will appear in the future to help convince composition teachers that their field, in the words of Richard Lloyd-Jones, "does support a body of knowledge and serious study."

It is with pleasure that I acknowledge the help I have received while editing this book. My thanks to E. Leigh Secrest and the TCU Research Foundation for providing the money for publication; to the ten authors (each my first choice), who did not, I suspect, initially realize the difficulty of the task I asked them to perform; to Jim W. Corder, for not only writing one of the essays, but for providing wise advice and encouragement along the way; to Judy Oelfke, for designing the book and keeping me calm during moments of crisis; to Phyllis Drake, that most charming and efficient of all secretaries, for her patient typing and re-typing of parts of manuscripts; to Linda Woodson and Lynn Levin for their help with the proofreading; and, finally, to Priscilla, who makes all that I do possible.

Gary Tate

ABBREVIATIONS

ADE Bulletin Published by the Association of Departments
of English, 62 Fifth Avenue, NY 10011 (MLA)
AP   *American Psychologist*
ASch   *The American Scholar*
ASHA   *American Speech and Hearing Association* (the
journal)
CCC   *College Composition and Communication*
CE   *College English*
CEA   College English Association
EE   *Elementary English*
EJ   *English Journal*
EQ   *English Quarterly* (Canadian Council of Teachers
of English)
ERIC   Educational Resources Information Center
(Documents can be ordered by using the number
listed by citations in this book.) Order from: Docu-
ment Reproduction Service, P. O. Box 190, Ar-
lington, Virginia 22210.
FEN   *Freshman English News*
HBR   *Harvard Business Review*
HER   *Harvard Educational Review*
JEGP   *Journal of English and Germanic Philology*
JEL   *Journal of English Linguistics*
JETT   *Journal of English Teaching Techniques*
JGE   *Journal of General Education*
JL   *Journal of Linguistics*
LL   *Language Learning*
MM   *Media and Methods*
NCTE   National Council of Teachers of English
P and R *Philosophy and Rhetoric*
PMLA   *Publications of the Modern Language Association*
QJS   *Quàrterly Journal of Speech*
RTE   *Research in the Teaching of English*
SM   *Speech Monographs*
ST   *Speech Teacher*
TESOL   Teachers of English to Speakers of Other Lan-
guages
TSLL   *Texas Studies in Literature and Language*

INVENTION:

A TOPOGRAPHICAL SURVEY

RICHARD YOUNG

University of Michigan

INVENTION IS THE RHETORICAL ART concerned with discovering the subject matter of discourse. Every writer confronts the task of making sense of events in the world around him or within him — discovering ordering principles, evidence which justifies belief, information necessary for understanding — and of making what he wants to say understandable and believable to particular readers. He uses a method of invention when these processes are guided deliberately by heuristic procedures, that is, explicit plans for analyzing and searching which focus attention, guide reason, stimulate memory and encourage intuition.

Of course, it is possible to discover content without the conscious use of such plans. If the writer proceeds less systematically — relying on intuition and habit formed by long experience — and does it effectively, we say he has a knack for dealing with ideas and experience. A knack becomes an art when what he does is made explicit in the form of reusable heuristic procedures. When this happens, the processes can be taught as well as learned.

Or, to be more precise, certain aspects of the processes can be taught. The procedures themselves can be taught, as can their use in conscious thought; but one cannot teach direct control of the imaginative act or the unanticipated outcome. What can be taught is not, however, trivial; no one would question the importance of careful thought in the composing process. Furthermore, the use of heuristic procedures can coax imagination and memory; the intuitive act is not abso-

1

lutely beyond the writer's control; it can be nourished and encouraged.

It is important to distinguish between rule-governed procedures and heuristic procedures lest we make the error of thinking that because invention is a systematic activity it is necessarily a mechanical one. A rule-governed procedure specifies a finite series of steps which can be carried out consciously and mechanically without the aid of intuition or special ability and, if properly carried out, infallibly produces a correct result — for example, the procedure for making valid inferences in syllogistic reasoning. A heuristic procedure provides a series of questions or operations whose results are provisional; it helps us guess more effectively — for example, the procedure used by journalists for gathering information for an article, the familiar who? what? when? where? how? and why? It does not infallibly lead to a comprehensive and useful account but it makes data-gathering more efficient and increases the likelihood that the account will be adequate. Although systematic, heuristic search is neither purely conscious nor mechanical; intuition, relevant experience and skill are necessary for effective use. The use of heuristic procedures is, by implication, an acknowledgement that the psychological processes involved in invention are too unpredictable to be controlled by rule-governed procedures.

G. Polya's *How to Solve It* (2nd ed.; Garden City, N.Y.: Doubleday, 1957) and Richard Young's "Notions of 'Generation' in Rhetorical Studies," *Studies in Language and Language Behavior*, Center for Research on Language and Language Behavior, Ann Arbor, Univ. of Michigan (Feb., 1968), 546-56 (ERIC:ED 021238) develop and illustrate these distinctions. An important theoretical treatment can be found in George A. Miller, Eugene Galanter, and Karl H. Pribram, *Plans and the Structure of Behavior* (New York: Holt, Rinehart and Winston, 1960).

The recent surge of interest in invention has brought with it several important theoretical studies, many more methods of invention and techniques for teaching them, and a few, too few, evaluations of their adequacy. What follows is a three-part survey of the principal developments:

I. a bibliography of historical studies from ancient Greece to the present;
II. discussions of four major methods of invention — neo-classical invention, Kenneth Burke's dramatistic method, D. Gordon Rohman's pre-writing, and Kenneth Pike's tagmemic invention;
III. discussions of various contexts necessary for understanding and teaching these methods — specifically, discussions of the methods in a problem-solving context, on a scale determined by relative adequacy, in the composing process, and in the teaching process.

I

The History of Invention

Understanding invention requires, among other things, that we understand the history of invention. One reason for this is that some of the most significant work in the 2500-year life of the discipline was done at its inception. Plato and Aristotle, and later Cicero and Quintilian, defined what are still by and large the basic issues, at least in Western rhetoric. We cannot understand what is happening unless we understand what happened. Furthermore, without a knowledge of history, we have no way of knowing what is genuinely new, what is redundant, what is promising, what has been tried before and found wanting. But perhaps more important than enabling us to understand and assess present developments, a knowledge of the history of invention provides us with conceptual systems which we can work within, or modify, or react against — an intellectually stimulating situation and probably necessary if the discipline is to grow. Douglas Ehninger's "On Systems of Rhetoric," *P and R*, 1 (Summer, 1968), 131-44, develops and illustrates this last point.

3

Histories of invention are rare. One of the few, and a useful one, is Elbert W. Harrington's survey, "Rhetoric and the Scientific Method of Inquiry," *University of Colorado Studies, Series in Language and Literature*, 1 (Dec., 1948), 1-64. A brief, chronologically structured discussion of both rhetorical and poetic invention can be found under "Invention" in the *Princeton Encyclopedia of Poetry and Poetics*, ed., Alex Preminger (Princeton, N. J.: Princeton Univ. Press, 1965), 401-2.

Numerous histories of rhetoric contain extensive discussions of invention and its relation to the other rhetorical arts, to other disciplines, and to society. Such histories are indispensable introductions to the art of invention, since its development cannot be understood apart from these relationships. The most valuable collection of historical studies on rhetoric is Joseph Schwartz and John A. Rycenga, eds., *The Province of Rhetoric* (New York: Ronald Press, 1965); it contains an extensive bibliography. Short historical surveys of rhetoric can be found in Richard C. Jebb, "Rhetoric" in *Encyclopaedia Britannica*, 11th ed., XXIII, 233-37; Thomas O. Sloan, "Rhetoric" in *Encyclopaedia Britannica*, 15 (1974), 798-805; Edward P. J. Corbett, "What Is Being Revived," *CCC*, 18 (Oct., 1967), 166-172; and Corbett's "A Survey of Rhetoric," in *Classical Rhetoric for the Modern Student* (New York: Oxford Univ. Press, 1965), 535-568. Lester Thonssen, A. Craig Baird, and Waldo W. Braden provide a more detailed survey in *Speech Criticism* (2nd ed.; New York: Ronald Press, 1970), 33-156. The Corbett and Thonssen texts contain substantial bibliographies.

More specialized studies of the various historical periods provide the most valuable discussions of invention. For studies of Greek and Roman rhetoric see James J. Murphy, ed., *A Synoptic History of Classical Rhetoric* (New York: Random House, 1972); Charles Sears Baldwin, *Ancient Rhetoric and Poetic* (New York: Macmillan, 1924); Donald Lemen Clark, *Rhetoric in Greco-Roman Education* (New York: Columbia Univ. Press, 1957); and William K. Wimsatt,

Jr. and Cleanth Brooks, "The Verbal Medium: Plato and Aristotle," in *Literary Criticism: A Short History* (New York: Knopf, 1959). "The Verbal Medium" is also available in Schwartz and Rycenga's *Province of Rhetoric*, 111-28.

For medieval rhetoric see: Charles Sears Baldwin, *Medieval Rhetoric and Poetic* (New York: Macmillan, 1928); James J. Murphy, *Rhetoric in the Middle Ages: A History of Rhetorical Theory from Saint Augustine to the Renaissance* (Berkeley, Calif.: Univ. of California Press, 1974); and Richard McKeon, "Rhetoric in the Middle Ages," in R. S. Crane, ed., *Critics and Criticism: Ancient and Modern* (Chicago: Univ. of Chicago Press, 1952), 260-96. McKeon's study is particularly useful for the study of invention; the extensive footnotes contain valuable references. This too is available in Schwartz and Rycenga's *Province of Rhetoric*, 172-212.

For rhetoric in Renaissance England, the definitive work is Wilbur Samuel Howell, *Logic and Rhetoric in England, 1500-1700* (New York: Russell and Russell, 1961). Howell's "Renaissance Rhetoric and Modern Rhetoric: A Study in Change," is also valuable; it is available in his *Poetics, Rhetoric, and Logic: Studies in the Basic Disciplines of Criticism* (Ithaca, N. Y.: Cornell Univ. Press, 1975), 141-62; and in Schwartz and Rycenga, *The Province of Rhetoric*, 292-308. Sister Miriam Joseph's *Rhetoric in Shakespeare's Time: Literary Theory of Renaissance Europe* (New York: Harcourt, Brace and World, 1962) contains discussions and illustrations of the use of classical invention for both information retrieval and literary analysis.

For developments in eighteenth-century England, the definitive work is Wilbur Samuel Howell, *Eighteenth-Century British Logic and Rhetoric* (Princeton, N. J.: Princeton Univ. Press, 1971). There is no comparable study for the nineteenth century. However, Albert Kitzhaber's *Rhetoric in American Colleges 1850-1900* (unpublished doctoral dissertation, Univ. of Washington, 1953) deserves to be better known since it chronicles the emergence of the as-

5

sumptions which have dominated freshman composition for a century, including those which have subverted the study of invention.

The growing interest in rhetoric and invention is apparent in the following works. Taken together they give a fair sense of developments during the last fifteen years — the centrifugal forces generated by a new awareness of the rhetorical tradition, the efforts to exploit sophisticated theories in composition courses, the opportunities for the scholar and teacher to do new and useful work, the confusion. The emphasis on invention in all these discussions suggests the importance of the art to modern rhetoric, whatever forms it may take.

Wayne C. Booth's "The Revival of Rhetoric," *PMLA*, 80 (May, 1965), 8-12, argues for a modern rhetoric in an intensely rhetorical age and notes the growing interest among English teachers. (The article is also available in Martin Steinmann, Jr., *New Rhetorics* [New York: Scribner's, 1967], 1-15.) Edward P. J. Corbett's "Rhetoric and Teachers of English," *QJS*, 51 (Dec., 1965), 375-81, summarizes a generation of efforts to improve the effectiveness of freshman composition culminating in the re-emergence of rhetoric. Robert M. Gorrell's "Teaching of Rhetoric," in *The Encyclopedia of Education*, 7 (1971), 549-54, discusses the shifting definitions of rhetoric, work in disciplines related to rhetoric, the history of rhetoric, and its revival and recent trends.

An important influence in the revival of both rhetoric and invention is Daniel Fogarty's *Roots for a New Rhetoric* (New York: Teachers College, Columbia Univ., 1959) — the "roots" being the work of Aristotle, the General Semanticist S. I. Hayakawa, I. A. Richards and Kenneth Burke. Edward P. J. Corbett's "A New Look at Old Rhetoric" in Robert M. Gorrell, ed., *Rhetoric: Theories for Application* (Champaign, Ill.: National Council of Teachers of English, 1967), 16-22, reinforces Fogarty's argument that classical rhetoric offers one possible basis for a modern rhetoric. In an important article, "A Plea for a Modern Set of Topoi," *CE*, 26 (Nov.,

6

1964), 111-17, Dudley Bailey suggests that Coleridge's concept of "method" could provide the basis for a rhetoric adequate to the times and consistent with what remains viable in classical rhetoric. Karl R. Wallace, "The Substance of Rhetoric: Good Reasons," *QJS*, 49 (Oct., 1963), 239-49, argues that modern rhetoricians have ignored the content of discourse, which is, in public argument, concerned with values and moral choices. James M. McCrimmon, "Will the New Rhetorics Produce New Emphases in the Composition Class?" *CCC*, 20 (May, 1969), 124-30, discusses application in composition classes of some recent developments in invention and stylistics.

In "Very Like a Whale — A Report on Rhetoric," *CCC*, 16 (Oct., 1965), 138-43, Robert M. Gorrell calls attention to the diversity of thought and the fluidity of the present situation and suggests several features which characterize the emerging rhetoric. Richard Ohmann's "In Lieu of a New Rhetoric," *CE*, 26 (Oct., 1964), 17-22, discusses the relationship of contemporary theories to older ones and how the composition curriculum might respond to rhetorical theory. Gorrell's article and Ohmann's can be read as prolegomena to Richard L. Johannesen, ed., *Contemporary Theories of Rhetoric: Selected Readings* (New York: Harper and Row, 1971), an exceptionally rich and well-integrated collection of theoretical statements, several of which are accompanied by detailed commentaries. Johannesen's "Some Trends in Contemporary Rhetorical Theory" is a useful summary of present theoretical concerns; his footnotes and the bibliography at the end of the text are a good point of departure for research in modern rhetoric, especially because of their numerous references to work in speech. A similar anthology, Douglas Ehninger, ed., *Contemporary Rhetoric: A Reader's Coursebook* (Glenview, Ill.: Scott, Foresman, 1972), is also valuable for understanding the current situation.

II

Neo-classical Invention

It is strange that the composition teacher's unflagging search for solutions to the problems of freshman composition brought him so late to his old home, particularly when we consider his perennial complaint that his students have nothing to say. If we ignore the unacknowledged residues of classical invention in the various patterns for developing paragraphs and essays (comparison, contrast, definition, etc.), it is safe to say that until recently composition texts have been innocent of classical influence. This in spite of the duration, richness and continuing usefulness of the classical tradition.

It is doubly strange when we consider that the classical tradition has remained a lively art in the discipline of speech, where a significant body of research on the theory and pedagogy of invention has developed, much of it relevant to the teaching of composition. For annual bibliographies, see the *Quarterly Journal of Speech*, 1947 to 1950, and since then *Speech Monographs*. Lester Thonssen, A. Craig Baird and Waldo W. Braden's *Speech Criticism* (2nd ed.; New York: Ronald Press, 1970) is also extremely useful, not only for its bibliographies but for its discussions of the history of rhetoric and recent developments in speech criticism.

For a discussion of the relevance of classical rhetoric to the teaching of composition, see Edward P. J. Corbett, "The Usefulness of Classical Rhetoric," *CCC*, 14 (Oct., 1963), 162-64. For a discussion of matters of mutual interest to speech and composition teachers, among which is invention, see Carroll C. Arnold, "Some Preliminaries to English-Speech Collaboration in the Study of Rhetoric," in *Rhetoric: Theories for Application*, ed. Robert M. Gorrell (Champaign, Ill.: National Council of Teachers of English, 1967), 30-36.

Classical rhetoric, the rhetoric of Aristotle, Cicero, and Quintilian, is the art of constructing persuasive arguments for popular audiences, specifically, deliberative, forensic, and epideictic, i.e., ceremonial, arguments. It is composed of five arts — invention, arrangement, style, memory, and delivery. Invention, first in importance and the first art used in the composing process, is designed to help one discover valid or seemingly valid arguments in support of a proposition. Invention usually begins with determining the *status*, or crucial issue, to be argued (a proposition of fact, definition, quality or procedure). This becomes the thesis of the argument. Once this is determined, the speaker or writer draws on the three available means of persuasion: *ethos* (an appeal based on his own moral character), *pathos* (an appeal to the audience's emotions), and *logos* (an appeal based on logic). All three appeals may be used in a single discourse; how they are used and which are emphasized depends on what Lloyd Bitzer has called the "rhetorical situation," i.e., it depends on the audience, the problematic situation that elicits the discourse, and the constraints on writer and audience ("The Rhetorical Situation," *P and R*, 1 [Jan., 1968], 1-14). Arguments in support of the thesis can be discovered systematically by the use of *topics*, or heuristic probes: logical arguments can be developed by definition, comparison, contrast, antecedents, consequents, contradictions and so on. Guides for emotional appeals and appeals to character are also provided by the method. For a summary of the distinctive features of classical rhetoric, see Gary Cronkhite's *Persuasion: Speech and Behavioral Change* (Indianapolis, Ind.: Bobbs-Merrill, 1969), especially 18-27.

During the last twenty years a neo-classical art of invention adapted for composition classes has begun to emerge. Among the earliest arguments for the use of classical invention in composition is "Looking for an Argument" (*CE*, 14 [Jan., 1953], 210-16) by Manuel Bilsky, McCrea Hazlett, Robert E. Streeter and Richard M. Weaver. Bilsky's *Patterns of Argument* (New York: Holt, Rinehart and Winston, 1956), an introduction to logic for writers, and Richard Weaver's *Rhetoric and Composition: A Course in Writing and Read-*

9

ing (2nd.; New York: Holt, Rinehart and Winston, 1967), appear to be extensions of the earlier work; both exploit a number of classical topics for constructing arguments. Since it is an introduction to logic, it is understandable why Bilsky's text would have little to say about either the writer or the audience. It is less understandable why there are no discussions of *ethos* and *pathos* in Weaver's book, since the concept of audience is at the center of classical rhetoric and since elsewhere Weaver's Platonism leads him into an extensive consideration of the character of the writer (for example, "Language Is Sermonic," *Dimensions of Rhetorical Scholarship*, ed. Roger E. Nebergall, [Norman, Okla.: Univ. of Oklahoma Dept. of Speech, 1963], 49-64).

Richard E. Hughes and P. Albert Duhamel's *Rhetoric: Principles and Usage* (Englewood Cliffs, N. J.: Prentice-Hall, 1962) is explicitly rooted in Aristotle's rhetoric. Like Weaver's text, it offers a substantial discussion of a sub-set of classical topics, but it also discusses *pathos* and *ethos*. Departing from the traditional order of presentation, which reflects a conception of the composing process, Hughes and Duhamel place the discussion of invention in the middle of the book, the assumption being that it should be deferred because of its difficulty. A brief review by Geoffrey C. Stokes can be found in *CCC*, 14 (May, 1963), 126.

Probably the best known, certainly the most thorough-going and uncompromising of the classical texts is Edward P. J. Corbett's *Classical Rhetoric for the Modern Student* (New York: Oxford Univ. Press, 1965; 2nd ed., 1971). The first edition is reviewed by W. Ross Winterowd in *CCC*, 17 (May, 1966), 115-16; the second by J. R. McNally, *P and R*, 6 (Spring, 1973), 125-26. The principle influences in Corbett's text, as in most of those which draw on the classical tradition, are Aristotle, Cicero, and Quintilian. An imaginative and well-executed modification of these sources is John H. Mackin's *Classical Rhetoric for Modern Discourse* (New York: The Free Press, 1969). Quintilian, Cicero and Aristotle are obviously present, but the inspiration for the book comes

10

from Plato's *Gorgias* and *Phaedrus*. The changes this produces in the conventional formulation of classical rhetoric are thoughtful and probably pedagogically useful; *logos*, *ethos*, and *pathos* are discussed in detail though idiosyncratically, *ethos* being combined with the art of arrangement, and *pathos* with the art of style. Mackin's work is particularly interesting since it explicitly sets invention in a problem-solving context; the motive for the act of invention arises not only from the need to develop an argument but from a prior need to understand and solve a problem confronting society — a thoroughly Platonic conception of invention, though Bitzer argues that it is implicit in Aristotle's work as well ("The Rhetorical Situation," *P and R*, 2). Unfortunately, Mackin offers no procedures to guide the analysis and formulation of problems. The book is reviewed by Gordon F. Hostettler in *CCC*, 21 (May, 1970), 204-05.

An extensive list and analysis of composition texts which make use of the classical topics can be found in Sister Janice Marie Lauer's *Invention in Contemporary Rhetoric: Heuristic Procedures* (unpublished doctoral dissertation, Univ. of Michigan, 1967). Several texts have since appeared which include simplified versions of the classical procedure; two of the more notable ones are Jacqueline Berke's *Twenty Questions for the Writer* (New York: Harcourt Brace Jovanovich, 1972) and W. Ross Winterowd's *The Contemporary Writer: A Practical Rhetoric* (New York: Harcourt Brace Jovanovich, 1975). Drawing on both modern and classical sources, they illustrate an eclectic tendency in recent texts.

The following works are valuable points of departure in the study of classical invention. Lane Cooper's *The Rhetoric of Aristotle* (New York: Appleton-Century-Crofts, 1932) is an inexpensive and particularly useful one-volume edition; it supplies explanations of numerous passages of the *Rhetoric* and references to more extensive commentaries. A convenient anthology of primary works containing a section on invention as well as a bibliography is Thomas W. Benson and Michael H. Prosser's *Readings in Classical Rhetoric*

11

(Bloomington, Ind.: Indiana Univ. Press, 1972). P. Albert Duhamel's "Traditional Misconceptions of Traditional Rhetoric" (in *Rhetoric: Theories for Application*, ed. Robert M. Gorrell [Champaign, Ill.: National Council of Teachers of English, 1967], 23-29) discusses the adaptation of classical rhetoric for modern use. Richard Hughes' "The Contemporaneity of Classical Rhetoric," *CCC*, 16 (Oct., 1965), 157-59, is a valuable argument on the nature and function of Aristotelian invention.

A discussion of some distinctive features of classical rhetoric can be found in Rodney B. Douglass, "An Aristotelian Orientation to Rhetorical Communication," *P and R*, 7 (Spring, 1974), 80-88. An adaptation of the classical concept of *status* can be found in Richard Braddock's "Crucial Issues," *CCC*, 16 (Oct., 1965), 165-69. Gary Cronkhite's *Persuasion: Speech and Behavioral Change*, 23-24, offers a brief explanation of the concept and additional references, as does James L. Kinneavy's *A Theory of Discourse* (Englewood Cliffs, N. J.: Prentice-Hall, 1971), 267-8, 301-6. A more extensive treatment of *status* is Otto Dieter's "Stasis," *SM*, 17 (1950), 345-69. Earl W. Wiley's "The Enthymeme: Idiom of Persuasion," *QJS*, 42 (Feb., 1956), 19-24, provides an introduction to enthymemic argument and its relation to the topics. Robert J. Brake's "A Reconsideration of Aristotle's Concept of Topics," *The Central States Speech Journal*, 16 (May, 1965), 106-12, presents what is probably the most conventional view of the topics. Paul I. Rosenthal's "The Concept of Ethos and the Structure of Persuasion," *SM*, 33 (June, 1966), 114-26, discusses the ethical appeal and its relation to the rhetorical situation. Perceptive discussions of Bitzer's concept of the rhetorical situation can be found in Richard E. Vatz, "The Myth of the Rhetorical Situation," *P and R*, 6 (Summer, 1973), 154-61; and Scott Consigny, "Rhetoric and Its Situations," *P and R*, 7 (Summer, 1974), 175-86.

The Dramatistic Method

In *A Grammar of Motives* (New York: Prentice-Hall, 1945), Kenneth Burke develops an extremely powerful method for analyzing human motives and motifs in human experience, which, broadly construed, include virtually everything men think and do. The heart of the method is a pentad of heuristic probes — act, scene, agent, agency and purpose. "Any complete statement about motives," Burke says, "will offer *some kind of* answers to these five questions: what was done (act), when or where it was done (scene), who did it (agent), how he did it (agency), and why (purpose)" (xv). The concepts, culled from the criticism of drama, are brought to bear on the human drama.

There is a natural tendency to identify the pentad with the journalist's procedure for developing an article — the procedure which asks who? what? when? where? how? and why? This is reasonable enough since the journalist, like Burke, is interested in the invariants in the analysis of human situations. But there are significant differences between the two procedures. Simple as it appears, Burke's procedure is capable of far more complex analyses. The terms and their referents can be combined in various "ratios" (e.g., act-scene, act-purpose, act-agency), ten ratios in all being possible. The relationships revealed in analyses using the ratios often provide original and important insights into behavior. Further complexity of analysis is possible by shifting points of view (e.g., machines are normally conceived of as *agencies,* yet combined they constitute the industrial *scene* with its own motivational properties). As Burke remarks, the pentad provides "a kind of simplicity that can be developed into considerable complexity, and yet can be discovered beneath its elaborations" (xvi). Since the "elaborations" are in part the result of the procedure and in part the result of the knowledge, imagination, and persistence of the user, the dramatistic method is a clear instance of what we earlier called a heuristic procedure.

13

Burke's grammar of motives, though not strictly speaking part of his rhetorical theory, is closely related to it. For Burke, the key term of the new rhetoric is "identification" ("Rhetoric — Old and New," *JGE*, 5 [April, 1951], 202-09):

> The key term for the old rhetoric was "persuasion" and its stress was upon deliberate design. The key term for the "new" rhetoric would be "identification" . . . . "Identification" at its simplest is also a deliberate device, as when the politician seeks to identify himself with his audience. In this respect, its equivalents are plentiful in Aristotle's *Rhetoric*. But identification can also be an end, as when people earnestly yearn to identify themselves with one group or other (203).

When one identifies himself with another, he becomes "consubstantial" with him while retaining his own identity (*A Rhetoric of Motives* [New York: Prentice-Hall, 1950], 20-3). The substance of another, i.e., his essential features, is understood by studying him in his dramatistic role; the pentad facilitates this understanding.

It has often been noted, by Burke as well as his critics, that his work is an extension of Aristotelian rhetoric, though the connection between his work and Aristotle's is not always apparent. The connection is most apparent in his concept of identification:

> As for the relation between "identification" and "persuasion": we might well keep it in mind that a speaker persuades an audience by the use of stylistic identifications; his act of persuasion may be for the purpose of causing the audience to identify itself with the speaker's interests; and the speaker draws on identification of interests to establish rapport between himself and his audience. So, there is no chance of our keeping apart the meanings of persuasion, identification ("consubstantiality") and communication (the nature of rhetoric as "addressed"). But, in given in-

stances, one or another of these elements may serve best for extending a line of analysis in some particular direction (*Rhetoric of Motives*, 46).

The function of the pentad, however, differs from that of Aristotle's topics, though the two are related. The topics are aids in discovering possible arguments in support of propositions; the pentad is an aid in discovering essential features of the behavior of groups or individuals. The topics are a rhetorical means for proclaiming substantial unity with others; the pentad reveals the motives implicit in rhetorical acts.

The following offer good discussions of key terms in Burke's rhetoric — identification, substance, and motive: Marie Hochmuth, "Kenneth Burke and the 'New Rhetoric,'" *QJS*, 38 (April, 1952), 133-44; Virginia Holland, *Counterpoint: Kenneth Burke and Aristotle's Theories of Rhetoric* (New York: Philosophical Library, 1959); Dennis Day, "Persuasion and the Concept of Identification," *QJS*, 46 (Oct., 1960), 270-73; Roy Armbrester, "Identification Within: Kenneth Burke's View of the Unconscious," *P and R*, 7 (Fall, 1974), 205-16; Don Abbott, "Marxist Influences on the Rhetorical Theory of Kenneth Burke," *P and R*, 7 (Fall, 1974), 217-33; Jane Blankenship, Edward Murphy, and Marie Rosenwasser, "Pivotal Terms in the Early Works of Kenneth Burke," *P and R*, 7 (Winter, 1974), 1-24. Joseph Schwartz's "Kenneth Burke, Aristotle, and the Future of Rhetoric," *CCC*, 17 (Dec., 1966), 210-16, discusses the nature of "new" rhetoric, Burke's contribution to it and his relation to Aristotelian theory. Identification is the central concept in Donald Byker and Loren J. Anderson's speech text, *Communication as Identification: An Introductory View* (New York: Harper & Row, 1975).

Burke's dramatistic analyses have centered on motivation in language behavior; for as he says, "language being essentially human, we would view human relations in terms of the linguistic instrument" (*Grammar of Motives*, 317). W. Ross Winterowd illustrates the use of the pentad in discourse analysis in his *Rhetoric and Writing* (Boston: Allyn and Bacon, 1965), 154-58; and in *The Contemporary Writer: A Practical Rhetoric* (New York: Harcourt Brace Jovanovich, 1975), 82-89. The former is reviewed by Robert H. Moore in *CCC*, 16 (Dec., 1965), 282-83.

The pentad may also be brought to bear on non-linguistic experiences, its function being to analyze data and retrieve information. William F. Irmscher (*The Holt Guide to English: A Contemporary Handbook of Rhetoric, Language and Literature* [New York: Holt, Rinehart and Winston, 1972], 27-45) modifies the terminology of the pentad and includes questions under each part: e.g., action — what happened? what is happening? what will happen? what is it? His treatment reduces the pentad to something very like the journalist's heuristic. He also suggests relationships between invention using the pentad and types of discourse; what happened and what is happening, for example, are related to narration. The book is reviewed by Garland Cannon, *CCC*, 25 (May, 1974), 213-18; and by Winston Weathers in *FEN*, 1 (March, 1972), 10-11.

Considering the richness of Burke's rhetorical thought and the power of the dramatistic method, it is surprising that there are no composition texts based entirely on his theory; Winterowd and Irmscher do us a service in making even part of the theory available in text form. There is no question that the pentad can be useful as a heuristic independent of the context of Burke's theory; and usefulness is an adequate justification for what they do. However, they pay a penalty for excerpting his work; separated from its context, the pentad loses some of its power, intelligibility, and reason for being. This is a difficulty in all eclectic texts. Techniques of invention are acroamatic; they are not wholly intelligible standing alone.

Pre-Writing

"Pre-writing" is frequently used as a synonym for "invention"; there are, however, good reasons for restricting the

use of the term to the method developed by D. Gordon
Rohman and others at Michigan State University. Rohman
appears to have been the first to use the term; at least it was
his work which made it popular. (See, for example, "Pre-
Writing: The Stage of Discovery in the Writing Process,"
CCC, 16 [May, 1965], 106-112.) Furthermore, the method is
sufficiently distinctive in its components, goals and theoretical foundation to require a special label. It is becoming
increasingly apparent that as new and significant methods of
invention emerge we need to develop a more adequate terminology which distinguishes various arts or methods of
invention from *the* art of invention, that is, the members from
the class.

Like classical invention, pre-writing presents a conception of the composing process that is essentially linear and
mentalistic. In defining the term Rohman says that

> Writing is usefully described as a process. . . . Different
> things happen at different stages in the process of put-
> ting things into words and words onto paper. . . . We
> divided the process at the point where the "writing
> idea" is ready for the words and the page: everything
> before that we called "Pre-Writing," everything after
> "Writing" and "Re-Writing." . . . What sort of "think-
> ing" precedes writing? By "thinking," we refer to that
> activity of mind which *brings forth* and develops ideas,
> plans, designs, not merely the entrance of an idea into
> one's mind; an active, not a passive enlistment in the
> "cause" of an idea; conceiving, which includes con-
> secutive logical thinking but much more besides; es-
> sentially the imposition of pattern upon experience
> ("Pre-Writing," 106).

Heavy emphasis is placed on the causal relation between
creative thought and good writing. The method appears to
grow out of the presupposition that, if the creative process
cannot be taught, it can nevertheless be coaxed by various
means — most notably by keeping a journal, by the practice

17

of principles derived from religious meditation, and by the use of analogy. Taken together, these devices constitute another definition of "pre-writing."

The principal goal of pre-writing is the self-actualization of the writer. "To what end do we teach writing?" asks Rohman:

> If it is to "program" students to produce "Letters and Reports for All Occasions," it is not only ignoble but impossible. . . . However, if it is to enlighten them concerning the powers of creative discovery within them, then it is both a liberal discipline and a possible writing program. . . . What we must do is place the principle of actualizing in the minds of students and the methods of imitating it in their hands ("Pre-Writing," 108).

This contrasts sharply with classical invention, the goal of which is discovery of the available means of persuasion in any rhetorical situation. The result of the composing process in classical rhetoric is a persuasive discourse; in pre-writing it is likely to be the informal essay, though nothing in the method precludes other types of discourse. Pre-writing's exclusive focus on the complex relations between writer, problematic world, and word is both a strength and a weakness. It does engage the writer in fundamental issues of the composing process; it also establishes clear and limited pedagogical objectives and offers the student techniques which can be mastered with relative ease. But in doing so it ignores important aspects of the rhetorical situation, most notably those associated with the audience.

Two ably-written texts embody and elaborate this approach: Clinton S. Burhans, Jr., *The Would-be Writer* (3rd ed.; Waltham, Mass.: Xerox, 1971) and Donald C. Stewart, *The Authentic Voice: A Pre-Writing Approach to Student Writing* (Dubuque, Iowa: Wm. C. Brown, 1972). The scope of Stewart's book is narrower than Burhans', which treats not only pre-writing, but writing and rewriting as well. Stewart's book is reviewed by Marjorie Donker in *CCC*, 24 (Feb., 1973), 47-8. A description of a course in which the method is used can be found in Stewart's "An Advanced Composition Course that Works," *CCC*, 25 (May, 1974), 197-200.

Michael Paull and Jack Kligerman's *Invention: A Course in Pre-Writing and Composition* (Cambridge, Mass.: Winthrop, 1973) can be associated with this method since it discusses the journal, the meditation, and, to a lesser extent, analogy. However, the section on pre-writing is more circumscribed, treating only immediate perceptions and their conceptualization. And substantial space is devoted to an elaborate series of exercises (happenings, production and analysis of non-representational art, etc.) which cannot be considered part of a formal method of invention, though they may be effective in developing knowledge and attitudes helpful in using such a method. Jean Dietz Moss reviews the book in *CCC*, 25 (Feb., 1974), 56-7. The approach is discussed in Michael Paull and Jack Kligerman's "Invention, Composition, and the Urban College," *CE*, 33 (March, 1972), 651-59; and Michael Paull's "Invention: Understanding the Relationship between Sensation, Perception and Concept Formation," *CCC*, 25 (May, 1974), 205-09.

A useful method and sound texts are adequate reasons for regarding pre-writing as a significant contribution to the art of invention. Another reason is that it is one of the few methods that have undergone rigorous testing in the classroom. Most of the numerous solutions proposed to problems of composition are more testimonials to our optimism than to rigorous scholarship; but large claims should be supported by strong evidence. Rohman's "Pre-Writing: The Stage of Discovery in the Writing Process" summarizes a project which sought to determine the effects of instruction in the pre-writing method; for the complete report, see D. Gordon Rohman and Albert O. Wlecke, *Pre-writing: The Construction and Application of Models for Concept Formation in Writing* (East Lansing, Mich.: Michigan State Univ., U.S. Office of Education Cooperative Research Project No. 2174,

1964); the report is available through ERIC: ED 001273. A subsequent study evaluated the effects of three approaches: (1) Rohman's version of the pre-writing method combined with a text on editing; (2) Burhans' version in *The Would-be Writer*; and (3) a more conventional approach to composition which offered no instruction in invention. The results are reported in Clinton S. Burhans, Jr., *Extended Testing of a Unified Experimental Course in Composition in a Variety of Materials and Formats* (East Lansing, Mich.: Michigan State Univ., U.S. Office of Education Cooperative Research Project No. 7-1149, 1968). The reports suggest that pre-writing not only increases the student's ability to form new conceptions which give meaning to his experience but, when combined with instruction in arrangement and style, produces more adequate writing than the conventional approach.

Various features of the pre-writing method grow out of Rohman's interest in Thoreau (see, for example, Rohman's "My Friend Henry," *CCC*, 23 [Dec., 1972], 373-77). But a second source is more significant for students of invention, that is, theoretical and applied work on creativity and concept formation. Among the works frequently cited by Rohman are J. S. Bruner, J. J. Goodnow and G. A. Austin, *A Study of Thinking* (New York: Wiley, 1956); J. S. Bruner, *On Knowing: Essays for the Left Hand* (New York: Atheneum, 1965); William J. J. Gordon, *Synectics: The Development of Creative Capacity* (New York: Harper and Row, 1961); and Arthur Koestler, *The Act of Creation* (London: Hutchinson, 1964). Such works are capable of providing theoretical underpinnings for methods of invention; and they are a valuable resource for the teacher who wants to develop his ability to analyze and evaluate particular methods, a useful skill since *ad hoc* and arbitrary methods are proliferating rapidly.

There is, however, another reason for calling attention to Rohman's emphasis on creative thought. For some time the composition teacher has struggled with a dilemma, a false one but nevertheless capable of impeding the development of more adequate theories and pedagogies. Vitalist assumptions, which have dominated our thinking about the composing process since Coleridge, appear to be inconsistent with the rational processes and formal procedures required by an art of invention. Vitalism leads to a view of writing ability as a knack and to a repudiation of the possibility of teaching the composing process; composition tends to dwindle into an art of editing. One of the principal contributions of pre-writing to modern invention is that it demonstrates that the dilemma is only apparent, for it offers an explicit, teachable method which does foster creative behavior.

Tagmemic Invention

Tagmemic invention is one recent result of a long effort by linguists of various persuasions to bring their discipline to bear on problems of composition. Though the effort began before World War II with a concern for a more adequate conception of usage, it did not gain real momentum until the 1950s when it was broadened to include problems of syntax. At this point, Harold Allen argues ("From Prairies to Mountains," *CE*, 26 [Jan., 1965], 260-66), the linguistic contribution to the teaching of composition appeared to have reached its limits — except in the case of psycholinguistics and tagmemics, both of which have the theoretical and analytical capacity to deal with language units larger than the sentence and with "pragmatics" (i.e., the psychological and social dimensions of language use).

The primary theoretical statement of tagmemics is Kenneth L. Pike's *Language in Relation to a Unified Theory of the Structure of Human Behavior* (The Hague: Mouton, 1967), which contains an extensive bibliography on tagmemic linguistics. For annotated bibliographies that include citations on tagmemic rhetoric and discourse analysis, see Kenneth L. Pike, "A Guide to Publications Related to Tagmemic Theory," in *Current Trends in Linguistics, Vol. III: Theoretical Foundations*, ed. Thomas A. Sebeok (The Hague: Mouton, 1966), 365-394; Ruth M. Brend, "Tagmemic

Theory: An Annotated Bibliography," *Journal of English Linguistics*, 4 (March, 1970), 7-45, and "Tagmemic Theory: An Annotated Bibliography, Appendix I,"*Journal of English Linguistics*, 6 (March, 1972), 1-16.

Since composition is but a specialized use of language, a theory about language behavior in general, Pike argues, should also be applicable to composing behavior. In "A Linguistic Contribution to Composition," *CCC*, 15 (May, 1964), 82-88, Pike asked if it would be possible "to explore a number of the axioms of such a language theory (i.e., tagmemics), in order to develop exercises based on these axioms about language structure but specifically designed to develop writing competence" (82), and then went on to suggest the groundwork for a new art of invention. Shortly thereafter, a series of articles appeared which explored and refined Pike's hypothesis: Pike's "Beyond the Sentence," Hubert M. English's "Linguistic Theory as an Aid to Invention," and Allan B. Howes' "A Linguistic Analogy in Literary Criticism," all of which appeared in *CCC*, 15 (Oct., 1964), 129-35, 136-40, 141-44. "Beyond the Sentence" offers a convenient introduction to the assumptions which constitute the nucleus of tagmemic invention; English's article reports on an early effort to use the method in the classroom; Howes' article suggests an application of one component of the discovery procedure in literary analysis. All three provide illustrations of the use of the method. Pike's "Language — Where Science and Poetry Meet," *CE*, 26 (Jan., 1965), 283-292, provides a further elaboration of tagmemic assumptions and illustrates their use in both linguistic and literary analysis.

In 1965, Alton L. Becker and Richard E. Young proposed that tagmemics could provide the basis for a modern art of rhetoric, one component being an art of invention growing out of the work cited above ("Toward a Modern Theory of Rhetoric: A Tagmemic Contribution," *HER*, 35 [Fall, 1965], 450-68). Young, Becker and Pike's *Rhetoric: Discovery and Change* (New York: Harcourt, Brace and World, 1970) is at

22

once an attempt to develop a rhetorical theory and a writing text; the first ten chapters are devoted to invention.

A brief summary of the chapters gives some idea of the nature and scope of the method. Chapters 2 through 7 discuss epistemological and linguistic assumptions underlying tagmemic invention, extended definition, the process of inquiry, and heuristic procedures for analyzing and formulating problems, for exploring problematic data and for testing hypotheses. Chapters 8 and 9 discuss some prerequisites for inducing psychological change and some characteristics of language behavior which arouse and allay defensive attitudes in readers. Chapter 10 develops a concept of intention based on kinds of psychological change in the audience.

Pre-writing focuses on the discovery of ordering principles and on psychological changes in the writer; classical invention focuses on finding arguments which are likely to produce psychological changes in the audience. Tagmemic invention focuses on both. The method is designed to help one carry out three activities when confronted with problematic experiences: retrieval of relevant information already known, analysis of problematic data, and discovery of ordering principles. It is also designed to help one discover features of the audience which facilitate communication. It is not designed to produce a particular mode of discourse; it draws on other rhetorics for instruction in discourse types, e.g., on classical rhetoric for instruction in traditional argument.

Rhetoric: Discovery and Change has been reviewed by Regina Hoover, *CCC*, 22 (Feb., 1971), 65-7; Garland Cannon, *Language*, 48 (Sept., 1972), 751-55; and R. J. Reddick, *Centrum*, 1 (Spring, 1973), 61-74. Simplified versions of the procedure can be found in Ray Kytle, *Prewriting: Strategies for Exploration and Discovery* (New York: Random House, 1970), 81-90; Joseph M. Williams, *The New English* (New York: The Free Press, 1970), 166-205; and W. Ross Winterowd, *The Contemporary Writer: A Practical Rhetoric* (New York: Harcourt Brace Jovanovich, 1975), 98-109.

23

Several works discuss various implications and applications of tagmemic invention. Among them: William Holtz, "Field Theory and Literature," in Robert M. Gorrell, ed., *Rhetoric: Theories for Application* (Champaign, Ill.: NCTE, 1967), 53-65; Richard Young, "Discovery Procedures in Tagmemic Rhetoric: An Exercise in Problem Solving," *Studies in Language and Language Behavior*, Center for Research on Language and Language Behavior, Ann Arbor: Univ. of Michigan (Sept., 1968), 187-203 (ERIC: ED 024951); Lee Odell, "Piaget, Problem-Solving, and Freshman Composition," *CCC*, 24 (Feb., 1973), 36-42, and "Responding to Student Writing," *CCC*, 24 (Dec., 1973), 394-400; Catherine Elizabeth Frerichs Lamb, *On Suffering Change: Towards a Theory of Instruction in the Art of Invention* (unpublished doctoral dissertation, Univ. of Michigan, 1974); and Kenneth Jurkiewicz, "How to Begin to Win Friends and Influence People: The Role of the Audience in the Pre-Writing Process," *CCC*, 26 (May, 1975), 173-76.

Two research projects have been carried out to determine whether instruction in tagmemic invention does in fact bring about significant changes in the student's conceptual ability and ability to communicate: Camillus Lee Odell, *Discovery Procedures for Contemporary Rhetoric: A Study of the Usefulness of the Tagmemic Heuristic Model in Teaching Composition* (unpublished doctoral dissertation, Univ. of Michigan, 1970). This study was summarized in Odell's "Measuring the Effect of Instruction in Pre-writing," *RTE*, 8 (Fall, 1974), 228-40. Richard E. Young and Frank M. Koen, *The Tagmemic Discovery Procedure: An Evaluation of Its Uses in the Teaching of Rhetoric* (Ann Arbor, Mich.: Univ. of Michigan, NEH Grant No. EO-5238-71-116, 1973); the report is available through ERIC: ED 084517. It is reviewed by W. Ross Winterowd in *P and R*, 8 (Summer, 1975), 183-87.

Like pre-writing, tagmemic invention draws substantially on cognitive psychology, especially work on cognition, creativity, and problem-solving. The following studies are particularly relevant to understanding the process of inquiry within which the various heuristic procedures of tagmemic invention function: Jerome S. Bruner, "Going Beyond the Information Given," in *Contemporary Approaches to Cognition* (Cambridge, Mass.: Harvard Univ. Press, 1964), 41-74, and "On Perceptual Readiness," *Psychological Review*, 64 (1957), 123-52; Leon Festinger, *A Theory of Cognitive Dissonance* (Stanford, Calif.: Stanford Univ. Press, 1957); J. P. Guilford, *The Nature of Human Intelligence* (New York: McGraw-Hill, 1967); George A. Miller, Eugene Galanter, and Karl H. Pribram, *Plans and the Structure of Behavior* (New York: Holt, Rinehart and Winston, 1960); and W. Edgar Vinacke, *The Psychology of Thinking* (New York: McGraw-Hill, 1952).

III

Problem-solving

Problem-solving is an important concept in the art of invention. Unfortunately, the introduction of the term into our critical vocabulary has been accompanied by disagreements over what it means. One reason for the disagreement is that the referent is not at all clear in the psychological literature from which the term is drawn. At the moment, there is no adequate psychological basis for sharply differentiating such seemingly disparate processes as problem-solving, decision making, creation, and invention. Furthermore, attempts to distinguish these processes on the basis of origin (e.g., external difficulty vs. internal need) and product (e.g., poem vs. management policy) quickly break down in application. For arguments to this effect, see J. P. Guilford, *The Nature of Human Intelligence* (New York: McGraw-Hill, 1967), 312-45; Donald W. Taylor, "Problem Solving," in the *International Encyclopedia of the Social Sciences*, 12 (1968), 505-11; W. Edgar Vinacke, *The Psychology of Thinking* (New York: McGraw-Hill, 1952), 160-94, 195-217, 238-61.

25

In articles on composition, the term has been used to refer to a wide range of activities in mathematics, gaming, manipulation of the physical environment, etc. that have been the subject of psychological studies; a number of these have bearing on rhetorical invention: see Sister Janice Lauer, "Heuristics and Composition," *CCC*, 21 (Dec., 1970), 396-404. It also is used to refer to a particular procedure for developing solutions to problems of decision making: e.g., Richard L. Larson, "How to Define Administrative Problems," *HBR*, 40 (Jan.-Feb., 1962), 68-80; and "Problem-solving, Composing, and Liberal Education," *CE*, 33 (March, 1972), 628-35. In the latter work, Larson proposes the procedure as a method of invention which can aid the writer in planning arguments on complex issues, reflecting on experience, discovering judgments, and evaluating the judgments of others.

Finally, problem-solving is used to refer to a generalized process of inquiry in which one moves from a perceived need or difficulty through the exploration of relevant data to the intuition of a potential solution and its testing, a process which can be manifested in behavior as diverse as writing a poem or essay, developing a management policy, or solving a problem in chess: e.g., Richard E. Young, Alton L. Becker, and Kenneth L. Pike, "The Process of Inquiry," in *Rhetoric: Discovery and Change* (New York: Harcourt, Brace and World, 1970), 71-88. Ann E. Berthoff, "The Problem of Problem Solving," *CCC*, 22 (Oct., 1971), 237-42, appears to argue for this last conception of problem-solving while repudiating other, more narrowly conceived conceptions as inappropriate for rhetorical purposes.

It makes a great deal of difference whether we regard the various procedures of invention as part of this generalized process of inquiry or apart from it. As part of the process they contribute to the discovery of new "truths," i.e., tested solutions to prior difficulties. Apart from it, they function merely as retrieval procedures providing the student with something, anything, to say; the issues of testing, truth, relevance to a larger psychological and social context disappear. Invention becomes merely another classroom exercise. The difference has been an important one throughout the history of invention: see Elbert W. Harrington, "Rhetoric and the Scientific Method of Inquiry," *University of Colorado Studies, Series in Language and Literature*, 1 (Dec., 1948), 1-64. The relation of this process to various heuristic procedures for facilitating it is important for another reason. Conceiving of rhetorical invention as a kind of problem-solving relates the discipline to other disciplines and encourages us to draw on relevant work therein. As Professor Harrington remarks:

> A broad view of invention simply means that the general aim of rhetoric is the same as the general aim of other courses in the curriculum. There should be no rhetorical spirit on the one hand and an academic spirit on the other. Besides teaching the techniques of writing and speaking, the rhetorician becomes a critic — a critic of methodologies at their best and a critic of resources which make our methodologies fruitful of results (64).

The Adequacy of Methods of Invention

It seems self-evident that the adequacy of the method taught has much to do with the effectiveness of the teaching. But on what basis does one decide the adequacy of a particular method? The question has received too little attention, although what has been done is significant. One criterion has already been mentioned in the section on problem-solving: if heuristic procedures are to be more than aids for retrieving information, they must be embedded in a process of inquiry which begins with a problem and ends with a tested solution.

Sister Janice Marie Lauer's *Invention in Contemporary Rhetoric: Heuristic Procedures* (unpublished doctoral dissertation, Univ. of Michigan, 1967), 141-57, provides two additional criteria for determining adequacy: comprehen-

27

siveness and efficiency. To determine comprehensiveness she asks (1) whether the method provides procedures for probing all the elements in the rhetorical situation (i.e., writer, audience and problematic experience); and (2) whether the method requires the writer to take more than one perspective on these elements. To determine efficiency, she asks (1) whether the method had simplicity of design; (2) whether it specifies a clear sequence of operations to be carried out by the writer; and (3) whether it has a "selector factor" (i.e., whether it provides a basis for following a particular direction of inquiry and for preferring one hypothesis to another).

W. Ross Winterowd's "'Topics' and Levels in the Composing Process," *CE*, 34 (Feb., 1973), 701-09, provides another criterion — whether the questions or operations which make up the heuristic procedure constitute a closed or open set, an open set being judged less adequate. Burke's pentad is a closed set, since the five terms exhaust the basic discriminations which can be made in that semantic system. By contrast Zebulon Vance Hooker, II's *Index of Ideas for Writers and Speakers* (Chicago: Scott, Foresman, 1965) provides 14,000 topics organized by the Dewey Decimal System; despite the very large number of topics, they constitute an open set — one can easily think of additional questions without drawing on another system. The operations called for in pre-writing and the topics of classical invention are also open sets.

Still another criterion is whether the psychological operations are fundamental, i.e., in some sense necessary to thought and inquiry, or whether they are arbitrary or designed for use only in particular, specialized situations. For example, two quite different arguments have been made that a sub-set of the classical topics is non-arbitrary. In "Language Is Sermonic" (in *Dimensions of Rhetorical Scholarship*, ed. Roger E. Nebergall [Norman, Okla.: Univ. of Oklahoma Dept. of Speech, 1963], 49-64; and in *Contemporary Theories of Rhetoric: Selected Readings*, ed. Richard L. Johannesen [New York: Harper & Row, 1971], 163-79),

28

Richard M. Weaver categorizes the Aristotelian topics and ranks them in order of their approximation to what is most permanent in existence; the ranking is based on Weaver's Platonic metaphysics. Genus-species definition, for example, ranks higher than cause-effect analysis since the former deals with unchanging essences and the latter with the changing physical world. Thus the system of topics reflects fundamental features of reality. "If one accepts the possibility of this or that ranking," Weaver argues, "one has to concede that rhetoric is not merely formal; it is realistic. It is not playing with counters; its impulses come from insights into actuality. Its topic matter is existential, not hypothetical" (Johannesen, *Contemporary Theories of Rhetoric*, 173). A useful analysis of Weaver's argument can be found in Richard L. Johannesen, Rennard Strickland and Ralph T. Eubanks' "Richard M. Weaver — On the Nature of Rhetoric: An Interpretation," in Johannesen's *Contemporary Theories of Rhetoric*, 180-95.

William F. Nelson in "Topoi: Evidence of Human Conceptual Behavior," *P and R*, 2 (Winter, 1969), 1-11, argues that the set of topics presented in John F. Wilson and Carroll C. Arnold's *Public Speaking as a Liberal Art* (2nd ed.; Boston: Allyn and Bacon, 1968), a modification of the set developed by Aristotle, are constants in conceptual behavior. Of the high-level semantic categories which the topics name, Nelson concludes that "it would seem there is a finiteness characterizing man's ability to categorize which, largely transcending the barriers of time, space, and cultural influence, renders a kind of stability and predictability to the patterns of human conceptual behavior" (9). For a study which casts doubt on the universality of the categories, see Emile Benveniste's "Categories of Thought and Language," in *Problems in General Linguistics, Miami Linguistics Series No. 8* (Coral Gables, Fla.: Univ. of Miami Press, 1971), 55-64.

Kenneth Burke's argument for the fundamental nature of the dramatistic method rests on two facts: First, its analytical power and ease of use are readily demonstrated.

> If you ask why, with a whole world of terms to choose from, we select these [i.e., act, scene, agent, agency, purpose] rather than some others as basic, our book itself is offered as the answer. For, to explain our position, we shall show how it can be applied.... Although, over the centuries, men have shown great enterprise and inventiveness in pondering matters of human motivation, one can simplify the subject by this pentad of key terms, which are understandable almost at a glance. They need never to be abandoned, since all statements that assign motives can be shown to arise out of them and to terminate in them (*A Grammar of Motives* [New York: Prentice-Hall, 1945], xv-xvi).

Second, it shares features with other well-established inquiry procedures. Daniel Fogarty observes that its similarity to "the 'four ultimate causes' of Aristotle only reassured Burke of [its] basic nature." And he continues,

> The similarity with the alternate questions that Scholastic philosophers asked themselves is also striking: *Quis? Quid? Quibus auxiliis? Ubi? Cur? Quomodo? Quando?* (Who? What? With what assistance? Where? Why? How? When?) The fundamental rule of thumb that used to be taught to journalism students as a way of covering all the pertinent details of a news event indicates how functionally useful is this metaphysical classification. Sociological research, also, has provided a communication model based on studies in control, content, audience, situation, and effect — really extensions in application of the Lasswell "formula" (*Roots for a New Rhetoric* [New York: Teachers College, Columbia Univ., 1959], 62-3).

Kenneth Pike argues that "certain universal invariants underlie all human experience as characteristics of rational-

ity itself" ("Beyond the Sentence," *CCC*, 15 [Oct., 1964],
129). These invariants function as axioms in tagmemic invention. The case for their universality rests (1) on their demonstrated usefulness in the analysis of highly diverse linguistic data and (2) on the mind's inability to function without them. Commenting on their usefulness, Pike states that

> I have . . . been directly or indirectly involved in the
> training of 5,000 or more students in the initial phases
> of linguistics — especially in connection with the
> Summer Institute of Linguistics . . . which is carrying
> on analytical work in some 260 languages in a dozen
> countries. In order to train these students to analyze
> and write descriptions of these languages we found it
> necessary to develop . . . a body of theory general
> enough to apply to any language whatever out of the
> several thousand in the world. . . . ("A Linguistic Con-
> tribution to Composition," *CCC*, 15 [May, 1964], 82).

This argument, like the first one for the pentad cited above,
is pragmatic — the procedure is unlikely to have such a wide
range of applicability unless it embodies psychological
universals.

The second argument Pike offers is an attempt to show that
the mind cannot function without certain epistemological
principles: see "Science Fiction as a Test of Axioms Concerning Human Behavior," *Parma Eldalamberon*, 1 (June,
1973), 6-7. "For some years," Pike states, "I have been attempting to develop and explicate a theory of the structure of
human behavior which is grounded in a set of axioms (or
affirmations, or assumptions) about human nature — assumptions which I take to be sufficiently basic that the
elimination of any one of them from our personal structure
would destroy our humanity itself. . . . Yet how can they be
tested?" Testing the axioms of any theory is difficult since
they must be expressed in ordinary language; however, ordinary language carries with it the biases of prior uses of the
language, including the residues of other theories. "So we

31

must find a way which can be handled through ordinary language, which grapples directly with the necessity of components of the theory, and which can do so in spite of human bias" (6). The way he proposes is an ingenious use of John Stuart Mill's Method of Difference, a technique of experimental inquiry which Mill summarizes this way:

> If our object be to discover the effects of an agent A, we must procure A in some set of ascertained circumstances, as ABC, and having noted the effects produced, compare them with the effect of the remaining circumstances BC, when A is absent (*A System of Logic, Bk.* III, ed. J. M. Robson [Toronto: Univ. of Toronto Press, 1973], 391).

"My proposal," Pike says, "lies in the use of science fiction. Specifically, I would like an author to take a list of such components, cross out one of them, and ATTEMPT TO WRITE A NOVEL WITHOUT DRAWING EITHER EXPLICITLY OR IMPLICITLY ON THAT COMPONENT. If the author could succeed, he would have DEMONSTRATED THE NON-BASIC NATURE OF THAT COMPONENT" (6).

Since classical invention, the dramatistic method, and especially tagmemic invention all provide procedures for the analysis of complex hierarchical systems, it is to the point to cite Herbert A. Simon's "Architecture of Complexity," *Proceedings of the American Philosophical Society*, 106 (Dec., 1962), 467-82. Although Simon is not directly concerned with rhetoric, he does discuss problem-solving, social systems, and symbolic systems, all of which are relevant to invention. But of special importance here is the following statement:

> If there are important systems in the world that are complex without being hierarchic, they may to a considerable extent escape our observation and our understanding. Analysis of their behavior would involve such detailed knowledge and calculation of the interactions

of their elementary parts that it would be beyond our capacities of memory or computation (477).

That is, although it is impossible to prove that all complex systems are hierarchically structured, human beings appear to be incapable of understanding any other kind of system. The concept of hierarchy thus must be regarded as fundamental to any inquiry procedure. Simon's article provides an argument for the fundamental nature of certain operations in all three methods, most obviously of partition and tagmemic field analysis.

Invention and Conceptions of the Composing Process

Among the most important subjects of rhetorical study now being opened up is the composing process itself. See, for example, James W. Ney, "Notes Towards a Psycholinguistic Model of the Writing Process," *RTE*, 8 (Fall, 1974), 157-69; William D. Page, "The Author and the Reader in Reading and Writing," *RTE*, 8 (Fall, 1974), 170-83; Charles K. Stallard, "An Analysis of the Writing Behavior of Good Student Writers," *RTE*, 8 (Fall, 1974), 206-18; and Terry Mischel, "A Case Study of a Twelfth-grade Writer," *RTE*, 8 (Winter, 1974), 303-14. The last two studies are extensions of Janet Emig's pioneering monograph, *The Composing Processes of Twelfth Graders, NCTE Research Report No. 13* (Urbana, Ill.: National Council of Teachers of English, 1971).

It is no accident that the gradual shift in attention among rhetoricians from composed product to the composing process is occurring at the same time as the reemergence of invention as a rhetorical discipline. Invention requires a process view of rhetoric; and if the composing process is to be taught, rather than left to the student to be learned, arts associated with various stages of the process are necessary. For a discussion of some relationships between invention and composing, as well as a critique of overly simple conceptions of both, see David V. Harrington, "Teaching Students the Art of Discovery," *CCC*, 19 (Feb., 1968), 7-14.

33

A particular method of invention presupposes a particular conception of the composing process. The simplest and most widely shared conception appears to be that of a linear, unidirectional process capable of being divided into more or less discrete stages. We think first (e.g., choose a subject, gather relevant information about it), then write a draft, and then revise it, editing for style, usage, etc. D. Gordon Rohman's division of the process into pre-writing, writing, and rewriting stages has already been noted; and the five arts of classical rhetoric — i.e., invention, arrangement, style, memory and delivery — suggest a similar conception. Many might disavow such a conception when stated so baldly, arguing that it is really more complex but that simplification is desirable for pedagogical purposes. Even so, the most widely shared supposition seems to be that thinking comes first, then writing.

As reasonable as this conception may at first seem, there are alternative conceptions of the composing process and of how content is, can be, or should be generated by it. For example, the process can be viewed as moving generally from conceptual problems to editing problems but moving cyclically, the writer shifting his focus of attention repeatedly among matters of content, style, and structure during each cycle. In this conception, a method of invention is seen as useful throughout the process, from beginning to end. This cyclical conception grows out of the assumptions that problems of content are finally inseparable from problems of style and structure and that composing is inescapably a recursive, trial-and-error procedure; heuristic procedures only reduce the number of trials needed to achieve satisfactory results. For examples, see Peter Elbow, *Writing Without Teachers* (New York: Oxford Univ. Press, 1973), especially 3-75; and Richard E. Young, Alton L. Becker and Kenneth L. Pike, *Rhetoric: Discovery and Change* (New York: Harcourt, Brace and World, 1970), especially 9, 59, 76-7, 135-36. The conception, however, is not adequately exploited in the latter text.

34

Or the activity of writing itself can be seen as a heuristic for discovering content (e.g., Sheridan Baker, "Writing as Discovery," *ADE Bulletin*, 43 [Nov., 1974], 34-7; and Taylor Stoehr, "Writing as Thinking," *CE*, 28 [March, 1967], 411-21). Such a conception does not inevitably exclude formal methods of invention from the act of composing, but it tends to make them redundant. When no method of invention is used, the content of discourse emerges from immediately available knowledge in the writer's mind and unanticipated discoveries prompted by the activity of putting words on paper.

Just how putting words on paper encourages the discovery of content is not at all clear. However, one explanation, at least a partial explanation, may be that the grammatical patterns and patterns of arrangement used by every writer serve some of the same purposes as explicit methods of invention. For a discussion of patterns as topics, see W. Ross Winterowd's "'Topics' and Levels in the Composing Process," *CE*, 34 (Feb., 1973), 701-9, especially 705-6; and Frank J. D'Angelo, *A Conceptual Theory of Rhetoric* (Cambridge, Mass.: Winthrop, 1975), especially 35.

A clear example of the use of language patterns to discover content is Francis Christensen's grammatical procedure for producing cumulative sentences: "A Generative Rhetoric of the Sentence," *CCC*, 14 (Oct., 1963), 155-61. (The article is also available, along with related ones, in *Notes Toward a New Rhetoric* [New York: Harper and Row, 1967]). The cumulative sentence, Christensen says, is "dynamic rather than static, representing the mind thinking. . . . the mere form of the sentence generates ideas. It serves the needs of both writer and reader, the writer by compelling him to examine his thought, the reader by letting him into the writer's thought" (156). Some shortcomings of Christensen's procedure can be found in Sabrina Thorne Johnson's "Some Tentative Strictures on Generative Rhetoric," *CE*, 31 (Nov., 1969), 155-65; of interest here is her objection that the procedure is of little use in generating content except that arising from immediate observation.

Johnson's objection does not apply to the use of some other patterns, however. For example, the patterns which help to organize paragraphs — e.g., generalization-example, generalization-comparison — can be seen as structural counterparts of the classical topics. One need only translate the patterns into operations to have a procedure for developing paragraphs or still larger units of discourse, as W. Ross Winterowd has suggested in "The Grammar of Coherence," *CE*, 31 (May, 1970), 828-35. Richard L. Larson argues that the patterns which organize complete discourses can be similarly used: "Toward a Linear Rhetoric of the Essay," *CCC*, 22 (May, 1971), 140-46. Walter J. De Mordaunt makes a comparable point in "Logic and Originality in Freshman Themes," *CCC*, 10 (Feb., 1959), 24-6. And Charles Kay Smith's *Styles and Structures: Alternative Approaches to College Writing* (New York: Norton, 1974) is based on the premise "that patterns of writing enact patterns of thinking, that by finding and practicing different ways of writing we can literally think different things" (ix). One value of the notion that forms are or can be used to guide thought in the act of composing — whether consciously or intuitively — is that it reminds us of the close and complex relationships between linguistic structure and meaning and between the arts of arrangement, style, and invention.

All of the conceptions mentioned above — and they do not exhaust the possibilities — are "mentalistic"; they all assume a mind at work carrying out a process that is both rational and intuitive. A provocative alternative, and a radical one since it repudiates mentalism itself, is the hypothesis proposed by Robert Zoellner based on work in behavioral psychology: "A Behavioral Approach to Writing," *CE*, 30 (Jan., 1969), 267-320. If the conceptions mentioned earlier can be crudely characterized as think/write, think/write/think/write . . . and write/think, Zoellner's can be characterized as speak/write. Language behavior, he argues, is a response, not to prior thought, but to stimulation provided by the external environment, including other writers and speakers. The behavior *is* thought. Since students have a greater fluency in speaking than in writing because they practice it more, speaking can be used as a stage prior to writing and can provide the basis for moving through increasingly adequate written versions of a unit of discourse. Rather than the judge of the finished product, the teacher is the primary reinforcer of adequate responses. If unguided creativity marks one boundary of the art of invention, Zoellner's work surely marks another, for in repudiating mentalism he repudiates the possibility of deliberate thought guided by heuristic procedures. Which is to say he repudiates invention itself, at least as it is presently conceived.

For various qualifications, critiques and explications of Zoellner's position, see "On Zoellnerism," *CE*, 30 (May, 1969), 645-68; and "Comment and Rebuttal," *CE*, 31 (Nov., 1969), 199-230, particularly Zoellner's "Response: Mentalizing S. R. Rodent," 215-30. Terry Radcliffe's "Talk-Write Composition: A Theoretical Model Proposing The Use of Speech to Improve Writing," *RTE*, 6 (Fall, 1972), 187-99, extends Zoellner's argument and proposes an experiment for testing whether "pre-talking" improves writing ability. Douglas Porter elaborates on the behavioral contribution to teaching composition in "The Behavioral Repertoire of Writing," *CCC*, 13 (Oct., 1962), 14-17. James Deese, "Behavior and Fact," *AP*, 24 (May, 1969), 515-22; and George A. Miller, Eugene Galanter and Karl H. Pribram, *Plans and the Structure of Behavior* (New York: Holt, Rinehart and Winston, 1960) offer valuable discussions of some limitations in the behavioral approach to language behavior. Deese argues that behavioral psychology cannot provide an adequate account of the experience of understanding, which need have no overt manifestations. Miller, Galanter and Pribram demonstrate that the use of heuristic procedures can significantly increase the speed of memorization, and that memorization does not depend upon "piling up increments of response strength" (136). Both studies lend support to mentalism; and the latter supports the assumption that heuristic procedures can increase the effectiveness of psychological processes.

The scope of the composing process is largely determined by the functions of the method of invention. If, for example, the process has its inception in a thesis assigned by the teacher — a common practice in composition courses — and if invention involves merely finding relevant things to say about it, the scope is relatively narrow — narrower than if the thesis must first be established and then developed in response to and within the constraints of a rhetorical situation, as is the case in classical invention. Pre-writing and tagmemic invention, however, extend the scope of the process to include activities hitherto not usually regarded as part of rhetoric. The difference in function between these methods and the classical method is apparent in Francis Bacon's distinction between classical invention and another sort of invention which has by and large been the concern of logic and the sciences:

> The invention of speech or argument is not properly an invention: for to invent is to discover that we know not, and not to recover or resummon that which we already know; and the use of this invention is no other but *out of the knowledge whereof our mind is already possessed, to draw forth or call before us that which may be pertinent to the purpose which we take into our consideration.* So as, to speak truly, it is no *Invention*, but a *Remembrance* or *Suggestion*, with an application; which is the cause why the schools do place it after judgment, as subsequent and not precedent. Nevertheless, because we do account it a Chase as well of deer in an inclosed park as in a forest at large, and that it hath already obtained the name, let it be called invention: so as it be perceived and discerned, that the scope and end of this invention is readiness and present use of our knowledge, and not addition or amplification thereof.

(The Works of Francis Bacon, ed. James Spedding, Robert Leslie Ellis, and Douglas Denon Heath [New York: Hurd and Houghton, 1869], VI, 268-69.)

Helping the writer discover what he does not know in order to satisfy his own need to know is not the only function of pre-writing and tagmemic invention, but it is their primary function. The conception of the composing process which emerges is similar to St. Augustine's, who said of his own rhetoric that "there are two things necessary . . . a way of discovering those things which are to be understood, and a way of teaching what we have learned" *(On Christian Doctrine,* trans. D. W. Robertson, Jr. [Indianapolis, Ind.: Bobbs-Merrill, 1958], 7). Tagmemic invention extends the scope of the composing process to what appears to be the limit when it provides a heuristic procedure for analyzing and formulating problems which give rise to inquiry: Richard Young, "Problems and the Process of Writing," *Studies in Language and Language Behavior,* Center for Research on Language and Language Behavior, Ann Arbor: Univ. of Michigan, (Feb., 1969), 494-502 (ERIC: ED 029040).

The development of methods of invention designed to discover new concepts and ordering principles is an effort to respond to the fragmentation of the culture, new uncertainties about old truths, and new epistemologies which insist that the world one knows is in part the result of who he is. Modern rhetoric, S. M. Halloran argues in "On the End of Rhetoric, Classical and Modern," *CE*, 36 (Feb., 1975), 621-31,

> is distinguished by its emphasis on the responsibility of the speaker (or author) to articulate his own world, and thereby his own self (631).

Other arguments on the interaction of modern rhetoric with its social and philosophic context can be found in Lloyd F. Bitzer and Edwin Black, eds., *The Prospect of Rhetoric* (Englewood Cliffs, N. J.: Prentice-Hall, 1971); Richard McKeon's "The Uses of Rhetoric in a Technological Age:

Architectonic and Productive Arts," 44-63, is particularly notable.

From what has been said, it is apparent that methods of invention strongly shape not only our conceptions of the composing process but the process itself, the things we do in composing. And, by implication, they also influence how composing is taught. It is apparent that we cannot accurately speak of a single composing process in which various methods of invention can be substituted; there are several variants, each with distinctive capacities, limitations and appropriate uses.

Teaching Invention

Those seriously concerned with teaching rhetoric — and in particular invention, the most difficult of the rhetorical arts — must give more than ordinary attention to the processes of teaching and learning. The newness of the skills to be mastered, their complexity, and their subtlety combine to place heavy demands on the knowledge and imagination of the instructor.

The need for exceptional care in planning and teaching is borne out by several reports on efforts to teach invention. For example, Richard E. Young and Frank M. Koen conclude that when teaching methods of invention which incorporate a problem-solving approach, the instructor must initially present students with problematic data rather than allow them to select their own, for they have a tendency to select problems whose answers they already know or which are easy to solve. Both situations preclude the need for a formal art of inquiry and the motivation to master one. Once they have mastered the art and unlearned old strategies for academic success, they can select their own problems. See *The Tagmemic Discovery Procedure: An Evaluation of Its Uses in the Teaching of Rhetoric* (Ann Arbor, Mich.: Univ. of Michigan, NEH Grant No. EO-5238-71-116, 1973), especially 64-65; the study is available through ERIC: ED 084517.

Furthermore, Clinton S. Burhans, Jr., in *Extended Testing of a Unified Experimental Course in Composition in a Variety of Materials and Formats* (East Lansing, Mich.: Michigan State Univ., U.S. Dept. of Health, Education and Welfare Cooperative Research Project No. 7-1149, 1968), especially 31-44, argues that the *sequence* of skills taught must be considered carefully, since they are often presented in an order inconsistent with student needs. Development of the skills involved in creative inquiry and expressive writing, he argues, should precede development of more technical skills such as grammar, logic, library research, argument, etc.; without the former, students are neither willing nor able to acquire the latter. Catherine Elizabeth Frerichs Lamb's *On Suffering Change: Toward a Theory of Instruction in the Art of Invention* (unpublished doctoral dissertation, Univ. of Michigan, 1974) lends support to Burhans' position while arguing for the necessity of explicit "bridges" between less formal and more formal methods of invention.

To say that we need to attend to sequence and continuity guided by a clear sense of the structure of the subject and student needs is to say that we need a theory of instruction. One relevant theory is articulated in Jerome S. Bruner's *The Process of Education* (New York: Vintage Books, 1960) and *Toward a Theory of Instruction* (New York: Norton, 1966). Bruner develops four theorems which specify what a theory of instruction ought to do:

> First, a theory of instruction should specify the experiences which most effectively implant in the individual a predisposition toward learning — learning in general or a particular type of learning. . . .
>
> Second, a theory of instruction must specify the ways in which a body of knowledge should be structured so that it can be most readily grasped by the learner. . . .
>
> Third, a theory of instruction should specify the most effective sequences in which to present the materials to be learned. . . .

41

Finally, a theory of instruction should specify the nature and pacing of rewards and punishments in the process of learning and teaching (*Toward a Theory of Instruction*, 40-41).

Bernard Z. Friedlander's "A Psychologist's Second Thoughts on Concepts, Curiosity, and Discovery in Teaching and Learning," *HER*, 35 (Winter, 1965), 18-38, offers an important cautionary statement on Bruner's ideas.

Consistent with Bruner's work is the argument by the Commission on English (*Freedom and Discipline in English* [New York: College Entrance Examination Board, 1965], 87-92) for a composition curriculum based on Alfred North Whitehead's "The Rhythm of Education" and "The Rhythmic Claims of Freedom and Discipline" (*The Aims of Education* [New York: The Free Press, 1967], 15-28, 29-41). A critique of the Commission's report can be found in Glenn Matott's "Speculations on Sources of Confusion in Teaching Composition," *CCC*, 26 (May, 1975), 168-72.

One interesting implication of these theoretical and pedagogical efforts is that we are encouraged to view the various approaches to the composing process not as mutually exclusive but as organizable in mutually reinforcing sequences. Such a view allows us to acknowledge the truths in disparate approaches to teaching the process of inquiry and composing. One need not repudiate classical invention or any other formal procedure to embrace less formal methods which rely more heavily on the student's intuitive ability: for example, Ken Macrorie, *Telling Writing* (New York: Hayden, 1970); James E. Miller, Jr., *Word, Self, Reality: The Rhetoric of Imagination* (New York: Dodd, Mead, 1972); and Jean Guitton's elegant but little known text, *A Student's Guide to Intellectual Work* (Notre Dame, Ind.: Univ. of Notre Dame Press, 1964). They can be equally useful at different stages of the curriculum. Compendiums, such as W. Ross Winterowd's *The Contemporary Writer* (New York:

Harcourt Brace Jovanovich, 1975), also become, from this point of view, especially valuable because of the flexibility and range of options they offer the teacher.

STRUCTURE AND FORM IN NON-FICTION PROSE

RICHARD L. LARSON

Herbert H. Lehman College
City University of New York

WHEN TALKING OF "FORM" in composition, we can have in mind the structure of the complete piece of writing or the structure of identifiable parts of the piece — even typical features of the structure of sentences. In this essay I take up first various approaches to the structure of complete pieces and then — leaving aside the organization of parts that include more than one paragraph — I turn to studies of the design of individual paragraphs. About the latter, perhaps, more advice is given to students by textbooks and instructors than about any other topic in composition. I will try to suggest connections that can be made between theories about the structure of the paragraph and theories about the structure of the whole piece; I will devote about a third of this essay to theories about the structure of paragraphs and the ways of teaching the writing of paragraphs. Questions of form and order within sentences I leave to other essays in this volume.

I

Although there has recently come to be a large body of literature about invention in composing, and an even larger body of literature about syntax and the rhetoric of the sentence, form in complete essays has not been the object of much theoretical investigation. Classic essays on form, such as Kenneth Burke's discussion in *Counter-Statement* (Los Altos, California: Hermes Publications, 1953, pp. 124-149; accessibly reprinted in W. Ross Winterowd, *Contemporary*

Rhetoric: A Conceptual Background with Readings, New York: Harcourt Brace Jovanovich, 1975, pp. 183-198), focus more on form in literary writing than on form in expository or argumentative composition. Burke's general definition of form as "an arousing and fulfillment of desires . . . one part of [a work] . . . leads a reader to anticipate another part, to be gratified by the sequence" (Winterowd, p. 183) is useful, of course, for the discussion of writing in whatever mode, but the kinds of form that Burke enumerates — syllogistic progression, repetitive form, conventional form, etc, — are illustrated in his essay mostly from literary texts. Burke does cite syntactic, semantic, and rhythmic structures of nonfictive prose, but he says little about the overall design or structure of such prose. Still, a few recent theorists have begun investigations of form that may illuminate the design of much composition in prose. W. Ross Winterowd, for example, has defined form as *"the internal set of consistent relationships perceived in any stretch of discourse, whether poem, play, essay, oration, or whatever"* ("Dispositio: The Concept of Form in Discourse," *CCC*, 22 [February, 1971], 41: the essay is reprinted with some changes in his *Contemporary Rhetoric*, pp. 163-170, and the quoted passage is on p. 165 of the book.) Winterowd goes on to elaborate the view that perception of form includes recognition of the "deep structure" of an utterance, the surface structure in which it appears, and the other alternatives available for setting forth the substance of what is to be said (*Contemporary Rhetoric*, p. 166). But Winterowd's discussion focuses more on the language of literature and on connections between sentences (we will discuss these connections in our comments on theories of the paragraph) than on form in complete pieces of discourse, though Winterowd asserts (*Contemporary Rhetoric*, p. 170) that the "grammar of the sentence [is] the most productive analogical model for exploration of 'grammar' beyond the sentence." Winterowd's other major theoretical essay on form, "Beyond Style," *Philosophy and Rhetoric*, 5 (Spring, 1972), 88-110 (reprinted in *Contempor-*

ary Rhetoric, pp. 207-224), also looks primarily at literary texts, exploring the impact of different kinds of form on readers, and urging that the power of seemingly "incoherent" works casts doubt on conventional assumptions about the need for obvious form in literature.

Other commentators have made occasional contributions to a theory of form, but are often not looking into the fundamental characteristics of form in composition so much as advancing their preferences about forms that should be taught. Keith Fort, in his highly suggestive essay entitled "Form, Authority, and the Critical Essay," *CE*, 32 (March, 1971), 629-639 (accessibly reprinted in Winterowd, *Contemporary Rhetoric*, pp. 172-183), says that form "comprises those elements in an expression that reflect the attitude of the speaker and that tend to control the audience's relation to the expression's subject matter and the speaker." Thus defined, form to Fort reveals the attitude of a writer toward subject and listener — what we might paraphrase as a set of wishes about how the reader should view the writer and a set of assumptions about how the reader will and should want to respond. Fort's purpose in offering this definition, however, is not so much to initiate a full investigation of form as to deplore the usual demand for customary kinds of logic and argument in the writing (and teaching) of critical essays on literature. The insistence that writers of critical essays establish their authority over their texts by arguments structured in traditional patterns is, according to Fort, unduly restrictive; our tastes in critical essays — by professionals and students alike — on literary texts should accommodate greater variety in structure and in relationship among writer, subject, and audience. Making a somewhat similar appeal (though not only for essays in literary criticism), Walt Stevens, in "A Proposal for Non-Linear Disposition," *Western Speech*, 37 (Spring, 1973), 118-128, cites writers of poems and novels as well as theorists of rhetoric, well-known speechmakers, and social scientists to establish that failure of a work or a process to conform to familiar patterns of linear organ-

47

ization need not be damaging, but can lead to "individuality, novelty, variety, invention, or creativity." He is, like Fort, arguing in support of a particular outlook on form more than he is investigating principles of form.

Howard Brashers, however, does look to the discovery of formal principles mainly for their value in illuminating non-fiction prose. In his "Aesthetic Form in Familiar Essays," *CCC*, 22 (May, 1971), 147-155, Brashers identifies several techniques of design: contrast, gradation, theme and variation, restraint (and climax), and several typical patterns that bring such devices into unity: linear patterns, radial-circular patterns, and mytho-literary patterns (sequences of experiences "recognizable as a unit in a culture"). In discussing these techniques, Brashers explores how connections are made between parts of works, and how unity is achieved within variety of detail. But Brashers applies his analysis only to what he calls the "familiar essay" (other kinds of essays, he says, have other principles of form), and he has not pursued his investigations in subsequent published essays. Still, Brashers leaves us with numerous suggestions about the kinds of form that a reader may recognize in non-fiction prose.

Among these recent writers, only Willis Pitkin, Jr. has attempted to offer a general theory of the structure of discourse. In his most accessible article, "Discourse Blocs" *CCC*, 20 (May, 1969), 138-148, written early in his teaching career, Pitkin argues that discourse may be usefully viewed not simply as a collection of sentences and paragraphs, but as a hierarchical arrangement of "blocs" of thought, most of which can be subdivided into smaller blocs, and combined with other blocs to form larger blocs. The blocs are discovered, not by how long they are or by how they are punctuated, or by their appearance on the page, but by the function each serves in the discourse. At the top of the hierarchy, a bloc can presumably include several sentences (or paragraphs); near the bottom of the hierarchy, it may consist of a small part of a sentence.

Most blocs come in pairs; the blocs in each pair are related in one of four ways: by simple coordination (since it is possible to coordinate more than two items, there can be more than two blocs in a coordinate series); by complementation, in which one bloc starts a unit of thought and a second bloc completes the unit (e.g., question/answer, assertion/reassertion, cause/effect, negative/positive, premise/conclusion, etc.); by subordination, in which the first bloc mentions genus, the second mentions species; and by superordination, in which the first bloc mentions species, the second genus.

In his short essay, Pitkin is less than completely clear about how his complex hierarchical system assists the student of discourse or a working writer. But the relationship he calls "complementation" is an important one to emphasize in a theory of discourse, and one hopes to hear more from Pitkin about his view of discourse as a hierarchy of two-part blocs.

II

We have, then, a relatively slender body of theorizing about the conceptual bases for discussions of form and structure in prose. Possibly as a result, scholarship and pedagogy about arrangement and order in discourse have been largely concerned with enumerating useful plans for the presentation of ideas, and with describing ways for a writer to make connections between major ideas once that author has chosen an overall pattern for the essay. Rarely have writers dealing with order and form even considered the possible connections between the arrangement of ideas and the discovery of ideas to be arranged. Rarely, too, have writers examined the connections between the way ideas are arranged and the way those ideas are perceived by readers after they have been arranged. The connections between form and effectiveness of discourse have prompted serious inquiry mainly by a few psychologists little known among teachers of writing. Most discussions of form that are available to teachers of writing, then, are enumerations of plans and stock formulas from which writers can choose; when it comes to guidance in making the choices, the writer is pretty much left to his intuitive guesses.

The classic plan for organizing a piece of discourse — "classic" in the dual sense of being derived from theorists in classical antiquity and of being cited frequently in contemporary texts — is the pattern of the formal oration, or persuasive speech. The plan is most accessibly discussed by Edward P. J. Corbett in *Classical Rhetoric for the Modern Student* (Second Edition, New York: Oxford University Press, 1971), Chapter 3.

Summarizing the views of Cicero (*De Oratore*) and Quintilian (*Institutio Oratoria*) on structure, Corbett notes that the typical plan for a discourse included five parts: an introduction; a statement of the facts or circumstances that a reader of the discourse needs to know; the points that tend to support the writer's arguments; the points that tend to refute opposition to the writer's arguments; and a conclusion that brings together and restates, amplifies, or shows the significance of what has been argued. Possibly anticipating criticisms such as those voiced by Richard Young and Alton Becker in their article, "Toward a Modern Theory of Rhetoric: A Tagmemic Contribution," *HER*, 35 (Fall, 1965), 450-468 (reprinted in Martin Steinmann, Jr., ed., *New Rhetorics* [New York: Charles Scribners Sons, 1967], pp. 78-107) that this view of arrangement divorces form from content, "failing to consider the importance of the act of discovery in the shaping of form," Corbett cites the experiences of Ronald Crane (in *The Languages of Criticism and the Structure of Poetry*, [Toronto: University of Toronto Press, 1952]). Crane asserts that he had never been able to write anything that seemed to him unified, organically whole, "except in response to . . . a synthesizing idea," the perception of a "subsuming form," for his materials (Corbett, p. 301). From Crane's experience, Corbett infers the need for the writer to exercise a good deal of judgment and discretion in adapting the standard pattern to his or her purposes in addressing a particular audience on a particular occasion; Corbett insists on the need for adjusting form to ideas and circumstances, even as he offers extended and useful advice about the management of each part in the standard pattern.

That the arrangement of parts envisaged by classical theorists reflects a powerful insight into effective ways of putting arguments, however, is revealed in the advocacy by Young and Becker themselves of a structure different in name from but similar in essentials to that of the classical oration. In their original and fresh view of rhetoric, set forth in *Rhetoric: Discovery and Change* (co-authored with Kenneth Pike, New York: Harcourt, Brace, and World, Inc., 1970), they identify as one strategy for reconstructing the reader's "image" of a subject this arrangement of parts:

Introduction
Background
Argument
    (major premise
    minor premise
    conclusion
    superiority of argument offered to alternative positions)
Conclusion
    (summary of argument and statement of its implications)

(pp. 234-235)

Young and Becker are careful to discuss ways for a writer to vary the basic strategy depending on what the reader knows and what the reader thinks of the writer and/or of the writer's views on the subject. But their discussion of form, quite brief in comparison to their discussion of heuristic techniques for invention and of ways for analyzing the reader's ideas and attitudes, in effect supports the views of Corbett about the usefulness of the classical paradigm.

There are eighteenth- and nineteenth-century antecedents for the pattern of oratorical discourse discussed by Corbett, in case the teacher wishes to consult "early modern" treatments of the standard oration. One of the best known is by Hugh Blair, Professor at the University of Edinburgh, whose *Lectures on Rhetoric and Belles Lettres* were widely read in the half century after 1780; the *Lectures* have been reprinted (ed. Harold Harding, Carbondale, Illinois: Southern Illinois University Press, 1965), and are excerpted in James Golden and Edward P. J. Corbett, eds., *The Rhetoric of Blair, Campbell, and Whately* (New York: Holt, Rinehart, and Winston, 1968). Blair's entire discussion of order (Lectures 31 and 32) is an elaboration of how the different parts of the oration might be handled, together with an admonition to restraint in the appeal to a listener's feelings — which Blair identifies as an optional, separate part of the discourse (coming between one's refutation of his opponent's views and one's conclusion). In his comments on the rationale for different sequences of arguments, Blair gets little beyond discouraging long, impassioned introductions and suggesting that a proposition likely to be resisted by the hearer should be approached gradually, while a proposition likely not to evoke disagreement may be asserted early and defended in the rest of the discourse.

One other "modern" source for the discussions in Corbett is the work of Richard Whately, a clergyman, whose *Elements of Rhetoric* flourished in the early nineteenth century. The *Elements*, like Blair's *Lectures*, have been reprinted (ed. Douglas Ehninger, Carbondale, Illinois: Southern Illinois University Press, 1963) — parts of it also appear in the volume by Golden and Corbett cited above — and may also be worth the attention of those interested in the antecedents of current treatments of organization. Whately's remarks on arrangement of topics are few, and are tied in to a discussion of how a speaker accepts (or transfers) the "burden of proof" of his argument and of how one refutes an opponent, but he introduces the two patterns (general to particular, and par-

STRUCTURE AND FORM IN NON-FICTION PROSE

ticular to general) that are highlighted in many texts on writing to this day. And, perhaps his most important contribution, he enumerates several kinds of introductions (inquisitive, paradoxical, corrective, preparatory, narrative) that a discourse can have — introductions that survive, with slightly different names, in current texts (including Corbett, who on pages 304-308 names and illustrates each of Whately's principal types of introduction).

Corbett, recently, and Blair, Whately, and other rhetoricians from earlier centuries offer their patterns, they would admit, largely for argumentative or persuasive discourse. But argument or persuasion is only one of the possible aims of discourse, as James L. Kinneavy argues in *A Theory of Discourse* (Englewood Cliffs, New Jersey: Prentice-Hall, Inc., 1971). Kinneavy identifies four kinds of discourse, differentiated by aim: persuasive discourse; reference discourse (for giving information, recording scientific research, or exploring problems); literary discourse; and expressive discourse (for recording the feelings of an individual or the aspirations and convictions of a group). He asserts that discourse serving each one of these aims tends to have its distinctive patterns of organization. In persuasive discourse, Kinneavy finds essentially the pattern discussed by Corbett. And in the various forms of reference discourse he discerns a number of different patterns, e.g., "inverted induction" — giving the generalization first, followed by the details that lead to it — in "scientific" discourse, and problem-solving in "exploratory" discourse. (See pp. 151-166, *passim.*) Yet Kinneavy acknowledges that the effort to connect particular forms with particular aims of discourse can lead to oversimplification. Though informative or factual discourse, for instance, is organized to achieve accuracy, comprehensiveness, and surprise in the reader, different examples of such discourse may follow different organizational plans (including narration, description, classification, evaluation — which Kinneavy calls the "modes" of discourse), and may even be ordered according to "literary" or "expressive" or "persuasive" principles. Kinneavy discusses the organization of "literary" discourse mainly with concepts taken from linguistics and semantics, rather than with concepts customarily employed to describe organization. And he does not discern any typical patterns in what he calls "expressive" discourse. Since his discussion of the "modes" of discourse is yet to be published, it is hard to assess his contributions to our knowledge of the structure of discourse. His discussion demonstrates, however, that even a rigorous division of the "aims" of discourse does not substantially enlarge our theoretical understanding about patterns of arrangement.

Among modern theorists of rhetoric, one of the more emphatic in resisting theoretical reliance on generalized patterns (advocated irrespective of subject and audience) and more subtle in recognizing the possible consequences of different ways to arrange ideas is Chaim Perelman, whose *The New Rhetoric: A Treatise on Argument* (trans. John Wilkinson and Purcell Weaver, Notre Dame: University of Notre Dame Press, 1969) concludes with some reflection on how the arrangement of arguments affects readers. Perelman lists some "points of view" to be taken in the development of a plan for a persuasive discourse and in the analysis of the values in any plan: "the argumentative situation itself, by which is meant the influence of the earlier stages of the discussion on the argumentative possibilities open to the speaker"; the "conditioning of the audience, which comprises changes of attitude brought about by the speech" as it progresses; and "the reactions occasioned in the audience by its perception of the order or arrangement adopted in the speech" (p. 491). Perelman examines briefly, as Corbett does, some of the effects on audiences that can be achieved in an introduction, and he explores some of the values of different ways for sequencing arguments. But his discussion is, like those of most rhetoricians, primarily concerned with persuasive argument, and it offers more of theoretical considerations and possibilities than it does of direct guidance in the selection and working out of plans for arrangement.

54

Perelman's major value for the teacher of writing is in his insistence upon the interaction of audience and arrangement — an insight that will apply to virtually any composed piece.

But for specific, empirically based guidance in the selection of order in arrangement, as distinguished from theoretical discussions based upon classical oratory or other principles, there are few studies to recommend. Among those few are two volumes by Carl I. Hovland, Irving Janis, and Harold H. Kelley, psychologists working at Yale. One of their books, *The Order of Presentation in Persuasion* (New Haven: Yale University Press, 1957), reports the results of particular experiments in the arrangement of persuasive arguments with audiences that had different orientations toward the subject of the argument. Hovland's more general discussion of the subject is an earlier volume, *Communication and Persuasion: Psychological Studies of Opinion Change* (New Haven: Yale University Press, 1957; pages 1-18 are reprinted in Steinmann, ed., *New Rhetorics*, pp. 35-57). This volume details the interdisciplinary foundations of studies on persuasion and opinion change, describes the difficulties confronting those who undertake research on opinion change — the number of variables to be dealt with other than the content and structure of the communication, for example — and examines the various elements in persuasive communication. The elements Hovland and his colleagues list are familiar: the communicator; the stimuli transmitted in the communication (content and organization of ideas); the audience (including predispositions and individual personality features) and the responses of that audience (how far the responses are overt, how far opinion change is retained for periods of time). Those interested in observing directly the interdisciplinary dimensions of empirical studies in rhetorical form would find the work of Hovland and his colleagues revealing. Such readers might also wish to note, however, the criticisms of "scientific" studies of persuasion in Charles Larson and Robert Sanders,

"Faith, Mystery, and Data: An Analysis of 'Scientific' Studies of Persuasion," in *QJS*, 61 (April, 1975), 178-194.

The slenderness of scholarly studies about arrangement of parts in discourse is perhaps suggested by a short passage in the essay contributed by Wayne Brockriede to the report of the Speech Communication Association's National Developmental Project on Rhetoric. Brockriede notes his puzzlement over the discovery that Harry Truman's 1947 speech announcing the Truman Doctrine did not follow the strict argumentative plan of a logical brief, and recalls considering whether the structure of the speech might successfully be described by analogy to counterpoint in music. He summarizes his reasons for believing that contrapuntal structure might be effective in situations such as Truman's, but concludes the discussion only by suggesting that his hypotheses could be subjected to experimental investigation. (See Wayne Brockriede, "Trends in the Study of Rhetoric: Toward a Blending of Criticism and Science," in Lloyd Bitzer and Edwin Black, eds., *The Prospect of Rhetoric* [Englewood Cliffs, New Jersey, 1971], pp. 134-135.) It is precisely these kinds of questions, theoretical and empirical, that scholars interested in form in discourse have hardly begun to investigate.

III

The discussions of form at which we have looked in Section II often appear to view the composed piece as a succession of discrete units, each more or less self-contained, open to being arranged in different orders and not necessarily disclosing a progressive sequence of thought that follows a movement begun in the opening sentences in the piece. Other discussions in modern rhetorical theory, however, suggest ways in which an essay, looked at as a total unit, may be said to exhibit a plan that evolves, or develops, from commitments or choices made at the outset by the writer. Perception of how that plan unfolds enables one to see the essay as an organic unit, beginning with an idea and working through a describable plan toward completion of the statement of that idea.

In its simplest form, this view of the essay as the unfolding of a plan initiated by the writer's view of his subject is most easily illustrated by the listing of "methods of development" (enumeration, analysis, comparison/contrast, general to particular, and particular to general) discussed in standard composition texts as ways for achieving a writer's purpose. An example, no more informative but no less useful than most others, might be a familiar text such as McCrimmon's *Writing with a Purpose* (6th edition, Boston: Houghton, Mifflin Company, 1976), in which chapter 3 sets forth the more common plans available and gives examples of each. Another, but much more original and revealing, discussion of the customary methods of development is that by Frank D'Angelo in his book, *A Conceptual Theory of Rhetoric* (Cambridge, Massachusetts: Winthrop Publishing Company, 1975). D'Angelo argues (pp. 56ff.) that such patterns of organization as definition, description, classification, and so on, are manifestations in form of some procedures for thinking, for invention, to which D'Angelo gives extended attention before he takes up problems of arrangement. In connecting the typical patterns of arrangement with procedures for thinking — and eventually with ways of putting together sentences, i.e., with expression — D'Angelo does much to bring out the unity of rhetorical theory and the dangers of separating arrangement from invention and from style.

D'Angelo (who notes, but does not discuss extensively, the possibility that teachers should heed such "nonlogical" patterns of arrangement as fantasy, dream, reverie, etc.) also contributes two useful suggestions about ways of looking at the total movement of discourse. One, drawn from scholars of myth and fairy tale, D'Angelo identifies as the analysis of "paradigmatic" structure — the search for paradigms of form in similar kinds of discourse. D'Angelo illustrates the kinds of paradigms that can sometimes be found in narrative pieces, and then locates other kinds of paradigms, for instance the enumeration of instances of a generalization, in so-called expository discourse. The paradigms that D'Angelo locates are rather familiar, but his comments on paradigmatic form obviously assist our search for ways of seeing the evolving shape of total units of discourse.

D'Angelo's other suggestion about viewing the structure of discourse draws heavily upon the work of Francis Christensen, about whose work we shall have more to say in discussions of theories of the paragraph. D'Angelo notes the applications of Christensen's work to the whole essay that have been attempted by people such as Michael Grady ("A Conceptual Rhetoric of the Composition," *CCC*, 22 [December, 1971], 348-354), who argues that essays can be conceived as sequences of structurally related paragraphs, each paragraph functioning in relation to the whole discourse much as a sentence functions as part of a paragraph. D'Angelo prefers to look at a total discourse as a sequence of structurally related sentences bound to each other, and to the lead sentence of the discourse, through coordination or subordination, and he offers an extended analysis of a political commentary from a newspaper to illustrate this "syntagmatic" view of structure. While the detailed discriminating of coordinate and subordinate sentences in a complete essay may seem to obscure the development of a discourse more than D'Angelo's paradigmatic analysis does, his presentation of both approaches to the study of form enables readers to attain a better understanding of some issues currently being raised in analysis of form than can be obtained from any other recent brief discussion of written rhetoric. (See also D'Angelo's article, "A Generative Rhetoric of the Essay," *CCC*, 25 [December, 1974], 388-396.)

The observation of paradigms in the progress of a writer's thought has also been advocated by Richard L. Larson in his article, "Invention Once More: A Role for Rhetorical Analysis," *CE*, 32 (March, 1971), 668-672. Although the article is intended to direct students toward a way of discovering ideas, its focus is on the form in which ideas appear in the work of professional writers. In effect, the article substantiates D'Angelo's contention that plans of organization are tightly related to procedures and habits in thinking; it asserts that patterns followed in thinking can themselves be discovered inferentially from the plans that organize professional writers' work. Calling these plans "movements of mind," Larson argues that most successful pieces of discourse will exhibit discernible "movements," that these movements are not necessarily identifiable from the short list of organizational plans presented to writers in most textbooks, and that attempting to duplicate the movements of mind followed by professional writers is, for the student writer, a useful procedure in learning how to develop ideas.

One paradigm in particular worth the student's attention is discussed by Larson in a subsequent article, "Problem-Solving, Composing, and Liberal Education," *CE*, 33 (March, 1972), 628-635. In this article, through an analysis of Swift's *A Modest Proposal*, Larson attempts to disclose the elements of the problem-solving process and to show how this process informs and organizes Swift's essay. Arguing that the problem-solving process underlies the structure of much writing by intellectual, social, and political theorists, Larson encourages teachers to introduce students to the process as both a way of finding their ideas about a topic and a way of giving a rough structure to those ideas in composing a first draft. Larson works in this essay with a somewhat narrower model of problem-solving than Young, Becker, and Pike advance in their book, *Rhetoric: Discovery and Change*, but the narrower model may nonetheless be a useful paradigm for students to practice and follow in learning how to advance deliberative discourse.

In a subsequent essay, "Toward a Linear Rhetoric of the Essay," *CCC*, 22 (May, 1971), 140-146, Larson elaborates the proposition that professional essays reveal typical movements of mind, arguing that any essay can be perceived as a sequence of steps taken in order to reach a particular goal, and that the individual steps in the sequence can be described in such a way that a student of organization can almost diagram the action of the piece. Larson works with theories adapted from the British philosopher J. L. Austin by Richard Ohmann, most notably in Harold Martin, Richard Ohmann and James Wheatley, *The Logic and Rhetoric of Exposition* (3rd Edition, New York: Holt, Rinehart, and Winston, 1969). For a more recent discussion of "speech-act" theory in composition, see Alan Lemke, "Writing as Action in Living," *CCC*, 25 (October, 1974), 269-274. These theories hold — to oversimplify them grossly — that an utterance not only makes a statement (or asks a question, or gives a command, or reveals strong emotion), but also performs a particular act in the context in which it occurs (e.g., stating, conceding, promising, predicting, threatening). Larson suggests that the successive acts performed by the successive sentences in a discourse can be identified, and the pattern established by the succession of acts can be described. He calls this pattern the "linear plan" for the discourse, distinguishing this plan from the outline advocated in many texts on composition by insisting that a linear plan identifies and clarifies the overall principle of forward motion in the essay. This is the principle by which an essay reaches, through successive steps, the particular argumentative or persuasive goal sought by the writer. If the steps are well ordered and well taken, the result of their having come in their particular succession will be a feeling in the reader of satisfaction or conviction of the rightness of the conclusion — or at least a feeling of respect for the writer's argument. The planning of any piece of writing thus involves much more than the replication of a previously discerned general pattern of discourse. It requires the choice of an order specially tailored to the subject, to the writer's view of that subject, to the goal sought by the writer, to the reader(s), and to the situation within which it will be perceived.

Implicit in this discussion of inferring plans from pieces of professional writing are the generalizations that for the working writer the process of writing is partly the process of choosing an appropriate plan, and that the available plans, while perhaps not infinite in number, are quite varied. How, then, does the working writer stay on the track? Particularly if he is working out his plan as he devises material (the task of inventing and the task of arranging, as we have suggested, are not truly separable), how does he determine whether he is carrying his reader along and satisfying him that the promised job is being done? Guidance in testing one's discourse is not widely available in the literature on form, but one essay that offers help is Robert Gorrell's "Not by Nature: Approaches to Rhetoric," *EJ*, 55 (April, 1966), 409-416, 449. In this essay, Gorrell observes that when a writer sets pen to paper and begins writing, he or she limits the options that are available for continuing the essay, and establishes a commitment to the reader concerning the subject to be discussed, the comment to be made about that subject, and the manner in which the comment will be developed. In the rest of the essay, the writer must carry out, or discharge, that commitment, and the reader must be able to observe how the commitment is being carried out; otherwise the reader will experience puzzlement and (by implication) the writer will fail of his purpose. Gorrell enumerates the ways — when identified at a high level of abstraction, the ways are few — by which a writer can move in carrying out his commitment; he identifies in general terms the kinds of steps that the writer can take, besides offering that writer some advice on how to test the effectiveness with which the successive steps are taken. Like most of the articles discussed in this section, this piece offers an analysis of some professional writing to illustrate both the commitments made by a writer and the procedures employed by the writer in discharging those commitments. Gorrell's is one of the essays a teacher might turn to for help in analyzing — and teaching — an approach to structure that even inexperienced writers should be able to adopt with profit.

IV

The preservation of form, of course, is not simply a matter of choosing a recognized pattern or working out, while inventing one's material, a plan for its presentation. The writer also has the task of welding the sections of the piece, however neatly progressive, into a coherent whole. The standard texts are full of advice on achieving coherence: build one of the key ideas from the conclusion of one part of the paper into the opening of the next part; employ recognized transitional connectives; occasionally sum up in a short transitional paragraph where the essay has been, and indicate where it next will go; and so on. There has even been an occasional study of how well-known writers connect together paragraphs in their discourse. One such study is Donald Ross, Jr.'s brief article, "Composition as a Stylistic Feature," *Style*, 4 (Winter, 1970), 1-8, in which Ross compares the reliance on connective words and repetition of key words in passages by Thoreau, Emerson, and Carlyle. (Ross's essay perhaps illustrates how one might apply the definition of "Style" offered by Young and Becker: "The characteristic route [a writer] takes through all the choices in both the writing and prewriting stages" [Steinmann, p. 104].) Ross's essay is useful, though it does not add much to our knowledge about form that the standard texts do not give us.

Few of these discussions of coherence, however, identify the kinds of relationships that connect individual ideas to each other in a fashion we might call coherent. One attempt at such identification is the essay by D. W. Cummings, John Herum, and E. K. Lybert, "Semantic Recurrence and Rhetorical Form," *Language and Style*, 4 (Summer, 1971), 195-207. The authors explore the kinds of interdependence between "postcedent" and "antecedent" sentences that make possible "good continuation" (possibly here the same as "coherence"). They review direct reference back from postcedent sentence to antecedent; they identify relationships in which an item in the postcedent is included within the same class as an item in the antecedent; and they cite instances in which a term in the postcedent is connotatively associated with a term in the antecedent. But Cummings and his associates, as they themselves admit, have just begun their work on the kinds of recurrences and cross-references that lead to coherence; their article does not deal with logical relationships among assertions.

Probably the most generally accessible short discussion of how coherence is achieved has been contributed by W. Ross Winterowd. In "The Grammar of Coherence," *CE*, 31 (May, 1970), 828-835, reprinted in his *Contemporary Rhetoric*, pp. 225-233, Winterowd offers, by analogy with the relationships according to which shorter sentences can be combined to form longer sentences, a suggested set of seven relationships by which sentences can be combined into paragraphs and — for our purpose more important — by which paragraphs and sections can be combined into essays, or chapters combined into books. The seven relationships are: coordinate, obversative, causative, conclusive, alternative, inclusive, and sequential. Winterowd does not push the discussion of these seven relationships beyond illustrating them — and arguing that they constitute techniques for generating ideas as well as for connecting them. Implied in his essay, however, as it had been asserted in Gorrell's, is the suggestion that the relationships employed — the paths of inquiry followed — need to be reasonably visible to the alert observer, and that by making the relationships visible the writer can control the movement and improve the impact of his whole discourse.

V

Winterowd's discussion of coherence leads us to our examination, occasionally anticipated earlier in this essay, of scholarship and theories about the formation, the composing, of paragraphs. It is the paragraph, far more than the total essay, to which theorists of rhetoric and writers about the teaching of composition usually give attention. Indeed,

63

scholarly and critical discussions of the paragraph since 1965 have shed far more light on their subject than have scholarly discussions about the organization of whole pieces.

The paragraph, in recent discussions, has been approached from three distinct perspectives. It has been approached, in effect, as an expanded sentence: a unit of discourse about which one can talk usefully in language comparable to that used about sentences. It has been approached as a self-contained unit of writing, with distinctive principles of structure that need to be understood and observed by all writers. And it has been approached as a subdivision in a total discourse — a unit whose length and form depend on the strategies of the writer in managing an entire piece, rather than on some rules governing what may appear in the space between one indentation and the next. We will examine briefly here the work of some proponents of these varied ways of viewing the paragraph.

This plan has the virtue of allowing us to begin with the work of Francis Christensen, whose "A Generative Rhetoric of the Paragraph," *CCC*, 16 (October, 1965), 144-156, following by exactly two years his "A Generative Rhetoric of the Sentence," initiated the flow of discussions of the paragraph in the last decade. In his earlier essay on the sentence, Christensen had said that the sentence modifiers which create what he called the "cumulative sentence" are related to the main clauses and to each other by coordination or by subordination, and he had developed a scheme for numbering these modifiers to reveal whether they are coordinate or subordinate and show for each subordinate modifier what it is subordinate to. In discussing the paragraph, Christensen applies the same procedures, calling the paragraph a "sequence of structurally related sentences," most of them related to a topic sentence or to each other by coordination or subordination, just as sentence modifiers are related to base clauses. Christensen identifies three principal kinds of paragraphs: coordinate sequences, subordinate sequences, and mixed sequences (sequences having some coordinate and some subordinate sentences), and, by numbering the sentences in sample paragraphs to show their level of subordination, he illustrates how these sequences work. It is Christensen's contention that awareness of whether a sentence is coordinate with, or subordinate to, a sentence preceding it will enable a writer to see when, if at all, his paragraph is losing coherence. Such analysis, Christensen claims, also can show when, if at all, additional sentences — coordinate or subordinate — are needed for the adequate development of the paragraph.

Christensen's recognition that sentences in paragraphs, like clauses in sentences, are related by coordination and subordination, while hardly profound, is useful. But his numbering of the levels of coordination and subordination in successive sentences is sometimes mysterious, and analyzing paragraphs by his method may do no more to generate thought on the part of a writer than the admonitions of older writers about the need for "adequate development" in a paragraph. Christensen's impact upon other theorists of the paragraph — inspiring followers and stimulating alternative views — has probably been as great as that of any theorist of composition in this generation. See, in particular, the "Symposium on the Paragraph" in *CCC*, 17 (May, 1966), 60-87.

Two followers of Christensen deserve notice, in addition to Willis Pitkin, whose work on the structure of discourse (work illustrated by analysis of paragraphs) we noted earlier. One is David Karrfalt, contributor to the "Symposium on the Paragraph," and author of a later essay entitled "The Generation of Paragraphs and Larger Units," *CCC*, 19 (October, 1968), 211-217. Karrfalt anticipated some of Pitkin's ideas by identifying paragraphs in which some sentences complete, or extend to a higher level of abstraction, the ideas in previous sentences (rather than being subordinate to — i.e., more specific and particular than — or coordinate with those sentences). Karrfalt calls this relationship of completion a "horizontal" relationship, and he also notes passages in which appear other sorts of sentences that cannot be accounted for

65

neatly by Christensen's theories. The other follower of Christensen to be noted here is Michael Grady, whose efforts to extend Christensen's view of the paragraph into a rhetoric of the whole essay were cited in reference to D'Angelo's advice about the structure of essays.

If Christensen and his followers have tried to extend their conceptual framework for the study of sentences so that it will illuminate paragraphs, other theorists, traditional and modern, treat the paragraph as a self-contained unit of composition without reference to the structure of sentences. Much of this work draws on writing about the paragraph that dates back to the time of Alexander Bain, who devised six influential rules for the construction of paragraphs. (See Paul Rodgers, Jr., "Alexander Bain and the Rise of the Organic Paragraph," *QJS*, 51 [December, 1965], 399-408, and, for an analysis of antecedents of Bain's thought, Ned A. Shearer, "Alexander Bain and the Genesis of Paragraph Theory," *QJS*, 58 [December, 1972], 408-417.) Some of the older theorists are excerpted in Virginia Burke's anthology, *The Paragraph in Context* (Indianapolis: Bobbs-Merrill, 1969), to which Burke has contributed a brief introduction sketching the history of paragraphs in English and tracing the concept of the paragraph as "a prose structure capable of organic internal arrangement." A particularly well-known exposition of these traditional views, one that has survived through several editions of his book, is in James McCrimmon's *Writing with a Purpose* (Chapter 4). McCrimmon argues that successful paragraphs should be characterized by unity, completeness, coherence, and adequacy of development; he reviews the obvious techniques (see Section IV, above) for assuring coherence in a paragraph that has the desired characteristics. He also insists, like most theorists, on the importance of the writer's including and developing a topic sentence as a way of helping to organize his ideas. (Even Christensen views the "topic sentence" as the first step in a well-ordered paragraph. But Christensen's "topic sentence" is simply the top of a sequence of related sentences — usually a more general or abstract sentence than those that follow, which are coordinate with or subordinate to the topic sentence.)

While McCrimmon's views of the characteristics needed in a paragraph are probably difficult to dispute, they tell the writer not much about how to attain these characteristics. Moreover, in an important piece of scholarship written just before his death, Richard Braddock analyzes the use of topic sentences in the writing of several professional writers and finds that the topic sentence is far less prominent in the work of these writers than texts such as McCrimmon's would lead us to suppose. Braddock concludes: "Teachers and textbook writers should exercise caution in making statements about the frequency with which contemporary professional writers use simple or even explicit topic sentences in expository paragraphs. It is abundantly clear that students should not be told that professional writers usually begin their paragraphs with topic sentences. . . . While helping students use clear topic sentences in their writing and identify variously presented topical ideas in their reading, the teacher should not pretend that professional writers largely follow the practices he is advocating" ("The Frequency and Placement of Topic Sentences in Expository Prose," *RTE*, 8 [Winter, 1974], 287-302).

Instead of sketching a profile of a well-constructed organic paragraph, Richard Young and Alton Becker at the University of Michigan, following out some of the implications of their tagmemic approaches to grammatical description, attempt through analysis of professional writing to discern recurrent patterns in the arranging of sentences into paragraphs that might be noted by writers interested in assuring that the structure of their paragraphs is regularly clear. Young and Becker identify a number of such patterns, among the most prominent being what they call TRI (Topic-Restriction-Illustration) and PSTRI (Problem-Solution-Topic-Restriction-Illustration). (See Alton Becker, "A Tagmemic Approach to Paragraph Analysis," *CCC* [December, 1965],

237-242, or Young and Becker's essay, "Toward a Modern Theory of Rhetoric," previously cited. For a useful, brief introduction to tagmemic theory that may help toward an understanding of the conceptual background of these articles, see Kenneth L. Pike, "A Linguistic Contribution to Composition," *CCC*, 15 [May, 1964], 82-88.) Young and Becker, like Winterowd, are exploring the applicability of grammatical theories to structures beyond the sentence; thus far, these explorations have not paid off richly for any theorist, but they may furnish sources for the next important theoretical statements we receive about the paragraph.

Also viewing the paragraph as a self-contained unit, but not seeking to discover recurrent patterns, Richard Larson, in an essay that predates by several years his discussion of "linear rhetoric," views the paragraph as a succession of sentences each of which performs an identifiable and separate action for the writer ("Sentences in Action: A Technique for Analyzing Paragraphs," *CCC*, 18 [February, 1967], 16-22). Arguing that an utterance is not only a locution conforming to rules of grammar, but an action performed in the service of some purpose, Larson lists a number of actions that a sentence can perform within a paragraph, and analyzes a number of paragraphs to reveal the successive actions performed by individual sentences. This procedure does not yield a heuristic for composing a paragraph, any more than the identification of possible linear plans yields a heuristic for designing an essay. What such analysis can do is disclose the options open to the writer as he moves sentence by sentence, and encourage the writer to think about which of these possible actions he wishes to perform at each step in the paragraph, and why. This method of analysis is also useful for the evaluation of paragraphs, since the role played by each sentence in the paragraph must be evident to the reader if that paragraph is to be fully understood. If the role of a given sentence is unclear, the paragraph loses force and coherence at that point, just as in Christensen's method of analysis a sentence that is not clearly coordinate or subordinate to a sentence above it signals a break in coherence and a failure of design in the paragraph.

What of the view that the paragraph should be treated as a subdivision of the total discourse of which it is a part? Except for isolated early glances (such as that by E. H. Lewis — p. 17 in Burke) and modern suggestions (such as those of Winterowd and Young and Becker — whose analyses of the subject are not fully developed), studies of the paragraph in the perspective of the whole discourse have been infrequent. The most important of the studies which have appeared is that by Paul Rodgers, Jr.: "A Discourse-Centered Rhetoric of the Paragraph," *CCC*, 17 (February, 1966), 2-11. Rodgers argues that to view the paragraph as a self-contained unit leads to incomplete vision, because many considerations — of tone, of emphasis, of appearance on the printed page, to name a few — affect the length and shape of professional writers' paragraphs. He further argues that in fact professional writers punctuate their discourse into paragraphs as part of their efforts to achieve the desired total effect in their pieces, not in conformity to predetermined rules for the construction of paragraphs. The essence of Rodgers' argument is given in this passage:

> Paragraph structure is part and parcel of the structure of the discourse as a whole; a given [unit of discourse] becomes a paragraph not by virtue of its structure but because the writer elects to indent, his indentation functioning, as does all punctuation, as a gloss upon the overall literary process under way at that point. Paragraphs are not composed; they are discovered. To compose is to create, to indent is to interpret. (p. 6)

Rodgers supports his contentions with an analysis of an essay ("Style") by Walter Pater, showing that ordinary observations about paragraphing will not explain how Pater paragraphed his essay, because Pater sought special effects of tone and emphasis in the division of his discourse. Rodgers' study is distinctive and important; if heeded, it might discourage teachers from assigning and grading paragraphs as separate units, and encourage them instead to help students plan and compose complete pieces of writing, in that process deciding how they want to divide their essays in order to achieve a desired effect. Rodgers implies that students might be asked in their assignments to write papers, rather than paragraphs. Rodgers is in no way arguing that paragraphs, as finally presented to the reader, should lack structure, or that other theorists' methods of analyzing the structure of paragraphs will not work. He says, instead, that paragraphs collaborate, and that for the practicing writer what is done in one paragraph may depend significantly on what is happening on either side of that paragraph, or elsewhere in the discourse. Decisions about how one paragraph will finally appear, he implies, should take that interdependence into account. (See also Rodgers' contribution — pp. 72-80 — to the "Symposium on the Paragraph," previously cited, and his article, "The Stadium of Discourse," *CCC*, 18 [October, 1967], 178-185.) In this connection we can note a small bit of research by Young and Becker which implies that readers can spot reasonable ways in which to break a discourse into paragraphs. It must be, suggest Young and Becker, that there are in any discourse semantic clues that a reader can pick up to show when one sequence of thought has been terminated and another begun, because in experimental tests readers have shown that they could agree on the placing of most paragraph breaks in passages typed without any paragraph indentations. (The experiments are cited briefly in "Toward a Modern Theory of Rhetoric," Steinmann, p. 100.) This work of Young and Becker further encourages studies that may show how the structure of paragraphs and the structure of a whole piece interact. These studies, too, if carried on may enlarge our understanding of structure and planning in discourse.

Much important work on form and structure in units of discourse beyond the sentence, then, remains to be done.

The array of critical and pedagogical pieces on these topics to date highlights problems and uncertainties, but provides few of the kinds of insights recently offered, for example, to students interested in heuristics for the discovery of ideas and to students seeking rhetorical applications of knowledge about grammar. We have, in studies of form, largely a record of search for formulas and patterns in discourse, and a record of advice on the properties that well-ordered discourse ought, in the *a priori* judgment of theorists, to exhibit. But the reasons for the effectiveness of different patterns, the ways in which their parts interact, the most useful techniques of deciding upon particular sequences of steps in composing — in short, many of the fundamental topics one has to address in choosing a form for a composition — have been dealt with slightly, hesitantly, or not at all.

The gap is serious, because, as James Coomber points out, many students do not grasp the structure or the main ideas in materials they read, and that inability may be connected to weaknesses in the organization of students' writing ("Perceiving the Structure of Written Materials," *RTE*, 9 [Winter, 1975], 263-266). We need investigations of structure and form in prose to help us with the teaching of reading as well as writing.

Confronting the dearth of knowledge about form, the teacher might wisely exercise caution. Instead of talking about "good organization" in the abstract, or advocating one plan of organization in preference to all others, the teacher should recognize the interconnections of form and content, and help students quietly in the subtle and personal task of choosing a form that suits well their ideas and emphases. Since reliable criteria for such choosing are not available, flexibility and sensitivity to the values of different structures are attitudes to cultivate. Form may not *be* the message, but it interprets the message while relaying it. And we all need, basing our best judgment on sensitive reading of our drafts or finished essays, to consider *how* our message is relayed and interpreted through its form.

71

APPROACHES TO THE STUDY OF STYLE

EDWARD P. J. CORBETT

Ohio State University

STYLE HAS BEEN A CONCERN of rhetoricians from the beginning of rhetoric in fifth-century Athens. During the long history of rhetoric, the concern for style has had its ups and downs. There were rhetoric texts preoccupied almost exclusively with style; there were periods, on the other hand, when the emphasis shifted so heavily toward *res* that the study of *verba* was neglected and even deplored. But the fascination with the stylistic aspects of discourse never really died; it faded at times, but it invariably revived. Today, stylistic study is the most advanced and flourishing area of the so-called "new rhetoric." Evidence of the prosperous state of stylistic study is everywhere to be found. In addition to the growing number of articles on style in our professional journals, we now have two journals devoted exclusively to articles on style: *Style*, founded in 1967, and *Language and Style*, founded in 1968. Evidence of the sheer volume of work on style can be found in the Annual Bibliography on Style appearing each year in *Style*. The Annual Bibliography for 1972, for instance, covered 153 pages in the Winter 1974 issue of *Style*. A peek at recent issues of *Dissertation Abstracts* reveals the great number of graduate students who have turned, for the subjects of their dissertations, to the many unplowed fields of style.

Two factors that have contributed significantly to the flourishing stylistic scene are the computer and linguistics. It took a long time for us humanists to overcome our antipathy for electronic hardware and to recognize it as a helpful tool for literary studies. The production of computer-assisted concordances and word-lists probably first led humanists to recognize that what the computer had to offer was relief from the tedium of manual tabulating and the means of achieving accuracy, objectivity, and completeness of data. For many years what hampered the development of descriptive studies of style, comparable to descriptive studies of grammar, was simply that, aside from the statistical information about sentence length and paragraph length compiled by such assiduous counters as Edwin Lewis and Lucius Sherman in the last decade of the nineteenth century, there was a dearth of raw data about stylistic features available to scholars. But thanks to the help of the computer, we now have valuable banks of information about the style of literary texts, such as Sally Sedelow's work on Milton's *Paradise Lost*, and about the style of workaday prose, like the corpus of over a million words that Henry Kucera and W. Nelson Francis drew from 500 samples of pedestrian American prose in 1967 (see their *Computational Analysis of Present-Day American English* [Providence, R.I.: Brown University Press, 1970]).

The computer will continue to facilitate the production of additional concordances and of attribution studies, like those of Alvar Ellegard on the Junius letters and of Frederick Mosteller and David L. Wallace on the Federalist Papers, and of further stylistic studies of literary prose, like Louis Milic's *A Quantitative Approach to the Style of Jonathan Swift* (The Hague: Mouton, 1967). Fortunately, we humanists do not have to be computer experts to be able to make use of the computer. We have to gain just enough elementary knowledge about computers to be aware of the kinds of information a computer can spit out and to be able to explain fully and clearly to a programmer what kind of information we want to gather. As a good basic article on the capabilities of the computer for stylistic studies, I would recommend Robert S. Wachal's "On Using a Computer" in *The Computer and Literary Style*, ed. Jacob Leed (Kent, Ohio: Kent State University Press, 1966), pp. 14-37.

If the contribution of modern linguistics to stylistics is not obvious to you, it will be obvious before this bibliographical survey reaches its conclusion. A convenient summary of the contributions that various linguistic schools have made to stylistic studies can be found in Nils Erik Enkvist's "On the Place of Style in Some Linguistic Theories" in *Literary Style: A Symposium*, ed. Seymour Chatman (New York: Oxford University Press, 1971) and in Julie Carson's article "Proper Stylistics" in the Spring 1974 issue of *Style*. Ms. Carson regards Archibald Hill, Samuel R. Levin, and Richard Ohmann as the most representative of the linguist-analysts in America. As she says, "Hill came to stylistics as a structuralist; Ohmann, as a transformationalist. And Levin got caught in the crossfire." Enkvist maintains that although traditional grammar was "amorphous and flexible enough to swallow stylistic considerations *ad libitum*," the study of style was "on the whole, a marginal, rather than a central pursuit" of both structural and transformational grammarians. Nevertheless, Enkvist recognizes some valuable contributions to stylistic studies in the works of such structuralists as Zellig Harris, Bernard Bloch, Kenneth Pike, Martin Joos, and Archibald Hill, and largely because of the work of Richard Ohmann, he is disposed to regard transformational grammar as the most promising of the linguistic systems for stylistic studies. "If style is choice," says Enkvist, "then transformational grammar is, I take it, the grammatical model that so far most fully maps out the system and range of this choice."

This essay will also discuss some of the contributions that speech-act theory is making to stylistic studies and that various theories of conceptual rhetoric are likely to make to the analysis of linguistic units larger than the sentence. What we are witnessing in the studies of inter-sentence relationships and of larger units than the sentence is a movement toward holistic criticism, a truly rhetorical kind of criticism that relates the syntagmatic and paradigmatic features of a text not only to the dynamics of the whole text but also to the author, the audience, and the universe of discourse. If this movement toward a holistic kind of analysis continues, the apprehensions that some literary critics have about the limitations of purely linguistic analysis may be allayed. Those apprehensions were well summarized by Elias Schwartz in "Notes on Linguistics and Literature," *College English*, 32 (November, 1970), 190:

> What distinguishes the language of literature is not some inherent feature, but its function in relation to the whole of which it is a part. This function is not marked in the language so used; it inheres rather in the relation of that language to the total structure of the poem, a structure which is aesthetic, not linguistic. There is no such thing as a distinctive literary language. And if this is true, though linguists tell us a great deal about language, they can tell us nothing about literature.

The linguist is equipped by training to describe and analyze the linguistic structures in a text and to classify the patterns of those structures, but he is not especially equipped by his training to utilize the data that he discovers and identifies in the critical interpretation of the whole text. For that reason, the current feeling is that the student of style will have to combine the expertise of the linguist, the rhetorician, and the literary critic.

Given the current state and the great volume of stylistic studies, I despaired of being able to adequately survey, in a relatively short essay, the literature on style. Even to touch on the most important books and articles on style is too vast a project. Clearly, I would have to carve out an even smaller section than that from the vast acreage. What might be manageable would be for me to concentrate on those books and articles that would, in my judgment, be most useful and usable to teachers of composition who might want to engage their students in a stylistic study of English prose on a fairly elementary level. That focus would exclude from the survey the highly technical literature in stylistics and most of the stylistic studies of belletristic texts. Even within those parameters, my choices of the books and articles to talk about would have to be arbitrary, and I suspect that ten minutes after this essay has been finally locked into print, I will think of half a dozen books or articles that should have been mentioned. But who of us is not liable to fallibility of judgment and myopia of vision?

I have grouped my selections under the headings Collections, Bibliography, History, Theory, and Methodology and Application. I sometimes had difficulty settling on a category for a particular entry. A basically theoretical article, for instance, sometimes slid over into methodology and application. I finally had to adopt the joint category of Methodology and Application, rather than a separate section for each, because most of the authors who started out by talking about methodology eventually exemplified the method by applying it to an analysis of a particular text. The numbers enclosed in brackets after some of the items mentioned in the essay indicate that the item is reprinted in one or more of the collections that will be discussed in the next section (see the appendix for the numbers assigned to these collections).

Collections

The available anthologies of articles on style fall into two general classes: those that reprint papers delivered at a single conference and those that reprint pieces that were previously published in journals or books. Some of the latter kind are not given over wholly to articles on style; only a section of the anthology presents articles on style.

There are two anthologies which present papers delivered at international conferences on style. The first of these, published in 1960 by the M.I.T. Press, is *Style in Language*, edited by Thomas A. Sebeok. Under eight distinct headings representing the three main viewpoints of linguistics, psychology, and literary criticism, this collection reprints twenty-six papers (six of them only in abstract) delivered at the 1958 conference on style held at Indiana University in Bloomington. Comments by the participants are reproduced at the end of each section, and an extensive bibliography is given on pp. 435-449. *Literary Style: A Symposium*, ed. Seymour Chatman (New York: Oxford University Press, 1971) reproduces the twenty-one papers delivered at a symposium on style that took place in Bellagio, Italy, in August of 1969. Some of the most distinguished stylisticians from America, England, and Continental Europe participated in this conference. Seymour Chatman presents his summary of the subsequent discussions of most of the papers immediately after the printed version of the paper. Of these two collections, I think teachers of composition would find more useful articles in the Chatman anthology.

In 1967, Houghton Mifflin published a distinguished collection of previously published articles on style, under the title *Essays on the Language of Literature*, ed. Seymour Chatman and Samuel R. Levin. The thirty-one essays in this collection are grouped under five headings: Sound Texture (4 articles); Metrics (6 articles); Grammar (6 articles); Literary Form and Meaning (7 articles); Style and Stylistics (8 articles). Although most of the articles in this collection treat of style as it applies to belletristic texts, teachers of composition will find at least ten of the articles useful for their purposes. This is the only anthology that reprints the two often-cited articles by Michael Riffaterre that will be discussed later on.

Glen A. Love and Michael Payne in their collection *Contemporary Essays on Style: Rhetoric, Linguistics, and Criticism* (Glenview, Ill.: Scott, Foresman, 1969) reprint twenty-five articles under the three headings indicated in the sub-title. If I were asked to recommend one anthology that would be most suitable for an introductory course on style on the undergraduate or graduate level, I would nominate the Love-Payne collection. It is the one that I first send my students to when they express an interest in the study of style.

Essays in Stylistic Analysis, ed. Howard S. Babb (New York: Harcourt Brace Jovanovich, 1972) reprints twenty-one essays, including some of the classic essays by Richard Ohmann, Morris Croll, and Josephine Miles. Professor Babb's wife has translated the three essays that were written in German and has also translated the passages in French and Latin in the essays by Croll and Riffaterre.

Donald C. Freeman has reprinted twenty-three essays in his collection *Linguistics and Literary Style* (New York: Holt, Rinehart, and Winston, 1970). The five essays appearing in the fourth section, Approaches to Prose Style, would be the ones most useful to the teacher of composition.

The anthologies in the next group have an historical bent. This orientation is reflected in the title of the collection that James R. Bennett, the editor of *Style*, put together in 1971 — *Prose Style: A Historical Approach Through Studies* (San Francisco: Chandler, 1971). Starting out with three essays that deal with the Continuity of the Sentence and the Paragraph, Bennett arranges the remaining articles according to the period they deal with: II. The Old English and Middle English Periods; III. The Renaissance Period; IV. The Restoration and the Eighteenth Century; V. The Nineteenth and Twentieth Centuries. Each section carries Suggestions for Research, and sections III, IV, and V present Selections for Analysis. One of the most valuable features of this diachronic collection of essays is the Annotated Bibliography on pp. 253-280.

Louis T. Milic's *Stylists on Style: A Handbook with Selections for Analysis* (New York: Scribner's, 1969) also has an historical range, but the fifty-seven short selections in which various authors present their views on style are arranged in reverse chronological order, from Robert Graves in 1961 to Caxton in 1490. The second part of this collection presents forty-three selections for analysis from British and American authors. In the second edition of his *Modern Essays on Writing and Style* (New York: Holt, Rinehart, and Winston, 1969), Paul C. Wermuth presents thirty essays on style and

79

writing by contemporary authors, but the forty Sample Passages for Analysis and Discussion represent an historical range. In his *Style in English Prose* (New York: Macmillan, 1968), Carl H. Klaus traces the development of prose style in his introductory essay "Reflections on Prose Style" (pp. 1-14), but the rest of the collection merely reprints short selections for analysis. Perhaps the most inexpensive of the historically-oriented anthologies is the 288-page *The Problem of Style* (Greenwich, Connecticut: Fawcett Publications, 1966), which was compiled by J. V. Cunningham. This 95-cent anthology carries thirty-five essays by such writers on style as Aristotle, Cicero, Longinus, Eric Auerbach, Morris Croll, René Wellek, Austin Warren, James Sledd, Frank Sullivan, and J. V. Cunningham himself.

The following anthologies have only a section of them devoted to style, but although they reprint considerably fewer essays on style than the anthologies devoted exclusively to style, the essays they do present are all pertinent to the composition classroom. In their *Teaching Freshman Composition* (New York: Oxford University Press, 1967), Gary Tate and Edward P. J. Corbett present five essays on style and two short bibliographies on style by James R. Bennett and Paul C. Doherty. In their later anthology, *Teaching High School Composition* (New York: Oxford University Press, 1970), they reproduce only three essays in the section on style, but they reprint Francis Christensen's "A Generative Rhetoric of the Sentence" and Bennett's annotated bibliography in two other sections of the book. In the section on style in his *New Rhetorics* (New York: Scribner's, 1967), Martin Steinmann, Jr. reproduces five of the oft-reprinted essays on style. In the most recent collection, *Contemporary Rhetoric: A Conceptual Background with Readings* (New York: Harcourt Brace Jovanovich, 1975), W. Ross Winterowd presents his own introductory essay on style (pp. 253-270) and seven previously published essays on style.

The value of collections like these is that they bring together a number of carefully selected pieces from widely scattered and sometimes inaccessible sources. Consequently, the teacher can add a number of these anthologies to his personal library and has available an ample body of material, in relatively inexpensive volumes, that he can prescribe as texts for a course he wants to teach. As recently as ten years ago, a teacher who wanted to teach a course in style would have had to send his students to bound periodicals in the library or to make xerox copies of the articles he wanted the students to read.

Bibliography

Not much needs to be said about the bibliographies of style. It will suffice to list them and say something about their scope, if their titles do not indicate their province. They fall into two general classes: selective listings published either as articles or as parts of books and book-length listings.

Four of the selective listings were mentioned in the previous section: (1) Thomas A. Sebeok's "Bibliography" in *Style in Language* (Cambridge, Mass.: M.I.T. Press, 1960), pp. 435-449; (2) James R. Bennett's "Annotated Bibliography" in *Prose Style: A Historical Approach Through Studies* (San Francisco: Chandler, 1971), pp. 253-280; (3) James R. Bennett, "An Annotated Bibliography of Selected Writings on English Prose Style," *CCC*, 16 (December, 1965), 248-255 [12, 13]; (4) Paul C. Doherty, "Stylistics — A Bibliographical Survey," *The CEA Critic*, 28 (May, 1966), 1, 3-4 [4, 12]. Doherty prefaces his list of forty-four items with a brief essay in which he discusses the two main schools of stylistic studies — the "normative" and the "individual," to use his terms.

To these alphabetical listings of selected books and articles can be added Josephine Miles's extensive bibliography at the end of her book *Style and Proportion: The Language of Prose and Poetry* (Boston: Little, Brown, 1967), pp. 164-212; R. C. Alston's "Rhetoric and Style: A Bibliographical Guide," *Leeds Studies in English*, New Series, 1 (1967),

137-159; James R. Bennett's, "Stylistic Domains: A Checklist," *Symposium in Rhetoric*, ed. J. Dean Bishop, Turner S. Kobler, and William E. Tanner (Denton, Texas: Texas Woman's University, 1975), pp. 18-24. The later the date of these selective bibliographies, the greater the chance that more recent stylistic studies are included in the listing.

Helmut Hatzfeld's *A Critical Bibliography of the New Stylistics Applied to Romance Literatures, 1900-1952* (Chapel Hill: University of North Carolina Press, 1953) was the first of the book-length bibliographies of style. But although this compilation carries some 2000 items, most of the entries, as the title indicates, deal with literary texts written in the Romance languages. We now have two other book-length bibliographies. The first of these and the one that would probably be most useful to teachers of composition is *Style and Stylistics: An Analytical Bibliography* (New York: Free Press, 1967) compiled by Louis T. Milic. Milic lists the more than 800 items in his bibliography under five categories: I. Theoretical; II. Methodological; III. Applied (i.e., studies of particular authors, works, periods, etc.); IV. Bibliographies (separate bibliographies and bibliographies that are parts of other works); V. Omnibus (reference works and collections of essays on style). Three handy indexes aid the student of style in finding a particular item or a particular class of items: Authors as Contributors, Authors as Subjects, Subjects and Topics.

English Stylistics: A Bibliography, compiled by Richard W. Bailey and Sister Dolores M. Burton (Cambridge, Mass.: M.I.T. Press, 1968), is comparable in its comprehensiveness to Hatzfeld's bibliography of stylistic studies in the Romance languages. Its more than 2000 items are divided into three parts: I. A list of bibliographical sources (28 items); II. Language and Style Before 1900 (pp. 5-46); III. English Stylistics in the Twentieth Century (pp. 47-173). Sister Dolores, who compiled the bibliography in Part II, subdivided her area into five periods: Classical, Medieval, Renaissance, Neoclassic, and Nineteenth Century. In a prefatory section,

Bailey provides a useful survey of modern stylistic activity and organizes his bibliography in Part III under topical headings.

For a year-by-year updating of these published bibliographies, Richard W. Bailey has been compiling the Annual Bibliography on Style that appears each year in the journal *Style*, which is published at the University of Arkansas and edited by James R. Bennett. The number of stylistic studies published in the last fifteen years is staggering.

History

As with most subjects, the study or the teaching of style can be enhanced by some acquaintance with the history of style. Most of the important studies of the history of style have appeared in books, but, as will be seen, treatments of a particular kind or period of prose style have also appeared in articles.

One of the earliest book-length treatments of English prose was George Philip Krapp's *The Rise of English Literary Prose* (New York: Oxford University Press, 1915), which traced the development of literary prose from Wyclif to Bacon. In *The Continuity of English Prose from Alfred to More and His School* (London: Oxford University Press, 1932), R. W. Chambers traced it back even further, to Alfred, and then forward through Aelfric to Thomas More. It is generally agreed, however, that the really pioneering studies of English prose style appeared in the series of essays that Morris W. Croll wrote in the 1920's to demonstrate his thesis that the development of "Attic Prose" and the Baroque Style represented a reaction to the development of "Ciceronian" prose style in the seventeenth century. Nine of Croll's essays, including "The Baroque Style in Prose," "'Attic Prose' in the Seventeenth Century," "Muret and the History of 'Attic Prose,'" and "Attic Prose: Lipsius, Montaigne, Bacon" have been conveniently gathered together in *Style, Rhetoric, and Rhythm: Essays by Morris W. Croll*, ed. J. Max

Patrick and Robert O. Evans, with John M. Wallace and R. J. Schoeck (Princeton, N. J.: Princeton University Press, 1966). George Williamson, in his *The Senecan Amble: A Study in Prose Form from Bacon to Collier* (Chicago: University of Chicago Press, 1951), revealed himself to be a Crollian. The thesis that he argues in a book notable for its turgid prose style but sound scholarship is that the dominant prose style of the seventeenth century was modelled on the "Senecan Amble," a term that the Earl of Shaftesbury used to describe the kind of curt, easy, succinct prose style that developed as part of the anti-Ciceronian movement and that helped to establish many of the characteristics of modern prose style.

Croll's views are not as sacrosanct as they once were. They first were attacked by R. F. Jones, who in articles like "Science and English Prose Style in the Third Quarter of the Seventeenth Century," *PMLA*, 45 (1930), 977-1009 and "Science and Language in England of the Mid-Seventeenth Century," *JEGP*, 31 (1932), 315-331, argued that it was the new Baconian science that influenced the development of English prose style. Croll's thesis is further challenged in the latest book-length treatment of the evolution of prose style, Robert Adolph's *The Rise of Modern Prose Style* (Cambridge, Mass.: M.I.T. Press, 1968). "Although my position," Adolph says, "is clearly closer to Jones than to Croll, the evidence suggests strongly that the ultimate influence on the new prose is neither 'science' nor 'Anti-Ciceronianism' but the new utilitarianism around which the values of the age are integrated."

Three of the more recent books on prose style are not so much historical treatments as they are analytical attempts to classify distinct types of prose style. In *Prose Styles: Five Primary Types* (Minneapolis: University of Minnesota Press, 1966), Huntington Brown distinguishes and exemplifies five types, which he labels the deliberative, the expository, the tumbling, the prophetic, and the indenture. In *Tough, Sweet, and Stuffy: An Essay on Modern American*

Style (Bloomington: Indiana University Press, 1966) — a book that will be discussed below in another connection — Walker Gibson classifies three distinct styles which he regards as being reflections of the *ethos* of the writers. One of the best and most convincing book-length treatments of the development of a single kind of prose style is Richard Bridgman's *The Colloquial Style in America* (New York: Oxford University Press, 1966). Bridgman makes a good case for his thesis that Henry James, Mark Twain, Gertrude Stein, and Ernest Hemingway were the authors mainly responsible for the development of a truly colloquial prose style in America.

Theory

Although a number of promising methodologies have been developed, we still lack a fully developed, coherent theory of style. The closest we have come to a poetics of style is perhaps Longinus's *On the Sublime*, but the theory presented in that noted treatise deals with only one variety of style — the style that "transports" listeners or readers — and a great number of components of style are not dealt with at all. The kind of metatheory of style that I have in mind is exemplified in Louis Milic's article "Rhetorical Choice and Stylistic Options: The Conscious and Unconscious Poles" in *Literary Style: A Symposium*, ed. Seymour Chatman (New York: Oxford University Press, 1971), pp. 77-88. In that article, Milic makes a distinction between *stylistic options*, those choices we make unconsciously and habitually about lexicon and syntax while in the act of writing, and *rhetorical choices*, those decisions we make consciously and deliberately when we review and evaluate what we have generated. It is Milic's contention that "stylistic options taken together are the style of the writer and represent the primary field of inquiry for the analyst of style." "Where I differ from most investigators," he says, "is in the conviction that they have erroneously treated all decisions constituting style as conscious rhetorical choices, representing the realization of artistic intentions or that they have mingled together habitual and artistic considerations." Accordingly, in his own book *A Quantitative Approach to the Style of Jonathan Swift* (The Hague: Mouton, 1967), Milic concentrates on the recurring stylistic features that he found in a large corpus of Swift's prose.

It is that kind of theory of style, with its implications for stylistic analysis, that has not yet been developed on a comprehensive scale. But I will review here some of the philosophical or linguistic orientations of stylisticians that might some day be incorporated into a comprehensive theory of style.

A number of Louis Milic's many articles on style have dealt with his objections to the usual bases for arriving at a typology of style, as in his "Against the Typology of Styles," in *Essays in the Language of Literature*, ed. Seymour Chatman and Samuel R. Levin (Boston: Houghton Mifflin, 1967), pp. 425-450 [3, 4], or with his attempts to classify the metaphysical underpinnings of the various schools of stylistic criticism, as in "The Problem of Style," a chapter in his *A Quantitative Approach to the Style of Jonathan Swift*, pp. 40-73 [15]. An article of the latter sort, which should be of special interest to the teacher of composition, is Milic's article "Theories of Style and Their Implications for the Teaching of Composition," *CCC*, 16 (May, 1965), 66-69, 126 [4, 12]. In this article, he posits three basic theories of style:

(1) The theory of ornate form or rhetorical dualism (the theory that claims a separate existence for form and content — "ideas exist wordlessly and can be dressed in a variety of outfits").
(2) The individualist or psychological monism ("style is the man").
(3) The organic theory, the Crocean aesthetic monism, which denies the possibility of any separation of content and form.

Milic contends that acceptance of the second or third of these theories leaves little for the composition teacher to do. If "style is the man," all we can do is urge the student to express himself naturally and not tamper with his style at all; if form is inseparable from meaning, then we cannot encourage our students to consider alternative or synonymous ways of saying something, because a change in the form results inevitably in a change of meaning. Although the dualistic view has its shortcomings, especially in its potential implication that style is merely the dress of thought, it is, Milic contends, the only one among the three basic theories that justifies a teacher's efforts to help his students improve their style. "In the college composition course," Milic says, "which represents for most students their first formal training in rhetoric, an awareness must be instilled of the existence of alternatives, of different ways of saying the same thing, of the options that the language offers."

A good example of the organic or Crocean view of the inseparability of style and meaning is found in Monroe E. Beardsley's frequently reprinted "Style and Good Style," which first appeared in *Reflections on High School English: NDEA Institute Lectures 1965*, ed. Gary Tate (Tulsa, Oklahoma: University of Tulsa, 1966), pp. 91-105 [4, 13, 14]. Beardsley clearly lines up on the side of the organicist view of style: "My argument is that a difference of style is always a difference in meaning — though implicit — and an important and notable difference of style is always a sizable difference in meaning. . . . Style is nothing but meaning. . . . Good style is logical congruity of explicit and implicit meaning." One of the consequences of this view is that "if a teacher advises a change of words or of word order, he is recommending a different meaning. And if he says one stylistic feature is better than another, he is saying that it is better to mean one thing rather than another." From this philosophical standpoint, Beardsley takes issue with many of the stylistic pronouncements in William Strunk and E. B. White's widely-used text *The Elements of Style* (New York: Macmillan, 1959).

87

In his earliest article on style, "Prolegomena to the Analysis of Prose Style" in *Style in Prose Fiction: English Institute Essays*, ed. Harold C. Martin (New York: Columbia University Press, 1959), pp. 1-24 [3, 4, 5], Richard Ohmann registered his dissatisfaction with this organicist view of style: "The [organicist] critic can talk about what the writer says, but talk about style he cannot, for his neat identity — one thought, one form — allows no margin for individual variation, which is what we ordinarily mean by style." Ohmann found that I. A. Richards's notion of "forms of thought" ["I see the tiger," "I kick the tiger"], as presented in *Interpretation in Teaching*, represented a happy compromise between dualism and monism, because it left form and content "neither quite joined nor totally separated." Ohmann adopted the view of style as *epistemic choice* ("a writer's method of dissecting the universe as expressed by the infinite number of choices he makes"), a view that resides somewhere in between the dualistic school and the style-is-the-man school. "If the critic," Ohmann says, "is able to isolate and examine the most primitive choices which lie behind a work of prose, they can reveal to him the very roots of a writer's epistemology." It was this theory of style as epistemic choice that informed Ohmann's study of George Bernard Shaw's style, *Shaw, the Style and the Man* (Middleton, Conn.: Wesleyan University Press, 1962).

Another influential early article by Ohmann was his "Generative Grammars and the Concept of Literary Style," *Word*, 20 (December, 1964), 423-439 [4, 6, 12, 14]. At the beginning of this article, Ohmann outlined twelve different kinds of stylistic studies and claimed that none of them could yield "a full and convincing explication of the notion of style" because they lacked "an appropriate underlying linguistic and semantic theory." It was in this article that Ohmann espoused transformational grammar as the most promising linguistic theory for stylistic study, mainly because it gets at the "syntactic component" in style and at the "alternativeness" among constructions. His analyses in this article of short passages from Faulkner, Hemingway, James, and Lawrence presaged some of the stylistic analyses that will be reviewed in the next section of this essay.

Two important articles by Michael Riffaterre laid the theoretical groundwork for the development of a methodology of style analysis: "Criteria for Style Analysis," *Word*, 15 (1959), 154-174 [3] and "Stylistic Context," *Word*, 16 (1960), 207-218 [3]. Riffaterre's intention was to make stylistics as much of a science as possible by devising a heuristic that would permit objective determination of the linguistic facts of a text. Seeing style as a departure from a linguistic norm, he proposed to make use of an "average reader" as an informant to identify a convergence or cluster of "stylistic devices" (those unpredictable, contrasting linguistic elements in a text) and to replace the overall linguistic norm with "stylistic context" as a norm. The notion of "stylistic context" was the novel element in Riffaterre's theory. In the 1959 article, he defined the stylistic context as "a linguistic pattern suddenly broken by an element which was unpredictable"; "the contrast resulting from this interference," he went on to say, "is the stylistic stimulus." In the 1960 article, he refined his definition of context and differentiated between an interior context (the context that creates the opposition constituting the stylistic device) and an exterior or macrocontext (the context that modifies this opposition by reinforcing or weakening it).

In "On Defining Style," *Linguistics and Style*, ed. John Spencer (New York: Oxford University Press, 1964), pp. 3-56 [4, 9], Nils Erik Enkvist, a professor of English Language and Literature in Finland, picks up on this notion of context. "Style," he says, "is concerned with frequencies of linguistic items in a given context, and thus with contextual probabilities. To measure the style of a passage the frequencies of its linguistic items of different levels must be compared with the corresponding features in another text or corpus which is regarded as a norm and which has a definite contextual relationship with this passage." Enkvist too differentiates between two kinds of context: a textual context (phonetic, phonemic, morphemic, syntactic, lexical, and compositional elements) and an extra-textual context (period, type of speech, literary genre, speaker/writer, listener/reader, situation and environment, etc.). "The aim of stylistic analysis," he says, "is the inventory of style markers [those linguistic items that only appear in one group of contexts] and a statement of their contextual spread."

In his headnote to the section on style in *Contemporary Rhetoric: A Conceptual Background with Readings* (New York: Harcourt Brace Jovanovich, 1975), pp. 253-270 [15], W. Ross Winterowd divides his own discussion of style into two parts: *pedagogical stylistics* ("teaching students to develop style") and *theoretical stylistics* ("concerned with theory, definitions, place of style in literary studies"). In his discussion of the prevailing theories of style, Winterowd questions the concept of style as choice. He observes that transformationalists speak of "obligatory transformations" and "non-obligatory transformations" and concedes that we might call the latter "stylistic transformations." But a complication is introduced by Charles Fillmore's notions of case and modality (see Charles J. Fillmore, "The Case for Case," in *Universals in Linguistic Theory*, ed. Emmon Bach and Robert T. Harms [New York: Holt, Rinehart, and Winston, 1968]). From the point of view of case grammar, *all* transformations are obligatory, and if so, the element of choice would be eliminated. Winterowd asks then, "What is it that we describe when we study style?" Like others, he sees transformational grammar as providing the best framework for the analysis of style, but in formulating his own schema of what we look at when we study style, he turns to speech-act theory as propounded by J. L. Austin in *How To Do Things with Words* (Cambridge, Mass.: Harvard University Press, 1962) and by John Searle in *Speech Acts* (Cambridge, England: Cambridge University Press, 1969). Searle divides Austin's *locutionary act* into two parts: the *utterance act* (the act of uttering strings of words) and the *propositional act* (consisting of referring [the subject] and predicating [the verb]). Positing that all aspects of the locutionary act can be subsumed under *transformations*, *lexicon*, and *figures of thought* (tropes such as metaphor, irony, and litotes rather than schemes like chiasmus, asyndeton, or alliteration, which would be studied under *transformations*), Winterowd proposes this schema of the proper objects of stylistic study:

Transformations

Intersentence
   Embedding
   Subordinating
   Conjunction
Intrasentence
   (units larger than the sentence, like the paragraph)

Lexicon

Parts of speech
   (content words, like nouns, verbs, etc.)
Structure words
   (conjunctions, prepositions)

Figures of Thought

Those figures which involve a shift in normal meaning

It is significant that Richard Ohmann, who has written extensively on style as epistemic choice and on the usefulness of transformational grammar for the analysis of style, has also in recent years been turning to speech-act theory for another basis of stylistic analysis. He has published at least three articles in which he points out the rhetorical and stylistic dimensions of speech-act theory: "Speech Acts and the Definition of Literature," *Philosophy and Rhetoric*, 4 (Winter, 1971), 1-19; "Instrumental Style: Notes on the Theory of Speech as Action," *Current Trends in Stylistics*, ed. Braj B. Kachru and Herbert F. W. Stahlke (Champaign,

Ill.: Linguistic Research, Inc., 1972), pp. 115-141; and "Speech, Action, and Style," *Literary Style: A Symposium*, ed. Seymour Chatman (New York: Oxford University Press, 1971), 241-254 [2]. Basically, the speech-act theorists view an utterance not so much as *expressing* something as *doing* something, and they distinguish three major kinds of act that the speaker or writer performs: the *locutionary act* — the sounds or the graphic symbols that the speaker or writer produces; the *illocutionary act*, the act that the speaker or writer performs *in* saying something — e.g. stating, promising, endorsing, questioning, etc.; the *perlocutionary act*, the effect of the act of speaking or writing on the hearer or reader — e.g. informing, frightening, enraging, puzzling, etc. What is particularly fruitful about this method of analysis is not only that it allows the critic to range freely from word to sentence to larger units of discourse but that it allows him to unite the provinces of the linguist as he looks at the locutionary act, the semanticist as he looks at the illocutionary act, and the rhetorician as he looks at the perlocutionary act. It moves us from the rather atomistic study of isolated units of language to the larger social, political, aesthetic, and pragmatic contexts of the language.

Winston Weathers's "The Grammars of Style: New Options in Composition," which occupied the entire Winter 1976 issue of *Freshman English News*, is likely to increase our tolerance of a wider and more unorthodox range of styles than we recognized or permitted our students to cultivate in the past. Weathers's thesis is that many students write well when they find a "grammar of style" that works best for them, either because it fits their "chemistry" of composition or because it suits what they have to say. Today, we have prose styles that fall outside the established "grammars of style" — discontinuity replacing continuity, non sequiturs replacing transitions, synchronicity replacing diachronicity, etc. Until recently, we tended to apologize for the Gertrude Steins, the John Barths, the William Burroughses, the Donald Barthelmes — as though they fell outside our stylistic mainstream but got away with their strange styles because of some sort of dispensation given them by the culture. Weathers's point is that if we confront our students with these "unorthodox" styles and encourage them to cultivate such styles, they might prove themselves in ways previously denied them.

That is not quite the point, but it is akin to the point, that Martin Joos made in his *The Five Clocks* (New York: Harcourt, Brace and World, 1962), in which he claimed that all of us are in command of a variety of styles or registers — to use his terms, *frozen, formal, consultative, casual,* and *intimate* — and that we shift back and forth among these styles to suit the occasion and our audiences. Some of Joos's registers — especially the *casual* and the *intimate* — are so individualistic and unorthodox as to qualify as idiolects, and still they communicate perfectly well in certain settings and with certain audiences.

It is perhaps time that we move away from our exclusive interest in the style of those pieces of discourse that are enshrined in the literary pantheon. There is colorfulness and eloquence to be found in the speech of common folk too. The current interest in various dialects and registers of the language may promote the study of the stylistic features of *vox populi* and the study too of the style of spoken discourse.

Methodology and Application

Since behind every methodology there is an implicit or an explicit theory, many of the items reviewed in this section might just as well have been discussed in the previous section on Theory, but I have chosen to discuss them in this section because the primary emphasis in them seems to be on methodology and/or application. Most of the items in this section propose a method of analyzing the style of a prose text that has already been composed, but in most cases, the method proposed can have at least an indirect effect on the synthetic process too — that is, in helping students generate stylistically improved sentences. However, a few of the

93

items discussed here — like the items by Christensen, the items describing imitation exercises, and the items on sentence-combining exercises — deal primarily with methods for generating rather than analyzing sentences. In many of the items that outline a method of analyzing style, the author goes on to demonstrate the method by applying it to some piecé of prose.

One of the questions many teachers ask is this one: "If I want to engage my students in analyzing prose style, what do I have them look at?" That is an elementary question, and many of the items discussed here suggest very specific features that the student should observe, tabulate, and classify. I dare say that many teachers have overlooked the "readability formula" that Rudolf Flesch proposed in his bestselling *The Art of Readable Writing* (New York: Harper & Row, 1949, revised edition 1974). In the very first sentence of this book, Flesch says, "To come right out with it, this is a book on rhetoric." And indeed it is. The first eight chapters of the book deal with the larger aspects of composition — invention, arrangement, and audience. But he devotes thirteen chapters of the book to style. And it is in the chapters on style that he sets forth his formula for measuring the readability of prose. His readability formula consists of two components: a human-interest rating and a reading-ease rating. The human-interest rating measures the percentages of "personal words" (proper nouns, personal pronouns) and "personal sentences" (dialogue, questions, commands, requests, incomplete sentences) found in a piece of prose. The more "personal" words and sentences, the higher the human-interest rating. The reading-ease rating measures the length of words and sentences. According to Flesch, the longer the words and the sentences, the harder the prose is to read. One of the criticisms levelled against Flesch's system is that if applied strictly, these formulas would rate the kind of prose found in the Dick-and-Jane readers as being the "most interesting" and the "easiest to read." Whether that criticism is justified or not, one must concede that Flesch's formulas do give the student something definite and specific to observe and tabulate, and teachers might consider using them as an easy entree into stylistic study.

In *Tough, Sweet, and Stuffy: An Essay on Modern American Styles* (Bloomington: Indiana University Press, 1966), Walker Gibson proposes his Style Machine as a paradigm for the analysis and classification of prose style. His formula outlines sixteen grammatical-rhetorical qualities to look for in measuring the relative toughness, sweetness, or stuffiness of passages of prose. He looks at such features as the size of words (in syllables), the length of sentences (in number of words), the structure of sentences (grammatical types), the use of articles (definite and indefinite), the proportions of nouns, verbs, modifiers, and imagery. Throughout the book, Gibson demonstrates his method by looking at 200-word samples of contemporary American prose and arriving at some characterization of the personality of the writer behind the prose. Gibson's model suggests more features to look at than the Flesch formulas do.

As the title suggests, Edward P. J. Corbett's "A Method of Analyzing Prose Style with a Demonstration Analysis of Swift's *A Modest Proposal*," in *Reflections on High School English: NDEA Institute Lectures 1965*, ed. Gary Tate (Tulsa, Oklahoma: University of Tulsa, 1966), pp. 106-124 [4, 12, 13] presents a method of analysis and then demonstrates the method by applying it in an analysis of a text familiar to most English teachers. Corbett suggests those features of diction (abstract/concrete, formal/informal, monosyllabic/polysyllabic, referential/emotive), of sentences (length and grammatical, rhetorical, and functional types), of paragraphs (length, methods of development, transitional devices) that an investigator can look at. Most of the analysis that follows the exposition of the method is given over to pointing out the rhetorical significance or effect of the raw data, most of which is given in statistical tables at the end of the essay. Corbett suggests that a great deal about the style of a prose piece can be learned simply by copying out a prose passage word for word, and he recommends that students be asked eventually to do an analysis of their own prose.

In "Teaching Prose Style Analysis: One Method," *Style*, 9 (Winter, 1975), 92-102, John F. Fleischauer describes, along with a week-by-week syllabus, an undergraduate course in prose stylistics that he offered at two different universities. His assignments included short oral reports on the style of a particular author and on published criticism of those writers, the reading of books and articles on general stylistic theory and of literary works themselves. The final paper in the course was a long one on the style of an author chosen by the student. He includes a bibliography of general works on style, of analyses of specific works or authors, and of the literary works studied in the course. Only one paragraph of the article tells us what kinds of things he had his students look at: "As for the technical matter of analysis, I asked the students to pick one paragraph which seemed to them to be typical (not outstanding) of the author after a thorough reading of the whole text. Then they identified the patterns in that passage, including sentence length and number, types of verbs and modifiers, conjunctions, clausal structures, images — whatever elements seemed both typical and significant based upon their reading of the whole work."

In a later article, "James Baldwin's Style: A Prospectus for the Classroom," *CCC*, 26 (May, 1975), 141-148, Fleischauer gives us more specific information about what he has his students look at when they analyze prose passages: average length and variety of length of sentences and paragraphs; kinds of verbs used (active, passive, *to be*) and their proportions; diction; kinds and positions of subordination; repetition and parallelism; parenthetical structures; sentence-openers. In his analysis of James Baldwin's "Notes of a Native Son," he frequently compares the characteristics of Baldwin's prose with those of such other contemporary writers as Arthur Miller, Jack Kerouac, J. Edgar Hoover, Eldridge Cleaver, William Buckley, and some anonymous prose-writers in *Atlantic*, *Newsweek*, and *U.S. News*. Like the other authors reviewed above, Fleischauer uses the method of counting and classifying various linguistic features of the text, and like Louis Milic, he looks more for recurrent features than for rare and unusual ones.

As early as his article "Generative Grammars and the Concept of Literary Style" [4, 6, 12, 14] in the December 1964 issue of *Word*, Richard Ohmann was showing us how he made use of transformational grammar to analyze the style of prose texts. In that article, he looked at short passages from Faulkner, Hemingway, James, and Lawrence and broke down the surface structures of their sentences into kernel sentences to show us the characteristic ways in which those authors constructed their sentences. Ohmann's article "Literature as Sentences," *CE*, 27 (January, 1966), 261-267 [3, 4, 5, 15] is an extension of that earlier article in *Word*. In the latter article, he analyzes a sentence from Joyce's "Araby," a sentence from Conrad's "The Secret Sharer," and a sentence from Dylan Thomas's "A Winter's Tale," converting the surface structures into the separate kernel sentences that reflect the deep structures of the sentences. In the last paragraph of the article, Ohmann says, "But I hope that in loosely stringing together several hypotheses about the fundamental role of the sentence I have indicated some areas where a rich exchange between linguistics and critical theory might eventually take place. To wit, the elusive intuition we have of *form* and *content* may turn out to be anchored in a distinction between surface structures and the deep structures of sentences. If so, syntactic theory will also feed into a theory of style."

A surprising number of analyzers of style have resorted to the transformational model in their analysis of sentence structure and have thereby given us some sense of what makes an author's style distinctive. One of the best examples of this kind of analysis is found in Curtis W. Hayes's "A Study in Prose Styles: Edward Gibbon and Ernest Hemingway," *Texas Studies in Literature and Language*, 7 (1966), 371-386 [6]. Like Ohmann, he regards transformational grammar as one of the best systems for analyzing and differentiating styles, and like Milic, he holds that a style can best be defined by its characteristic, habitual, recurrent linguistic features. He applied the transformational model to a hundred randomly chosen sentences from Edward Gibbon and Ernest Hemingway, and as a result of his analysis, he confirmed his own "intuitions" that Gibbon's style is "grand," "majestic," and "complex" and that Hemingway's style is "simple." He discovered, for instance, that whereas Gibbon averaged 4.3 transformations per sentence, Hemingway averaged 1.3 and that whereas Gibbon's sentences frequently had transformational expansions and embedded structures, Hemingway's rarely did. The comparative statistical tables included in the article further point up the differences between the two styles. My own intuition has been that Hemingway's style is not as "simple" as many people suppose — and indeed it isn't — but what this study does confirm is that Hemingway's style is "simple" in comparison with Gibbon's.

Before going on to review some of the methods which are more generative than analytical, I would like to look at a few more systems of analyzing prose that has already been composed.

In her book *Style and Proportion: The Language of Prose and Poetry* (Boston: Little, Brown, 1967), Josephine Miles is more interested in observing and tabulating lexical proportions than in studying syntactical patterns of whole sentences. She defines her method in these words: "The chief specified pattern then is the proportion, in a sequential text of one thousand lines of poetry (six to eight thousand words) and eight thousand words of prose, of adjective to noun to verb, the referential pattern; and of these to connectives, the grammatical pattern. These proportions, simply established, allow us to see the overall structure of the text — its dominant subordination or its dominant qualification, for example — more easily than a closer structure-by-structure scrutiny could do." On pages 204-5 of her book, she records in a chart the changes in the proportion of adjectives, nouns, verbs, and connectives used by sixty poets and sixty prose writers in English in the past five centuries. "Our prose," she says, "has moved in good array from much clausal subordination to much phrasal subordination to much adjectival assumption, through three standard styles — plain, middle, and high." On the basis of the part-of-speech proportions, she distinguishes three predominant contemporary styles:

(1) *predicative* (heavy on verbs, a statement-making style that creates situations — e.g. D. H. Lawrence)
(2) *connective-subordinative* (heavy on connectives — e.g. Bertrand Russell)
(3) *adjectival* (heavy on adjectives, a style that *presents* rather than *states* — e.g. Huxley [Julian? Aldous?])

Ms. Miles's system of observing the proportions of lexical items could be a useful one for those teachers who want to look more at diction than at syntax in a text.

An extremely interesting and useful article, using traditional grammar as its orientation, is Richard M. Weaver's "Some Rhetorical Aspects of Grammatical Categories," in *The Ethics of Rhetoric* (Chicago: Henry Regnery, 1953), pp. 115-127 [13]. His thesis is that "a language has certain abilities or even inclinations which the wise user can draw into the service of his own rhetorical effort. . . . Language is not a purely passive instrument, but owing to this public acceptance, while you are doing something with it, it is doing something with you or with your intention." In the first half of the article, he takes the three basic grammatical types of sentence — simple, complex, and compound — and shows the rhetorical potentialities of each type. For instance: "Whereas the simple sentence exhibits the co-existence of discrete classes, the complex sentence reveals the hierarchy between things by the process of subordination. Subordination makes inevitable the emergence of a focus of interest." In the second half of the article, Weaver goes on to discuss the grammatical and rhetorical aspects of

99

the parts of speech — noun, adjective, adverb, verb, conjunction, and preposition. I have never seen any other writer on style treat the rhetorical dimensions of the grammar of language in the way that Weaver does, and I highly recommend his article to teachers of writing.

Prompted by Weaver's article, Donald Davidson, in his "'Grammar and Rhetoric:' The Teacher's Problem," *QJS*, 39 (December, 1953), 425-436 [12], takes single sentences, from writers like Agnes DeMille, Thomas Babington Macaulay, W. H. Hudson, Aldo Leopold, and analyzes not only the grammatical structures of the sentences but their rhetorical effects. One could not imagine that so many significant observations could be made about the stylistic flavor of a single sentence. I recommend this article to teachers of writing and also the analyses that Davidson does of a single sentence by James Joyce and one by William Faulkner at the end of his *Twenty Lessons in Reading and Writing Prose* (New York: Scribner's, 1953), one of the best little rhetoric texts ever published in this country.

An unusually brilliant example of the analysis of a single paragraph of prose is provided by Ian Watt's "The First Paragraph of *The Ambassadors*: An Explication," *Essays in Criticism*, 10 (July, 1960), 250-274 [4, 5]. Starting out with the objectively observable idiosyncracies of Henry James's syntax and diction, Watt relates these features to their function in the paragraph, to their effects on the reader, to the character traits of Strether and the narrator, and ultimately to the cast of James's own mind. He attempts then to persuade us that the stylistic features of this one paragraph are not only characteristic of James's later prose but also indicative of James's complex vision of life and his conception of the novel as an art form.

Frank D'Angelo does a similar thorough-going analysis of five paragraphs, totalling ten sentences, from Thomas Wolfe's novel *You Can't Go Home Again* in his article "Style as Structure," *Style*, 8 (Spring, 1974), 322-364. D'Angelo outlines for us what his examination of these paragraphs will include: (1) a brief discussion of the literary context of the passage; (2) a word-for-word tabulation of sentence length, paragraph length, and discourse length; (3) a sentence-by-sentence description of the potentially significant linguistic and rhetorical features within each sentence; (4) a description of the potentially significant features of relationships between each sentence and all the preceding sentences; (5) a description of the structural features of the whole passage; (6) an interpretation of the passage, including an explanation of the linguistic and rhetorical features and the rhetorical method in terms of the interpretation; (7) a summary of the generalizations implied about the conventions and devices of this kind of description. One disadvantage of this arrangement is that D'Angelo has frequently to rehearse the same stylistic features as he moves from section to section. He says in the last paragraph of his article, "If the study of style is to advance beyond the identifying of easily classified features on the sentence level, much more attention will have to be devoted to holistic analyses of this sort."

Teachers who want to investigate figurative devices in prose may find the following three articles helpful: Laurence Perrine, "Four Forms of Metaphor," *CE*, 33 (November, 1971), 125-138 [15]; Rosemarie Gläser, "The Application of Transformational Generative Grammar to the Analysis of Similes and Metaphors in Modern English," *Style*, 5 (Fall, 1971), 265-283 [15]; Richard L. Graves, "A Primer for Teaching Style," *CCC*, 25 (May, 1974), 186-190. Perrine points out that every metaphor has two components: a literal term (the thing actually being discussed) and the figurative term (the thing to which it is compared). Proposing that both the literal term and the figurative term of every metaphor or simile are ultimately reducible to substantives, Perrine arrives at his four-part classification on the basis of whether these terms are expressed or implied:

Form 1. When both the literal term and the figurative term are expressed. Takes the form of "A is B." ("All the world's a stage," *As You Like It*).

Form 2. The literal term occurs but the figurative term must be inferred. ("Sheathe thy impatience; throw cold water on thy choler." *Merry Wives of Windsor*).

Form 3. Only the figurative term is named; the literal term must be inferred. For this reason, Form 3 metaphors can easily be mistaken for literal statements. ("Night's candles are burnt out." *Romeo and Juliet*).

Form 4. Neither the literal nor the figurative term is named; both must be inferred. ("I like to see it lap the miles." Emily Dickinson — here the literal term is represented by the pronoun *it*, whose antecedent is left unspecified).

In the latter part of his article, Perrine discusses the consequent problems students may experience in interpreting the metaphorical content of a passage.

Professor Gläser sets up a tree diagram of the semantic markers of the noun, and on the basis of this categorization of the semantic markers, she analyzes similes and metaphors as "violations" of the selectional rules for nouns. For instance, she considers these three sentences:

(1) John works as hard as a miner.
(2) John works like a horse.
(3) John works like a machine.

The first sentence compares John [+ human] with a miner [+ human] and is therefore not a simile. The second sentence compares John [+ human] with a horse [+ animal] and is a simile because the comparison involves nouns of different semantic features. The third sentence presents an even stronger simile, because while the second sentence matches two [+ animate] nouns, the third matches John [+ human, + animate] with a machine [+ artifact, + inanimate]. She reminds us that not all deviations from selectional rules create metaphors or similes. "Random selections of lexical items," she says, "are not yet a metaphorical string. Apart from the semantic proximity or remoteness of the categorical semantic markers, there must be a minimum of semantic correspondence between the idiosyncratic semantic features of the lexical items compared."

Whereas the articles by Perrine and Gläser deal with the analysis of tropes (shifts in the meanings of words), Richard L. Graves's article shows how he teaches students to recognize and compose various schemes (patterns of words), like anaphora, epistrophe, isocolon, antithesis, chiasmus, polysyndeton. Using an overhead projector, he flashes on the screen the name of the figure, a one-sentence definition of the figure, a diagram of the figure (if it lends itself to graphic representation), and one or more examples of the figure. Then he asks the student to compose a similar scheme of his own. Apparently, the use of the visual aids helps the students to conceive of the pattern of the scheme.

The Graves article marks the transition to those methods that engage students in generating their own sentences instead of just analyzing the prose that others have written. The most widely known and maybe the most influential of these methods was first introduced by Francis Christensen in two articles: "A Generative Rhetoric of the Sentence," *CCC*, 14 (October, 1963), 155-161 [4, 12, 13, 15]; "A Generative Rhetoric of the Paragraph," *CCC*, 16 (October, 1965), 144-156 [4, 12, 14, 15]. Christensen later published these two articles, with some revisions, in a collection of six of his articles, *Notes Toward a New Rhetoric* (New York: Harper & Row, 1967), and they have often been reprinted in other collections. In the article on the sentence, Christensen says, "The typical sentence of modern English, the kind we can best spend our efforts trying to teach, is what we may call the *cumulative sentence*." In defining a cumulative sentence then, he uses a cumulative sentence:

> The main clause, which may or may not have a sentence modifier before it, advances the discussion; but the

> additions move backward, as in this clause, to modify
> the statement of the main clause or more often to expli-
> cate or exemplify it, advancing to a new position and
> then pausing to consolidate it, leaping and lingering as
> the popular ballad does.

"The main clause [of the cumulative sentence]," Christensen goes on to say, "is likely to be stated in general or abstract
or plural terms. With the main clause stated, the forward
movement of the sentence stops, the writer shifts down to
the lower level of generality or abstraction or to singular
terms, and goes back over the same ground at this lower
level. . . . Thus the mere form of the sentence generates
ideas." In the latter part of this article, Christensen lays out a
number of sentences, some of them written by professional
writers, some of them written by students, in structured
layers that show the direction of movement and the levels of
generality in the sentences.

   The thesis of Christensen's article on the paragraph is that
the paragraph has a structure similar to that of the cumulative
sentence: the topic sentence is equivalent to the main or
base clause in the sentence, and the other sentences are
equivalent to the modifiers in the sentence. He defines the
paragraph as a sequence of structurally related sentences. By
a "sequence of structurally related sentences," he means a
group of sentences related to one another by coordination or
subordination. As in the article on the sentence, Christensen
lays out several paragraphs in layered structures so that we
can see how the various sentences of the paragraph are
related either by coordination or by subordination. But in
this article, he uses only paragraphs from expository writing,
probably because of his sensitivity to the charge that in "A
Generative Rhetoric of the Sentence" he had used sentences
only from narrative and descriptive writing.

   Judging from the testimony given by teachers in convention talks and in journal articles, the Christensen method
really works. Christensen later expanded his system into a

full-blown *Rhetoric Program*, complete with transparencies, that Harper & Row published in 1968. It might be fair to mention at this point Sabina Thorne Johnson's "Some Tentative Strictures on Generative Rhetoric," *CE*, 31 (November, 1969), 155-165 [15]. The heart of Ms. Johnson's reservations about the Christensen method is that she cannot accept his claim that form can generate content, "especially if the content is of an analytical or critical nature." "The weaknesses I see in student writing," she says, "the paucity of thought, the monotony of style and structure, the superficiality of analysis and explanation, the insensitivity — all indicate to me that what students need first is training in how to attack a topic. . . . More experimentally, I would also like to see whether and to what degree his method of building sentences can be made to carry over from the narrative and descriptive to the expository essay." Readers should see the reply to Ms. Johnson's strictures that Christensen's widow, Bonniejean McGuire Christensen, published in the May 1970 issue of *College English* and also A. M. Tibbetts's response in the same issue.

Teachers interested in the generative potentialities of transformational grammar should consult John C. Mellon's report of his experiment with 250 seventh-graders in *Transformational Sentence-Combining* (Urbana, Ill.: NCTE, 1969) [15]. The hypothesis upon which this experiment was based was that "practice in transformational sentence-combining would enhance the normal growth of syntactic fluency." After students had had some instructions in basic transformational grammar, they were asked to transform a series of separate kernel sentences according to directions explicitly given to them, embedding these transforms as constituents in other sentences according to a simple formula that was used in all the exercises and finally writing out the results of all the transforms in a single fully-developed complex sentence. As a result of these exercises, these junior high school students did make significant advances in syntactic fluency. Teachers who may want to engage their students in this kind of sentence-combining practice can make use of the kernel-sentence groups that Mellon reproduces in the appendix of his book.

For an extension of Mellon's method, teachers can consult Frank O'Hare's *Sentence Combining: Improving Student Writing without Formal Grammar* (Urbana, Ill.: NCTE, 1973). O'Hare too conducted an experiment with sentence-combining practice as a way to improve student writing, but without giving students any formal instruction in grammar. He started out by exercising students in smaller sub-skills and then led them, through progressively more difficult steps, to a more mature style. In his book, he gives explanations of his sentence-combining methodology and reproduces sample lessons and several sentence-combining problems.

I will conclude this section with a glance at some items dealing with imitation as a way to improve students' prose style. Edward P. J. Corbett, in his article "The Theory and Practice of Imitation in Classical Rhetoric," *CCC*, 22 (October, 1971), 243-250, gives a short summary of the history of imitative practices, and in his book *Classical Rhetoric for the Modern Student*, Second Edition (New York: Oxford University Press, 1971), pp. 510-538, he suggests three or four kinds of imitative exercises. In his article, "An Exercise in Prose Style," in *Rhetoric: Theories for Application*, ed. Robert M. Gorrell (Champaign, Ill.: NCTE, 1967), pp. 99-106 [13], Walker Gibson describes some imitative exercises that he has used with his students. On the first day of class, Gibson asks his students to write a few sentences describing the circumstances of their birth and early life. On the next day, he distributes dittoed samples of the students' prose and asks the class to define and classify the various voices heard in these excerpts. In the second step, Gibson distributes to the students, without revealing the authors' names, the first couple of paragraphs from autobiographical novels by Charles Dickens and Saul Bellow and asks the students to analyze the language of each selection to see how these different voices are created. In the third step, Gibson then asks his students to rewrite twice, according to specific instructions, the prose they wrote on the first day. On the first rewriting, for instance, they might be asked to turn half their verbs into the passive voice, half their sentences into subordinate clauses and to put half of these subordinate clauses before the subject of the main clause. "The point," Gibson says, "is to illustrate, even in this heavyhanded way, the fact of choice" — and also to illustrate how changes in diction and sentence structure effect changes in the voice of the writer.

In his article "Imitation and Style," *CCC*, 24 (October, 1973), 283-290, Frank D'Angelo describes an approach he uses in helping students to improve their style:

> The approach consists basically in having the students follow a sequence of steps which may be described briefly as follows: a preliminary reading of the model in order to get an overview of the dominant impression; a careful analysis of the model, which should include quantitative descriptions and a sentence-by-sentence description of the potentially significant linguistic features within each sentence; an interpretation of the passage, including an explanation of the linguistic features and the rhetorical effects; and finally a close imitation of the model.

Readers will recognize this approach as essentially the one that D'Angelo demonstrated with his analysis of five paragraphs of Thomas Wolfe's prose in the article from *Style* discussed above.

Winston Weathers and Otis Winchester devote an entire book of 143 pages to this kind of imitative practice: *Copy and Compose: A Guide to Prose Style* (Englewood Cliffs, N. J.: Prentice-Hall, 1969). The authors display thirty-seven different kinds of sentences and twenty-eight different kinds of paragraphs. The pattern of their method is to reproduce a sentence — or a paragraph — written by a professional writer, to analyze the structure of the sentence and point out some distinctive stylistic features of it, and then to ask the students to write a sentence or a paragraph according to the model. Admittedly, this kind of imitative exercise is a form of finger-exercise, and it asks for the composition of sentences in isolation from a context of occasion, purpose, and audience, but like practice exercises in the acquisition of any skill, this kind of practice can pay off when a writer is called upon to engage in some real-life writing.

Even as I conclude this survey of style as it relates to the teaching of composition, I am apprehensive about having overlooked some important books and articles. But I guess I will just have to be judged by what I remembered to include, not by what I neglected to mention. I derive some measure of assurance, however, from the realization that many of the books and articles mentioned in this survey are those most often cited in studies on style and most often reprinted in anthologies of essays on style. It is comforting sometimes to ride the bandwagon.

A LIST OF THE COLLECTIONS MENTIONED IN THE BIBLIOGRAPHICAL ESSAY

The collections are listed here in the order in which they are discussed in the essay. Numbers given within brackets after an item in the essay indicate that this item is reprinted in the collections bearing those numbers in this listing. For instance, the notation [1, 4, 6] after an item indicates that this item is reprinted in the Sebeok collection, the Love and Payne collection, and the Freeman collection.

(1) *Style in Language*, ed. Thomas A. Sebeok (Cambridge, Mass.: M.I.T. Press, 1960).

(2) *Literary Style: A Symposium*, ed. Seymour Chatman (New York: Oxford University Press, 1971).

(3) *Essays on the Language of Literature*, ed. Seymour Chatman and Samuel R. Levin (Boston: Houghton Mifflin, 1967).

(4) *Contemporary Essays on Style: Rhetoric, Linguistics, and Criticism*, ed. Glen A. Love and Michael Payne (Glenview, Ill.: Scott, Foresman, 1969).

(5) *Essays in Stylistic Analysis*, ed. Howard S. Babb (New York: Harcourt Brace Jovanovich, 1972).

(6) *Linguistics and Literary Style*, ed. Donald C. Freeman (New York: Holt, Rinehart, and Winston, 1970).

(7) *Prose Style: A Historical Approach Through Studies*, ed. James R. Bennett (San Francisco: Chandler, 1971).

(8) *Stylists on Style: A Handbook with Selections for Analysis*, ed. Louis T. Milic (New York: Scribner's, 1969).

(9) *Modern Essays on Writing and Style*, ed. Paul C. Wermuth, Second Edition (New York: Holt, Rinehart, and Winston, 1969).

(10) *Style in English Prose*, ed. Carl H. Klaus (New York: Macmillan, 1968).

(11) *The Problem of Style*, ed. J. V. Cunningham (Greenwich, Conn.: Fawcett Publications, 1966).

(12) *Teaching Freshman Composition*, ed. Gary Tate and Edward P. J. Corbett (New York: Oxford University Press, 1967).

(13) *Teaching High School Composition*, ed. Gary Tate and Edward P. J. Corbett (New York: Oxford University Press, 1970).

(14) *New Rhetorics*, ed. Martin Steinmann, Jr. (New York: Scribner's, 1967).

(15) *Contemporary Rhetoric: A Conceptual Background with Readings*, ed. W. Ross Winterowd (New York: Harcourt Brace Jovanovich, 1975).

MODES OF DISCOURSE

FRANK J. D'ANGELO

Arizona State University

GENERALLY, WHEN TEACHERS of composition speak about the modes or forms of discourse, they are referring to the four kinds of written prose: description, narration, exposition and argumentation. These categories, however, are not immutable forms or modes of expression, but rather a part of a complex of changing conventions.

The *Oxford English Dictionary* defines a mode as "a way or manner in which something is done or takes place" and as "a particular form, manner, or variety (of some quality, process, or condition)." Some synonyms often given for mode are *form* ("the contour and structure of something as distinguished from its substance"), *kind* ("a class or category of similar or related individuals"), *type* ("a taxonomic designation, such as the name of a species or genus"), and *genre* ("a category distinguished by a definite style, form, or content"). Almost all of these senses of the word have been employed by scholars and teachers when they use the term.

It is not my principal concern, however, to try to define the modes of discourse precisely, but rather to examine, describe, and evaluate those theories of and practical approaches to the modes that might be of some pedagogical value to the teacher of composition.

Classical rhetoricians distinguished between two primary forms of discourse: rhetoric and poetic. To Aristotle, the main characteristic of rhetoric was persuasion, whereas the main characteristic of poetry was imitation. Within this broad division of discourse into rhetoric and poetic, the classical rhetoricians distinguished three kinds of persua-

111

sive discourse (since rhetoric was conceived of basically as the art of persuasion): the deliberative, the judicial or forensic, and the epideictic. Deliberative discourse is that kind of discourse used to exhort an audience to perform an action or to refrain from performing an action in the future. Although Aristotle used the term in relation to political debate, Isocrates suggested that this kind of discourse had wider implications since we also deliberate in many non-political matters. Judicial discourse attempts to demonstrate the justice of some past action. It is generally considered to be the rhetoric of the law courts in which someone is attacked or defended against wrongdoing, but again it is clear that this kind of discourse is not to be limited to the courts of law, but can be employed in any situation in which one is accused of wrongdoing. Finally, epideictic discourse (sometimes referred to as ceremonial discourse) is the rhetoric of display. It is that kind of discourse that "adorns an occasion." It is the rhetoric of commemorative addresses. Each type of persuasive oratory was associated with a particular style: the grand style for moving, the middle style for pleasing, and the plain style for proving. The most significant work dealing with the three kinds of persuasive discourse obviously is Aristotle's *Rhetoric*. The Lane Cooper translation of *The Rhetoric of Aristotle* (New York: Appleton-Century-Crofts, Inc., 1932), pp. 16-78 is helpful to teachers and students because it provides definitions of terms, commentaries on difficult or obscure passages, and "supplementary examples for students of composition and public speaking." Donald Lemen Clark's *Rhetoric in Greco-Roman Education* (Morningside Heights, N.Y.: Columbia University Press, 1957), pp. 133-143 contains a good description of and commentary on deliberative, judicial, and epideictic discourse as well as a good discussion of their educational value.

A very important and much overlooked approach to the modes of discourse is that described by the Greek schoolmasters Hermogenes and Aphthonius and generally referred to as the *Progymnasmata* (pro gym NAS ma ta). The *Progym-*

nasmata were preparatory or preliminary exercises in speaking and writing used in the Roman schools around the first century B.C., as well as in the schools during the Middle Ages and the Renaissance. Donald Lemen Clark, in an article entitled "The Rise and Fall of Progymnasmata in Sixteenth and Seventeenth Century Grammar Schools," *Speech Monographs*, 19 (November, 1952), 260, describes these exercises as follows:

> The first two were narrative exercises in retelling FABLES and TALES from poetry and history. Next came the expository exercises of CHREIA and PROVERB, which taught the boys to develop a topic by iteration, enthymeme, contrast, illustration, example and the testimony of authority. REFUTATION and CONFIRMATION were argumentative exercises in analyzing such myths as that of Apollo and Daphne to show that the story was or was not obscure, incredible, impossible, inconsistent, unfitting, or inexpedient. The exercises of COMMONPLACE gave practice in enlarging on praise of virtue and dispraise of vice. The next exercises of ENCOMIUM and VITUPERATION taught how to praise a person or thing for being virtuous and to dispraise a person or thing for being vicious. The exercises of COMPARISON made but a slight step forward, showing which of two is better or worse. The exercise of IMPERSONATION, or PROSOPOPOEIA, required the pupil to compose an imaginary monologue which might appropriately be spoken or written by an historical, legendary, or fictitious person under given circumstances. The exercise in DESCRIPTION, in Greek ECPHRASIS, was designed to train the boys in vivid presentation of details of sight or sound. The THESIS was an exercise in deliberative oratory, arguing for or against a general question such as Should a man marry or seek office. The final elementary exercise, LEGISLATION, gave the boys practice in speak-

ing for or against a law, usually one from ancient history.

It is interesting to note that these minor "forms" can be accommodated to the three major kinds of persuasive discourse. For example, the fable, the tale, chreia, the proverb, thesis, and legislation can be considered kinds of deliberative discourse. Confirmation/refutation and commonplace are kinds of judicial discourse. And encomium, impersonation, comparison, and description are kinds of epideictic discourse. The importance of teaching these minor forms before teaching the three major kinds of persuasive discourse is that these exercises introduce students to the fundamental principles and forms of the three kinds of rhetoric. They are a series of graduated exercises designed to lead the student through set forms, through the processes of invention related to those set forms, and finally to the more advanced exercises.

The fact that these exercises have been designated "elementary" should not mislead the teacher of college composition into thinking that they have little value on the college level. Quintilian did not approve of the fact that the teaching of these exercises was taken over by the *grammaticus*; he felt that the teaching of the *progymnasmata* was an important part of the rhetorician's task. Besides, the best orators, such as Cicero, continued to work with these exercises (much as pianists might work with "finger" exercises) long after their formal training in the schools was completed.

The best primary source of the *progymnasmata* is Raymond E. Nadeau's "The Progymnasmata of Aphthonius in Translation," *Speech Monographs*, 19 (November, 1952), 264-285. Donald Lemen Clark's *Rhetoric in Greco-Roman Education* (New York: Columbia University Press, 1957), pp. 177-212 and M. L. Clarke's *Rhetoric at Rome* (New York: Barnes & Noble, Inc., 1963), pp. 7, 15-17, 121 provide useful descriptions of and commentaries on the exercises.

As far as can be determined, Alexander Bain (*English Composition and Rhetoric*, American Edition, Revised,

New York: D. Appleton and Co., 1890) was the first rhetorician to establish the traditional classification of the four forms of discourse. The modes of discourse approach to writing (Bain called them "forms" of discourse) is based on the idea that all writing can be classified on the basis of form. The traditional forms of discourse are usually considered to be description, narration, exposition, and argumentation. Each form is assumed to have its own function, its own subject matter, its own organizational patterns, and its own language. The primary function of descriptive writing is to evoke sense impressions of people and things. Its subject matter is the objects of sense experience. It organizes its materials in space and time. Its language is a combination of the denotative and connotative, the literal and the figurative, the objective and the impressionistic. Narrative writing is that kind of discourse which functions to tell a story or narrate an event. Its subject matter is people and events which it organizes in space and time. Like the language of descriptive writing, the language of narration often combines the denotative and the connotative, the literal and the figurative, the objective and the impressionistic. The function of expository writing is to inform or to instruct, to present ideas and general truths as clearly and as objectively as possible. Its subject matter is ideas and generalizations. Its organizational patterns are logical, the most predominant being analysis and classification. Its language is generally denotative and factual. Argumentative discourse is that mode of discourse which attempts to convince or persuade, defend or refute a particular issue or point of view. Its subject matter is issues about which there is considerable difference of belief and opinion. Its organizational patterns are deduction (especially syllogistic progression) and induction (especially the example). Its language may be factual or emotive, depending on the kind of appeal (logical, emotional, ethical) being used.

Both Alexander Bain and William B. Cairns (*The Forms of Discourse*, Boston: Ginn and Co., Publishers, 1896) were interested in basing the forms of discourse approach to writing on the laws of the mind. Bain's categories, incidentally, include a fifth mode, poetry. According to Bain, the mind can be divided into three faculties: the understanding, the will, and the feelings. The aims of discourse (to inform, to persuade, and to please) correspond to these three faculties. The forms of discourse are the kinds of composition that relate to the faculties of the mind, the aims of discourse, and the laws of thought. Thus description, narration, and exposition relate to the faculty of understanding, persuasion relates to the will, and poetry to the feelings (p. 19).

It would be easy for us to dismiss Bain's attempt to relate the forms of discourse to the faculties of the mind as a kind of naive psychology, but it must be remembered that in addition to being a rhetorician, Alexander Bain was an associationist psychologist who was interested in basing the principles of discourse on the best knowledge about the laws of the mind as known in his day. Bain himself is said to have contributed significantly to the associationist school of psychology, then currently in vogue. For one thing, he took the Greek distinction between the mind (or soul) and the body, together with the faculties into which the mind was supposedly divided, and tried to relate them more directly to the brain, to the sense organs, and to the nervous system. For another, he attempted to explain these mental processes by means of the laws of similarity (W. Edgar Vinacke, *The Psychology of Thinking*, New York: McGraw-Hill Book Co., Inc., 1952, p. 13). More importantly, as a rhetorician he had as a main goal the idea that in writing more emphasis should be placed on the relationship between thought and discourse, a goal that many of us might do well to heed today.

William Cairns also based his approach to the forms of discourse on the laws of thought as enumerated by associationist psychologists. Cairns delineated four basic principles of association: contiguity, continuity, likeness or contrast, and cause and effect. Cairns claimed that these principles are useful in constructing sentences as well as in organizing complete discourses. Passages of description are organized according to the principle of contiguity. Narrative passages are organized on the principle of continuity. Expository writing and argumentation are based on the principles of likeness or contrast and cause and effect (pp. 46-47).

There are differing points of view about the value of the traditional modes of discourse approach to composition. Those teachers who like this approach argue that it is useful for students to learn the principles (the organizational patterns, the stylistic techniques, and so forth) of composition that are appropriate to the various kinds of writing. Thus expository writing, for example, uses formal definition, analysis, classification, exemplification, comparison and the like, whereas narration and description use other methods of development. My own belief is that these various methods of development can be found *in any kind of writing*. For example, Shakespeare uses comparisons in his sonnet "Shall I Compare Thee to a Summer's Day?" Marvell uses syllogistic progression in "To His Coy Mistress," and Elizabeth Barrett Browning uses enumeration in her sonnet "How Do I Love Thee? Let Me Count the Ways." These are all illustrations of literary discourse that contain examples of patterns of development generally associated with expository prose. It is true that expository prose *tends* to use certain logical patterns of development and that argumentative, descriptive, and narrative prose *tend* to use other kinds of patterns. But these are at best tendencies and not hard and fast rules that a writer must follow. Another objection is that the forms of discourse overlap, that it is almost impossible to find a discourse that is pure in form, one that is either description or narration or exposition or argumentation. In addition, some scholars such as Richard E. Hughes, in "The Contemporaneity of Classical Rhetoric," *CCC*, 16 (October, 1965), 157-158, who follow in the classical tradition, maintain that there is one main mode and that one is argumentation. The other modes are really supportive of argumentation and may be subsumed under this mode. Still others suggest that we must be more careful in determining the basis of our classifications of the basic modes. While many would accept exposition and argumentation as basic forms, others would reject description and narration, contending that these are simply compositional techniques which inform all discourse.

Despite my reservations about traditional approaches to the modes of discourse, I believe that beginning teachers of composition can profit by studying the works of Alexander Bain and William Cairns. In the works of these scholars there is at least an attempt to give a rationale for the traditional modes approach based on psychological principles. Another text that has some merit, from a practical point of view, is Erle E. Clippinger's *Illustrated Lessons in Composition and Rhetoric* (Boston: Silver, Burdett and Co., 1912) because it divides the four main categories of discourse into subtypes of kinds of writing that are much more useful for the student to deal with than are the broader categories. For example, under narrative writing Clippinger deals with types such as the short story, the reminiscence, the general reminiscence, the narrative-expository sketch, and so forth. Closely related to the Clippinger book are books such as the Albert C. Baugh, Paul C. Kitchen, and Matthew W. Block *Writing by Types*, 2nd ed. (New York: Appleton-Century-Crofts, Inc., 1937) which, although not based on the traditional modes, do try to give the student some specific kinds of writing to study and emulate. Some examples of these types are the critical essay, the feature article, the editorial, the interview, informal argument, the business letter, the character sketch, the short biography, and the familiar essay. The Baugh book, however, is essentially a reader, rather than a basic composition text which illustrates the principles along with the forms.

Since Alexander Bain, many scholars and teachers have been interested in the forms of discourse approach to writing, but some have become dissatisfied with the traditional classification of these modes. For example, in 1914 Sterling Leonard ("As to the Forms of Discourse," *The English Jour-*

nal, 3, April, 1914, p. 202) expressed his dissatisfaction in attempting to cope successfully with these modes in the classroom. Leonard writes: "The difficulty I have most often met in attempting to organize such courses has its roots in the present classification of the forms of discourse. For, useful as this doubtless is for sorting completed pieces of writing, it does not view the process of composition from the side of the thoughts or ideas the writer has to express, and particularly of his purpose in expressing these." Leonard's comments indicate that, despite Alexander Bain's attempt to relate thought to writing, in practice the forms of discourse approach to composition seems to place more emphasis on the "completed pieces of writing," the *products* of composition, than on the *processes* of composition.

Consequently, Leonard suggests a reclassification of the forms of discourse:

A Scheme of Reclassification For the Forms of Discourse

I. PRESENTATION OF FACTS

A) *Sense-Impressions* suggested to give the reader a new and interesting bit of experience: the forms of simple *objective narration* and *description.*

B) The same type of material but chiefly such matters as machines, processes, and so on, stated in order to give the reader useful information, the form of *simple explanation.*

II. INTERPRETATION OF FACTS

A) Conclusions as to character — mood and motive and so on; and the complications of cause and effect in human action developed into *plot*: the interpretive forms of *narration* and *description.*

B) Generalizations — conclusions as to the *relations* and the *significance* of the bodies of fact presented as information in I, B: the forms *interpretive exposition* and *argument.*

Leonard's reclassification of the forms of discourse is not really a new classification at all. It is, rather, a regrouping and a change in emphasis in the order of presentation of the material for pedagogical purposes. Leonard's avowed purpose in using the forms of discourse approach to writing is to help his students think clearly. Thus they are assigned a sequence of modes or combinations of modes arranged in ascending order of difficulty and abstraction. They begin by writing themes based on sense impressions. Then they are encouraged to explore the material, to explain it, to analyze it and to interpret it. Finally, they are asked to evaluate facts and information and to determine their significance.

Leonard's suggested reordering of the modes makes good pedagogical sense. He would have the student begin with the more "concrete" modes, such as description and narration, and base their writing on these modes, on sense impressions, for example, and on bits of narrative that increase in complexity and generality. Then the student moves on to the more abstract modes which deal with generalization and interpretation.

Thus far I have been discussing, for the most part, classroom approaches to the modes of discourse.

At least one empirical study, J. C. Seegars, "Form of Discourse and Sentence Structure," *The Elementary English Review*, 10 (March, 1933), 51-54, points out that there is some empirical justification in having students write in the traditional modes. This study questions the assumption of some teachers that the techniques of discourse should be taught without regard to the form of discourse used. The study was conducted with elementary school children who were asked to write essays using the four traditional forms of discourse. Their papers were then examined to determine the relative number and kinds of dependent clauses used as a result of writing in the various modes. The study concluded that the form of discourse does have a definite influence on the kind of clause structure. Argumentative writing employs a large number of substantive clauses, conditional clauses, and
120

clauses of cause. Expository writing also favors substantive clauses and conditional clauses, but it contains an almost equal proportion of adjective clauses and time clauses. Description and narration use a large number of time clauses, substantive clauses, and adjective clauses. As should appear obvious, this study has limitations, being based on dubious grammatical categories and outworn modes. Nevertheless, it does suggest that students may gain facility in the use of various kinds of sentence structure by being asked to write in different modes. It also suggests that in assigning and grading papers teachers would do well to consider the mode of discourse.

If the traditional four modes of discourse do not work well for some teachers and scholars, others seem to feel that some kind of classification of the modes is necessary no matter how weak the divisions. A few scholars seem to hearken back to the classical distinction between rhetoric and poetic by dividing all discourse into scientific and poetic, or referential and expressive. This classification is usually based on the kind of language employed in the discourse. Although this approach to the modes of discourse seems to offer a more objective basis for classifying the modes, the fact is that this approach to the modes also has its weaknesses. One of the first scholars in modern times to make this distinction between the modes was I. A. Richards, who, in *Science and Poetry* (London: Kegan Paul, Trench, Trubner & Co., Ltd, 1935), pp. 61-74, set up a fundamental opposition between what he called statements and pseudo-statements. A statement, Richards maintained, could be identified by its truth value; a pseudo-statement by its effect in organizing attitudes. In *Principles of Literary Criticism* (New York: Harcourt, Brace and Co., 1938), pp. 261-271, Richards had already set up a similar opposition of modes by concluding that scientific discourse uses referential statements, whereas poetic discourse employs emotive statements. Richards seems to have been following the lead of the logicians in setting up this dichotomy.

But Philip Wheelwright, in *The Burning Fountain*, New and Revised Edition (Bloomington: Indiana University Press, 1968), pp. 59-68, calls this distinction "an unworkable over-simplification." There are simply too many other linguistic possibilities between the logical statement and the pseudo-statement, contends Wheelwright. Similarly, Susanne Langer ("'Expressive Language' and the Expressive Function of Poetry" in *On Expressive Language*, ed. Heinz Werner, Worcester, Mass.: Clark University Press, 1955) argues that scholars who study special "poetic" uses of language are confused about the nature of poetry. All kinds of language are used in poetry, states Langer, not just the emotive or expressive. Poetry contains literal statements, statements with rich associations, commands, exclamations, and so forth. None of these, however, is intrinsically poetic. What makes them expressive is their "conventional" use in the work of art as a whole. The whole work is a symbol system the totality of which has an expressive function (pp. 3-5). Joe Adams ("Expressive Aspects of Scientific Language" in *On Expressive Language*) confirms Susanne Langer's assertions with the complementary view that "no strict line can be drawn between expressive language and scientific language."

Wheelwright contends that we should not conceive of referential language and emotive language as independent variables. We must think of them rather with presupposition. An utterance can be both referential and emotive, for the negative of referential is non-referential, not emotive; and the negative of emotive is non-emotive, not referential. On the basis of these new distinctions, Wheelwright presents a new scheme of "four interactive modes of discourse" which may be illustrated as follows (pp. 69-70):

MODES OF DISCOURSE

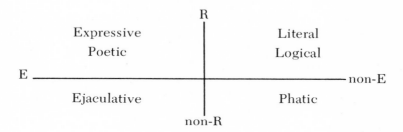

Expressive discourse is both referential and emotive. Poetic discourse is one kind of expressive discourse. Literal discourse is the discourse of everyday language when its use is primarily referential. Logical discourse is the ideal toward which literal discourse tends. Ejaculative discourse is the discourse of strong feelings and emotions ("Oh, damn!"). Phatic discourse consists of conventional expressions, such as "Good morning," which are not really felt (p. 70).

The strictures presented by Susanne Langer, Philip Wheelwright, and Joe Adams suggest to the composition teacher that expressive language and referential language should not be discussed in isolation from the uses of such language in actual discourse, and that the ends of the discourse must always be kept in mind.

A more ambitious scheme to reclassify the modes of discourse has been made by Leo Rockas in *Modes of Rhetoric* (New York: St. Martin's Press, 1964). Rockas' system appears in outline form as follows:

MODES OF RHETORIC

I. The Static Modes
   A. Description
   B. Definition

II. The Temporal Modes
   A. Narration
   B. Process
III. The Mimetic Modes
   A. Drama
   B. Dialogue
IV. The Mental Modes
   A. Reverie
   B. Persuation

Rockas' goal is noteworthy: to combine the literary modes with the rhetorical modes in one grand design. The A categories constitute the concrete modes (description, narration, drama, and reverie), whereas the B categories make up the abstract modes (definition, process, dialogue, and persuasion). Each of these modes is placed into one of four pairs, each pair containing a concrete mode and an abstract mode. The relationship between these seemingly disparate modes is explained by the superordinate categories which subsume each of the pairs: the static, the temporal, the mimetic, and the mental. The sequence of modes is from those which are abstracted from time and space to those embedded in past, present, and future actions (pp. ix, x). This scheme suggests that Rockas is on the verge of moving away from a static concept of the modes of discourse as the products of composition to the more dynamic concept of the modes as processes of the human mind.

I'm not too certain how valuable Rockas' modes are for the composition teacher. The first two categories, the static and the temporal modes, are eminently suggestive of two of Kenneth Burke's categories (the static and the progressive) in his discussion of form in *Counter-Statement*. As a logical sequence of patterns that we want our students to emulate, I think the first two categories work fine. But when we get to the mimetic and mental modes, we seem to be confronting categories different in kind. It's difficult for me to relate description, for example, to drama or to reverie. There can be descriptive passages in a character's speech, but in what way is description a "kind" of writing in the same way that drama or even reverie is? I would conclude, therefore, that teachers of composition will find some value in Rockas' discussion of description, definition, narration, and process, and even persuasion (though on a different level of structure), but that they will find the other categories not too useful to work with.

George Bramer, in an article entitled "Like It Is: Discourse Analysis for a New Generation," *CCC*, 21 (December, 1970), pp. 347-355, maintains that although Rockas' system has attractive features, it "cannot promote discourse that tells it like it is" nearly as well as other systems. Bramer offers in its place a theory whose main features are schematically presented below:

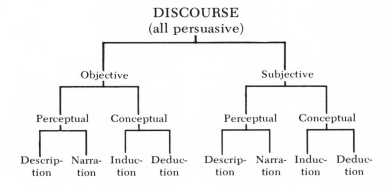

Bramer's theory considers persuasion as fundamental (an echo of Richard Hughes' contention that the four forms of discourse can be subsumed under the Aristotelian mode of persuasion). All of the other modes, therefore, are subdivisions of persuasion. The two main divisions are the objective and the subjective. Each of these is divided into the perceptual (or concrete) and the conceptual (or abstract). The subdivisions of these categories (description, narration, induction, deduction) constitute the modes of discourse. The concrete or perceptual modes are description and narration. There are two kinds of description: objective (or technical) and subjective (or imaginative). Similarly, there are two kinds of narration: objective (expository) and subjective (imaginative). The abstract or conceptual modes are induction and deduction. Bramer does not delineate these, but presumably he sees these modes as operating in both imaginative and non-imaginative discourse. Objective discourse is public and verifiable; subjective is not. The language of objective discourse is denotative and literal. The organizational patterns are logical. The language of subjective discourse is connotative and figurative. The organizational patterns are non-logical. Although Bramer warns that real language probably falls in an area between the objective and the subjective, one cannot help but notice the resemblance between Bramer's main categories and those of I. A. Richards.

Bramer's division of the modes into objective and subjective makes good pedagogical sense, but I'm not certain that I agree with (or perhaps even understand) his placing of induction and deduction on the same plane as description and narration. Description and narration can proceed inductively and deductively. Induction and deduction cannot be confined to expository or argumentative discourse. Nor am I certain that I agree with Bramer's perceptual and conceptual categories. Cannot description and narration operate in both the perceptual and conceptual domains? It is true that description and narration are concrete modes, but the processes of description and narration are perceptual only in the presence of the object of perception. In its absence, the processes can be conceptual as well as perceptual.

James Moffett, in *Teaching the Universe of Discourse* (Boston: Houghton Mifflin, 1968), has proposed several new ways of classifying discourse. One scheme is based on the idea that the structure of discourse is a set of relations among a speaker (first person), a listener (second person) and a subject (third person), p. 10. There are accordingly four kinds of discourse based on the increasing distance in time and space between the speaker and his audience (p. 33):

MODES OF DISCOURSE

Reflection — Intrapersonal communication between two parts of one nervous system.

Conversation — Interpersonal communication between two people in vocal range.

Correspondence — Interpersonal communication between remote individuals or small groups with some personal knowledge of each other.

Publication — Impersonal communication to a large anonymous group extended over space and/or time.

Moffett recapitulates this progression in the form of another scheme which emphasizes the increasing distance in time and space between the speaker and his subject (p. 35).

MODES OF DISCOURSE

What is happening — drama, recording
What happened — narrative, reporting
What happens — exposition, generalizing
What may happen — logical argumentation, theorizing

You will note that the four traditional forms of discourse become realigned in terms of increasing levels of abstraction (drama, narrative, exposition, argumentation), in terms of the relative distance between the speaker and the subject (What is happening, what happened, what happens, what may happen), and in terms of a sequence of activities closely tied in with the student's cognitive development (recording, reporting, generalizing, theorizing), pp. 35-36.

Bringing all of these schemes together, Moffett comes up with a grand design that he calls the spectrum of discourse (p. 47):

THE SPECTRUM OF DISCOURSE

Interior Dialogue (egocentric speech)   P
Vocal Dialogue (socialized speech)
   Recording, the drama of what is happening.
                              PLAYS O
Correspondence
Personal Journal   E
Autobiography
Memoir
   Reporting, the narrative of what happened. FICTION T
Biography
Chronicle
History
   Generalizing, the exposition of what happens. ESSAY R
Science   Y
Metaphysics
   Theorizing, the argumentation of what will, may happen.

As Moffett himself explains, "this linear model falsifies a lot" because aspects of each of these levels can be found on the other levels. Nevertheless, any scheme is necessarily an abstraction, and Moffett's scheme at least presents a plausible way of tying in a sequence of modes with a sequence of logical and psychological activities. The movement is from the immediate audience to an audience removed in space and time. The temporal movement is from present to past to future. There are also additional movements from the personal to the vicarious, the nonverbal to the verbal, the oral to the written, and from subjective response to objective analysis. The value of Moffett's approach to the modes of discourse is that a curriculum could be set up on almost any level of education in which students would be required to handle linguistic and rhetorical structures in increasing levels of abstraction, difficulty, and sophistication.

Perhaps the most significant approach to the modes of discourse presented in recent years is one articulated by James Kinneavy in a recent book entitled *A Theory of Discourse* (Englewood Cliffs, N.J.: Prentice-Hall, Inc., 1971). Following Alexander Bain, Kinneavy contends that each mode of discourse corresponds to a different kind of thinking, and that each is related to a different view of reality. Furthermore, the reason for the existence of these modes can be found in the human uses of language and the purposes to which this language is put. Thus Kinneavy is as much concerned with the "aims" of discourse as he is with the modes of discourse (pp. 36-38).

Kinneavy's theory of discourse owes much of its theoretical justification to communications theory. Kinneavy depicts the components of the process of communication as part of a triangle. The aims of discourse are based on the four elements of the communications triangle: the speaker or writer (the encoder), the audience or reader (the decoder), the outer world (the reality), and the text itself (the message). These four components are depicted below in the form of the communications triangle:

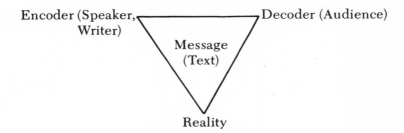

If the emphasis is on the speaker-writer (the encoder) and the speaker-writer's aim is self-expression, then the result is *expressive discourse*. If the stress is on eliciting a particular response from an audience and the speaker-writer's aim is to convince or persuade, the result is *persuasive discourse*. If the emphasis is on the subject matter or reality talked about and the aim of the speaker-writer is to present a picture of that reality as clearly and as logically as possible, the result is *referential discourse*. Finally, if the stress is on the internal ordering of the formal characteristics of the text and the speaker-writer's aim is to give pleasure, then the result is *literary discourse*. These four modes — the expressive, the persuasive, the referential, and the literary — constitute the basic forms of discourse (pp. 38-39).

Expressive discourse includes such forms of writing and speech as conversations, gripe sessions, protests, diaries, journals, prayers, religious credos, myths, manifestoes, declarations of independence, contracts and constitutions. Persuasive discourse embraces oratory, political speeches, sermons, propaganda, advertising, editorials, marriage proposals, safety warnings, and the like. Referential discourse has three main subdivisions: exploratory discourse, scientific discourse, and informative discourse. Exploratory discourse includes panel discussions, interviews, questionnaires, dialogues, diagnoses, tentative definitions, and seminars. Scientific discourse embodies descriptive analysis, literary criticism, history, and taxonomy. Informative discourse includes news stories, textbooks, articles, essays, summaries, and weather reports. The fourth basic mode, literary discourse, admits of such forms as the short story, the novel, drama, poetry, movies, songs, jokes, puns, the limerick, and T.V. shows (pp. 39-40).

Listed below is an overall view of Kinneavy's scheme (p. 61):

EXPRESSIVE

Examples:
Of Individual
  Conversation
  Journals

Diaries
Gripe sessions
Prayer
Of Social
Minority protests
Manifestoes
Declarations of independence
Contracts
Constitutions of clubs
Myth
Utopia plans
Religious credos

REFERENTIAL

Examples:
Exploratory
Dialogues
Seminars
A tentative definition of . . . .
Proposing a solution to problems
Diagnosis
Scientific
Proving a point by arguing from accepted premises
Proving a point by generalizing from particulars
A combination of both
Informative:
News articles
Reports
Summaries
Non-technical encyclopedia articles
Textbooks

LITERARY

Examples:
Short Story
Lyric
Short Narrative

    Limerick
    Ballad, Folk Song
    Drama
    TV Show
    Movie
    Joke

PERSUASIVE

Examples:
    Advertising
    Political speeches
    Religious sermons
    Legal oratory
    Editorials

Kinneavy's scheme is in many ways suggestive of Moffett's "The Spectrum of Discourse." Like Moffett's scheme, Kinneavy's model considers the speaker-listener relationship as well as the speaker-subject relationship. It also considers the degree to which the audience is removed in time and space. And it suggests a wide range of continuities: from the immediate to the remote, from present to past to future, from the personal to the vicarious, and from subjective response to objective analysis.

Kinneavy's scheme can be used as a way of organizing a book of readings or of working up an entire curriculum. The rationale for such a curriculum is built into the model itself. The aims of discourse provide the rationale not only for each mode, but for the curriculum as a whole. Because the aims of discourse are grounded in the nature of reality, they coincide with our aims in everyday life (to instruct, to convince or persuade, to please, etc.). One possible approach is to begin with expressive discourse, move on to literary discourse, then on to referential discourse, and finally conclude with persuasive discourse. Whatever the plan, however, we can envisage a sequence of linguistic and rhetorical forms and

132

subject matter ranging from the personal to the objective, from the less difficult to the more difficult.

One of the more interesting ways of classifying modes can be found in a text by Winston Weathers and Otis Winchester, called *The Attitudes of Rhetoric* (Englewood Cliffs, N.J.: Prentice-Hall, Inc., 1970). The authors argue that the writer's attitude toward his subject and his audience constitutes an important part of his message. "A writer does not simply discuss a subject; he discusses a subject in a particular way, from a particular perspective in a given state of mind. His attitude toward his subject is a part of his consideration—and ours. It makes a great deal of difference to us, in our understanding and comprehension of a piece of writing, if the writer has discussed his subject with *anger* or with *joyfulness*, with *compassion* or with *dogmatism*. His attitude is a part of his message" (p. v.).

Weathers and Winchester classify nine different kinds of discourse based on attitude:

THE ATTITUDES OF RHETORIC

1. The confident attitude
2. The judicious attitude
3. The quiet attitude
4. The imperative attitude
5. The impassioned attitude
6. The compassionate attitude
7. The critical attitude
8. The angry attitude
9. The absurd attitude

The confident attitude is based on the idea that the writer is secure in the knowledge that what he has to say is right. He presents his ideas in a forceful and unqualified manner. The judicious attitude is a reasonable one. The writer is willing to debate, to consider both sides of a question. He presents his ideas not as fixed opinions but as plausible conclusions. The quiet attitude is one in which the writer tries to communicate his sense of well-being, his feeling that despite the anxieties and turmoils in the world, at this particular moment he is at peace, at one with the world and with his subject. The imperative attitude is one that seeks solutions to problems and that leads to action. The writer's main task is to move his readers toward constructive action. The compassionate attitude is based on feeling and empathy for others. The writer wants to communicate that he too is a human being, with all of the joys and fears, successes and failures of his fellow man. The critical attitude is one in which the writer feels that he should point out errors and illuminate fallacies. Although the writer is skeptical and critical, his goal is to achieve change, reform, and improvement. The angry attitude is characterized by a fighting spirit, a need to right a wrong. No time for leisurely discussion and debate or for objectivity. The writer wants to communicate his outrage, his dismay at this particular moment. Finally, the absurd attitude is one in which the writer sees the essential inconsistencies and paradoxes in a situation. He sees the world as irrational, and he cannot understand how anyone can take any matter seriously.

Attitude is directly related to a writer's style, maintain Weathers and Winchester. They deplore the fact that some teachers ask their students to handle every subject in a "plain, dispassionate style." A writer can best reveal his changing attitudes toward his subject and his audience by varying his style. To deal with every subject in the same way is to reveal a point of view that is rigid, unbending, and uncompromising. This approach to discourse, it seems to me, has especial value in that it directly relates the study of kinds of discourse to the study of style and tone. In this view, a mode is a deliberately adopted temper of mind or disposition revealed in a particular style.

In a recent article entitled "The Spectrum of Rhetoric," *CCC*, 25 (May, 1974), pp. 181-185, Daniel Marder suggests that "we can view all rhetoric as a spectrum of persuasiveness" (an echo of Richard Hughes and George Bramer) ranging from "simple descriptions of objects or reports of observations at one end and the most esoteric poetry at the other end." Marder contends that all discourse is an attempt on the part of the speaker or writer to seek agreement. Although he does not go into any detail in delineating the parts of this spectrum of discourse, he does depict the extremes. At one end, there is the kind of discourse that appeals to the audience's logic; at the other end, there is "a shading of reason into highly symbolic and psychological modes of expression." Marder's most important assumption is that "if all discourse can be seen as a spectrum of effort to bring isolated beings into agreement or harmony, then aesthetics, at least verbal aesthetics, and science are aspects of rhetoric, and the principles or laws governing all discourse may be sought.... Assuming the oneness of all discourse amid its variety, we may discover that a single purpose directs it and that the purpose is human unification."

What then can we conclude about the value of a modes of discourse approach to composition? Although at times the various ways of classifying kinds of writing seem simply the result of a need or an impulse to get our experience in order, at other times such classifications seem to represent linguistic, psychological, and cultural processes at work on the writer's attitudes and intentions. Whether the modes of discourse are taken as genres, as aims, as attitudes, or as conventions, they must not be thought of as unchangeable and immutable archetypes. They are rather a cluster of changing conventions classified for specific purposes. At its best, the modes of discourse approach to writing forces us to attend more closely to differences in rhetorical purpose, attitudes, values, and audience. At its weakest, it may develop into a mere formalism, with undue emphasis on static conventions, rather than with a more proper emphasis on the processes of discourse.

BASIC WRITING

MINA P. SHAUGHNESSY

The City University of New York

I

THE TEACHING OF WRITING to severely unprepared freshmen is as yet but the frontier of a profession, lacking even an agreed upon name. "Remedial" writing is out of favor for good reasons: it seems inaccurate to speak of beginners, whether on the tennis court or in a writing class, as remedial and the students we are concerned with have generally had but token instruction in writing; the medical metaphor suggests a disease, and indeed students assigned to "remedial" classes do get sent to writing "labs" or "clinics" where their problems are "diagnosed"; but worse, it is a soiled word with unhappy associations that go back to grade school, where many college remedial students began the losing game of "catching up."

Still, the word persists. "English for the disadvantaged" and "handicapped" English are worse; "compensatory" is only slightly more neutral; and "developmental" or "basic" writing tends to get translated into "remedial" when the chips are down. I will use "basic writing" in this essay, but "remedial" will slip in often.

There is another problem with identifying the subject: even where programs and teachers use the word "remedial," we cannot be at all certain that they mean the same thing by it. One school's remedial student may be another's regular or even advanced freshman. The English A that Sabina Thorne Johnson describes so impressively in her article about remedial English at Berkeley, "Remedial English: The Anglocentric Albatross?" *CE*, 33 (March, 1972), 670-685, or the persona paraphrasing recommended by Phyllis Brooks for the same students in "Mimesis: Grammar and the Echoing Voice," *CE*, 35 (Nov., 1973), 161-168, would doubtless strike many teachers from inner-city colleges as unrealistic for their "remedial" classes. Nor can we assume that courses called "freshman composition" are *not* remedial, for many schools, particularly several two-year colleges, have eradicated all labels that carry the old connotations even though their students have the old problems. We cannot be guided by the type of institution either. Some two-year colleges accept no remedial students and some four-year colleges with open admissions policies now have over fifty per cent of their freshmen in remedial classes. Finally, there are distinctions to be made across time. Most colleges have always had some freshmen who couldn't write as well as their peers and often such students ended up in classes that were called remedial, or more crassly, "bonehead" English. L. W. Michaelson's "'Bonehead' Grammar," *Education*, 80 (Jan., 1960), 283-285, catches something of the quality of the course and of the attitudes that shaped it. But this type of course was waning, along with Freshman English, when the new remedial population began to appear in the sixties. In 1964, the first year of the War on Poverty, the headings "cultural deprivation" and "cultural differences" appeared for the first time in *Education Index*. By the next year, they were among the most heavily itemed headings in the *Index*. We can date the "new" remedial English from then.

Given the confusion of terms, therefore, I must try to define the population of writers I have in mind when I refer to basic writing students. Patricia Cross in *Beyond the Open Door: New Students to Higher Education* (San Francisco: Jossey-Bass, 1971) has provided the fullest portrait of the "new" students who entered colleges under the open admissions revolution of the sixties. Among the students she describes are many, however, whose skills are beyond the level I would call basic. Nonetheless many of the traits she mentions are familiar — non-academic interests, pragmatic educational goals (credentials and vocational preparation),

138

and fear of failure (although I would prefer to say the expectation of failure in academic situations without necessarily implying a lack of confidence and sense of self in other settings). I would add to this list certain features that define their writing. First, they tend to produce, whether in impromptu or home assignments, small numbers of words with large numbers of errors (roughly from 15 to 35 errors per 300 words) that puzzle and alarm college teachers when they see them for the first time, errors with the so-called regular features of standard English (the past tense of regular verbs, for example, or the plural inflections of nouns), misspellings that appear highly idiosyncratic; syntactic snarls that often seem to defy analysis, and punctuation errors that reflect an unstable understanding of the conventions for marking off the boundaries of sentences and little or no acquaintance with the uses of colons, semi-colons, parentheses, or quotation marks. Second, they seem to be restricted as writers, but not necessarily as speakers, to a very narrow range of syntactic, semantic, and rhetorical options, which forces them into either a rudimentary style of discourse that belies their real maturity or a dense and tangled prose with which neither they nor their readers can cope.

From these features alone we can infer much about their backgrounds. We can infer that they have never written much, in school or out, that they have come from families and neighborhoods where people speak other languages or variant, non-prestigious forms of English and that, while they have doubtless been sensitive to the differences between their ways of speaking and their teachers', they have never been able to sort out or develop attitudes toward the differences that did not put them in conflict, one way or another, with the key academic tasks of learning to read and write and talk in standard English. This situation in turn generated such a maze of misunderstandings of every kind throughout their school years that the one attitude a teacher has come to expect when he steps into his basic writing class is an attitude of mistrust. It is a mistrust only peripherally related to the ideological mistrust of the "establishment" that was cultivated in the sixties. It is rather a less deliberate but more deeply conditioned pessimism about the possibility of ever learning anything or ever being understood in school. It comes from experience, the experience of not having been noticed nor respected nor heard in too many classrooms, the experience of becoming used to not understanding what books and teachers are saying, of being passed on but never encouraged, of feeling dumb and bored in school. The typical silence of those first days of class is the silence of seasoned watchers of teachers who are trying to determine whether this class is going to be different from all the others and, if not, what strategy will best insure survival.

To recount the conditions that led to the entry during the sixties of large numbers of these students into college classrooms is not within the scope of this essay, but it is important to note that there were urgent conditions, both political and economic, that led administrators to create, often without much forethought or grace, entire remedial wings to their departments or even separate departments that were charged with the task of bringing these deeply unprepared men and women (usually with only a semester or two of low-intensity teaching) to a level of competence that placed them at no great academic disadvantage in regular college classes.

The teachers of these special courses, who were drawn usually from the untenured, junior ranks of English departments, set out to accomplish this task without knowing much about their students or the skills that were to be acquired so swiftly. Having little sense at that point of the ways in which the imperatives of the academy might collide with the social imperatives of the sixties, they simply started trying to teach their students to write. Usually they did first what *their* English teachers had done — or what they wished they had done — and then, as the classroom delivered its data, began to move outward, trying what seemed to be working for others, modifying, inventing, elaborating, but rarely stopping (or having the time to stop) to formulate theories or carry on systematic research.

It was a situation in which teaching clearly *had* to make a difference. So long as one's students could write the kind of prose that gets people through high school there was no pressing need for them to improve. Their writing would not be an embarrassment in academia — merely more of the depersonalized, institutional prose everyone was used to. A sobering analysis of the origins of this prose can be found in Carl Nordstrom, Edward Friedenberg, and Hilary A. Gold's *Society's Children: A Study of Ressentiment in the Secondary School* (New York: Random House, 1967). But here were young adult students, many of them with an experience of the world outside academia and with hard responsibilities in that world which their teachers had not encountered and probably never would. But they could write, neither in their own voices nor in what Friedenberg has called the "pasteurized prose" of high schools. Nor was it clear to teachers just why their errors and reluctancies did not give way easily under instruction.

Doubtless the richest materials from this period of groping and discovery are unpublished and unpublishable — teachers' journals, class materials (some of which is working its way into textbooks now), departmental memos on pedagogical issues, in-house evaluations, and the records of conference sessions with students. But in English there is no tradition of observation and cumulative publication, as there is in the sciences. Teachers and administrators of writing programs seldom keep systematic files of student writing or of conferences. They keep grade books and return the data to their students. Team research is rare. There are few case studies of student writers (none, to my knowledge, of basic writers), no longitudinal descriptions of writing progress that would enable us to credit successive approximations of good writing or determine sequences of instruction that might help avoid what I. A. Richards once called English teachers' "hugger-mugger, promiscuous leave-it-to-nature style in which the seeds of all things are being strewn over the would-be student's mind." (*Speculative Instruments*, New York: Harcourt, 1955), 106.

Without an accumulation of published information across a range of experiences with the new students, we are left with a highly circumscribed literature, essentially the bits and pieces of information that make their way back from a frontier, tempting us to premature judgments about the students and how or what they are learning. The literature consists largely of articles and dissertations which concentrate on two subjects: the students, how they write and what they appear to need; and programs and methods, what they are or how well they are working. I will describe each of these categories briefly, suggesting articles or studies that a basic writing teacher might find useful.

So far, we know the new students mainly through statistical reports on attrition rates, grade-point averages, performance on nationally normed tests, and responses to questionnaires. One wishes for more studies of the sort Rex M. Newton has undertaken in "An Exploratory Study of a Small Group of Disadvantaged Students' First Year on a College Campus" (Diss. Univ. of Oregon, 1971), in which he recorded and interpreted the behavior of a small group of students for a year. His findings remind us that far more central than statistics on attrition to an understanding of the students is the fact of their being in a new environment which appears to them unrelated to anything in their own backgrounds.

Statistics tell us little directly about the students as writers or even as learners. Surprisingly little effort has been made to analyze the content of their essays, perhaps out of a concern for their privacy. Yet Marie Jean Lederman's memorable piece on the self-images of remedial and composition students who were asked on a placement test, "What would you like to come back as if you were re-born tomorrow?" has a resonance few tests could yield. ("A Comparison of Student Projections: Magic and the Teaching of Writing," *CE*,

34 [Feb., 1973], 674-689). Adrienne Rich, in an essay describing her experiences as a SEEK and open admissions teacher, "Teaching Language in Open Admissions: A Look at the Context," *Harvard English Studies*, 4 (1971), 257-273, has written with exceptional insight of her students' backgrounds and responses to literature. Robert Cumming, in the same issue (pp. 245-255), has given a sensitive account of the literature that "worked" in his classes. The students have written of themselves, often in powerful, generous ways in the transient anthologies that writing classes generate. I recommend the *Basic Writing Anthology* (New York: English Department of City College of N. Y., 1972) because it is the one I know and have used in classes. But beyond this there is little direct description of the students. One seeks a portrait with the depth and complexity of Richard Hoggart's *The Uses of Literacy* (New York: Oxford, 1970), a description of working class culture in England, or a volume such as the Schoolboys of Barbiana wrote in their *Letter to a Teacher* (New York: Random House, 1971), a classic expression of the disadvantaged student's mistrust of the educator and his respect for an education.

Few attempts have been made to describe the writing of the new students. John A. Higgens, in "Remedial Students' Needs versus Emphasis in Text-workbooks," *CCC*, 24 (May, 1973), 188-192, has surveyed writing errors among remedial students at York College and reports that spelling, diction, and sentence logic pose greater problems for the students than grammaticality. He then goes on to demonstrate that current text-workbooks do not address the students' needs. We also have little information about the high school preparation of the students, but it seems safe to assume that their instruction has been not only inadequate but often alienating. A 1963 study of University of Nevada students, Robert McQueen, A. Keith Murray, and Fredericka Evans' "Relationships between Writing Required in High School and English Proficiency in College," *Journal of Experimental Education*, 31 (Summer, 1963), 419-423, shows a clear correlation between the amount of writing done in high school and performance in Freshman Composition. Little has been done to gather from the students themselves their recollections of learning to write in school, but Bonnie Rubenstein's "Say Something in English," *Junior College Journal*, 38 (Oct., 1967), 7-12, with its record of student responses to the word "English," suggests that we might learn much simply by asking students to describe how they learned to write.

While it is clear from direct experience if not from surveys that remedial-level students are reluctant writers, it does not follow that they are not motivated to learn to write. Many of them see the usefulness of this skill not only for college work but in the careers they hope to follow. They may, however, be skeptical about the possibility of acquiring the skill in an English class. (A good case might be made for a very different argument: namely, that teachers are not highly motivated to require writing of students in non-English courses, and that many English teachers still view an assignment to basic writing as a punishment.) Gerald A. Silver, in his study "A Comparative Investigation of Motivation in the Achievement of Remedial and Non-Remedial Students at Los Angeles City College" (Diss. Univ. of California, 1961), found among 608 remedial and non-remedial students few motivational differences between the two groups but did find that faculty members had a tendency to consider students with high verbal and quantitative skills as highly motivated. Geraldine McMurray Bartee, in another study of student perceptions, "The Perceptual Characteristics of Disadvantaged Negro and Caucasian College Students" (Diss. East Texas State Univ., 1967), found no support for the assumption that disadvantaged freshmen have lower self-concepts than other students. In fact, in her research a control group of "advantaged" students showed the lowest self-concept of all the groups, and two of the Negro groups of disadvantaged freshmen showed the highest self-concept scores. Such findings point to the need for a better understanding of the ways in which both students and teachers

perceive the task of learning to write and how these perceptions serve to supply or cut off the energies needed to do
their work.

It has been difficult so far to discover what makes a difference in basic writing teaching. The four-year colleges have
produced practically nothing in the way of program evaluations, although many colleges have described their programs
as successful. Among the two-year colleges, LeRoy Joseph
Dare reports in his "A Study of Remedial Programs in Public
Two-year Colleges" (Diss. Univ. of North Carolina, 1970)
that the few colleges who have made studies of their programs are often unwilling or unable to produce statistical
data. Meanwhile individual reports on programs are seldom
decisive. Thomas J. Farrell has ably reviewed the literature
of evaluation in his own study of the general program at
Forest Park Community College, "Opening the Door: An
Analysis of Some Effects of Different Approaches to Educat-
ing Academically High-risk Students at Forest Park Community College, 1971-1972," (Diss. St. Louis Univ., 1973).
John E. Roueche and R. Wade Kirk have written about junior
college programs that have made a difference in *Catching
Up: Remedial Education* (San Francisco: Jossey-Bass, 1974).
But such studies are evaluations of the over-all remedial
efforts of colleges and tell us little about how or how well the
students in these programs learn to write.

Where teachers have attempted to evaluate specific
methods of writing instruction, the results have generally
shown no significant difference among approaches. Allan
Lee Slay's "A Comparison of the Effectiveness of Pro-
grammed, Handbook, and Non-Formalized Grammar Instruction in Remedial College Freshman English Composition" (Diss. St. Louis Univ., 1968) found some progress
among all groups but no statistically significant differences
in writing skills among them. Richard M. Bossone and Max
Weiner, in "Three Modes of Teaching Remedial English: A
Comparative Analysis" (New York: City University of New
York, 1973), found little improvement under any method.

145

Doris G. Sutton and Daniel S. Arnold, comparing the grade-point averages and attrition rates of students in conventional and individualized (writing lab) remedial courses, reported in "The Effects of Two Methods of Compensatory Freshman English," *RTE*, 8 (Feb., 1974), 241-249, that over a two-year period the writing lab students did somewhat better than the conventionally trained students, but the differences, while statistically significant, were not impressive.

Where teachers have reported positive results with specific techniques or course designs (as they have for a range of strategies including card playing, pattern practice, simulation gaming, etc.), their experiments have rarely been replicated. One suspects they are rarely noted. Lucille G. Shandloff's study of the relation between teacher practice and research in written composition suggests little connection between the two. ("The Relationship of Freshman Composition Curriculum Practices in Florida Public Community Junior Colleges to Research in the Teaching of Written Composition" [Diss. Florida State Univ., 1973]).

Despite some excellent individual studies of programs or methods, one is left after reviewing the literature with the sense that there is something premature, repetitive, and unavoidably reductive about our attempts so far to evaluate instruction in writing. Few teachers have been trained for this kind of research. Few schools or programs are organized to generate or process information about their effectiveness, with the result that the individual researcher is overburdened by clerical and administrative duties that quickly discourage experimentation. Furthermore, writing is a slow-developing skill that should be measured over longer periods than a semester, but no system for collecting longitudinal data on writing performance exists to my knowledge in any program. We lack information and the habit of getting information about individual students that would enable us to isolate outside influences such as previous training or career commitments from methods of instruction. We lack adequate (i.e. precise and economical) instruments for measuring writing and then for controlling the unruly variables that swarm about the classroom situation. In the jargon of the systems analysts, we have difficulty measuring output (writing) and even greater difficulty relating output to input (teaching). Finally, we lack a tradition of collaborative research, within colleges as well as among them, that would enable us to combine resources and conduct more systematic experiments. Nowhere in the profession of teaching writing is the frontier more wide open.

Teachers must nonetheless keep pursuing their hunches and describing what "works," even though they lack the means to prove it. And this is largely what the literature in basic writing is — a miscellany of articles on what has been working, or appears to the teacher to have been working, in a variety of places with a variety of teachers and pedagogies. We find among the articles much that has been going on in Freshman English for years. The magic adjective "innovative" should be withheld until one has reviewed Gary Tate and Edward P. J. Corbett's *Teaching Freshman Composition* (New York: Oxford, 1967) and Michael F. Shugrue's summary of curricular programs that were developing in the early sixties under the support of the Office of Education, "New Materials for the Teaching of English: The English Program of the USOE," *PMLA*, 81 (Sept., 1966), 3-38.

Three concentrations among the articles on basic writing seem important to note: an emphasis upon creating what is often called a "humanistic" environment in the classroom; an interest in working out detailed sequences of instruction accompanied by unit tests; a concern with the pre-writing or beginning stages of the composing process. I will suggest readings in each of these areas.

Because he knows little about his students — what they know, what they can be expected to find difficult, what their individual silences or reluctancies may mean — the basic writing teacher needs a classroom that encourages open response. Yet, given the amount of work the student must do in order to reach even minimal proficiency within the timetable of the college, the teacher cannot afford to risk the way-wardness and easy solipsism that often follow the collapse of the teacher-centered class. Jerome Bruner, in an essay with the misleading title "The Uses of Immaturity," *Intellectual Digest*, Feb., 1973, stresses the importance of employing the socially mature elements in student character for better learning. He recommends collaborative approaches to learn-ing, especially among open admissions students. Basic writ-ing teachers, if one is to judge by the attention they give in their articles to classroom organization, would agree that the teacher-centered model which most of their students as-sociate with school is ineffective. It triggers stereotyped responses that impede learning and is especially unsuited for the highly social activity of writing.

Despite these inadequacies, the traditional classroom, as well as the relationships it fosters, is difficult to replace. Kenneth A. Bruffee has alerted us in "The Way Out: A Critical Survey of Innovations in College Teaching," *CE*, 31 (Jan., 1970), 457-470, to the ways in which the old au-thoritarianism reappears in the garb of the "decentralized" class, demonstrating that the real barriers to innovation lie within students and teachers and can be removed only by a deeper understanding of the learning process itself and by skill in organizing people to work collaboratively at learning. In "Collaborative Learning: Some Practical Models," *CE*, 34 (Feb., 1973), 634-643, Bruffee offers four models for teaching literature and composition. M. L. J. Abercrombie, reporting in *Anatomy of Judgement* (New York: Basic Books, 1960) on a course she developed to improve the diagnostic judgment of medical students, reviews the fundamental research on the use of group learning in teaching judgment, much of which has obvious relevance to teaching writing. She has also provided a useful short survey of practical methods of group teaching in university education, *Aims and Techniques of Group Teaching*, 3rd ed., (London: Society for Research into Higher Education, 1974, available through Pendragon House, Palo Alto, California).

Implicit in the move to open colleges to students who are not prepared for college work is the assumption that it is both practicable and possible to prepare them once they arrive at college. Support for this assumption can be found in the writings of several learning theorists, most particularly in John Carroll's "A Model of School Learning," *Teachers College Record*, 64 (May, 1963), 723-733, and Jerome Bruner's *Toward a Theory of Instruction* (Cambridge, Mass.: Harvard Univ. Press, 1966). Both writers hold that, given sufficient time and adequate instruction, most people (they would except those with severe learning disabilities and agree that the pace is reduced as learners get older) can learn any subject or master any task whatever its complexity. They may differ greatly, however, in the ways they learn and in the rate at which they learn. Aptitude, Carroll would say, is simply the *amount of time* required by the learner to attain mastery of a learning task, not a limit on the types of tasks a person can successfully undertake. Such a view shifts radically the way a teacher might view achievement, heightening his awareness of the content of instruction and of the importance of individual styles and rates of learning.

Even when teachers are unaware of the theories underlying so-called "mastery" learning, their approaches to teaching basic writing often parallel the approaches recommended by master theorists such as Benjamin S. Bloom in "Learning for Mastery," *Evaluation Comment*, 1 (May, 1968), published by the Center for the Study of Evaluation of Instructional Programs, Los Angeles. The approach involves breaking the course or subject into smaller units of instruction, each of which is then analyzed into a number of elements and arranged hierarchically for learning. There is frequent testing after each unit (called formative testing) to determine mastery or, where mastery is not achieved, to select a different approach to the lesson.

The analytic approach is not new. Good teachers always decide carefully "what comes after what" and tailor their methods of instruction to their individual students. Still, the mastery system is a more rigorous, conscious attempt at systematized instruction which encourages a scrutiny of the learning-teaching process much needed in basic writing, where many of the tasks yield to sharp definition and measurement. The approach can of course lead to gross simplifications of complex and little-understood skills, but wherever highly definable conventions and patterns are to be acquired (as they are in basic writing, where the conventions of both standard and academic written English usually make up a major part of the content), the principles of mastery learning appear applicable.

They underlie the approaches of many teachers, even those who are not acquainted with the term "mastery teaching." Gilbert Schechtman and William McGannon, in papers delivered at the March, 1975, CCCC Conference in St. Louis, described the mastery program in composition that has been developed at Olive-Harvey College, Chicago. Their report, "Mastery Learning," March 14, 1975, includes a sketch of a typical work week in a mastery writing course. The ambitious computer-assisted learning system now under development at Brigham Young University, described in a progress report by Victor C. Bunderson entitled "Team Production of Learner-Controlled Courseware," (Provo, Utah: Brigham Young Univ., May, 1973), will incorporate the main features recommended by Bloom for mastery teaching. Helen Mills, in "Individualized Instruction: A Shift in Perspective," an address delivered at the Workshop on Teaching Composition, Appalachia State University, May 10, 1974 (available in ERIC Reports), has described the evolution of her method of teaching the sentence and the paragraph through a sequence of individualized lessons.

Given the reluctance of many basic writing students to risk themselves on the written page and their ignorance of the ways of writers, it is not surprising that basic writing teachers have concentrated on understanding and teaching the art of getting started. Ken Macrorie's description of pre-writing in *Uptaught* (Rochelle Pk., New Jersey: Hayden, 1970) and

Peter Elbow's model of the writing process as he develops it in *Writing Without Teachers* (New York: Oxford Univ. Press, 1973) have by now had their effect upon basic writing teaching. In addition, basic writing teachers themselves have proposed imaginative ways of helping students gain access to themselves through written words. Many of their articles support some form of narrative or autobiographical writing as the most "natural" place for the inexperienced writer to begin. Don M. Wolfe, in "A Realistic Writing Program for Culturally Diverse Youth," in *Education of the Disadvantaged*, ed. A. Harry Passow (New York: Holt, 1967), 415-423, has made a strong argument for autobiographical writing. Harvey Wiener, in "Media Compositions: Prelude to Writing," *CE*, 35 (Feb., 1974), 566-574, has proposed media exercises that stimulate students to express their responses as a prelude to writing them down. Again in "The Single Narrative Paragraph and College Remediation," *CE*, 33 (March, 1972), 660-669, Wiener stresses the importance of beginning work on the essay with the form that allows for the greatest use of concrete detail from the writer's own experience. Michael Paull also locates "beginning" at the moment of perception and provides in "Invention: Understanding the Relationship between Sensation, Perception, and Concept Formation," *CCC*, 25 (May, 1974), 205-209, a sequence of steps for moving from that point into conceptualization.

It would be difficult to argue against the accumulation of experience in basic writing that suggests autobiographical content, expressive forms, and write-think or feel-think models of composing as most effective for beginning writers, even where the intent is to end up with formal academic writing. Certainly experience with children supports a method that encourages the development of both a personal and formal style of writing, with the personal coming first in the sequence of instruction. A pedagogy supporting this idea has been developed at the Institute of Education, University of London, in a project entitled "Writing Across the Curriculum," which has by now generated curricular materials as well as several important books, the latest of which is *Understanding Children Writing*, Tony Burgess, ed., (Middlesex, England: Penguin, 1972), an analysis of students of various ages writing both expressive and formal papers on a range of subjects.

Still, the special conditions of the remedial situation, that is, the need to develop within a short time a style of writing and thinking and a background of cultural information that prepare the student to cope with academic work, create a distinctive tension that almost defines the profession — a constant, uneasy hovering between the imperatives of format and freedom, convention and individuality, the practical and the ideal. Just where the boundaries between these claims are to be drawn in basic writing is by no means clear. Some would argue for a gradual exposure to academic subjects and skills through the extension of the remedial concern (but not the remedial structures and styles) into other courses, as in block programming and interdisciplinary curriculums, or into the entire college experience; others would press for a concentrated, direct approach to the distinctive tasks of academia, arguing that for students to lay claim to their critical and analytical powers and to cultivate the formal discursive style associated with academic work is no less "creative" or "personal" than the activities (poetry, stories, etc.) usually associated with those words.

The debate has not yet surfaced among basic writing teachers in formal or scholarly ways. It is more an undercurrent that unsettles staff meetings and most probably confuses students who must often move between semesters from one pedagogy to another. As I will suggest later, a better understanding of the nature of academic writing may help teachers move more effectively and imaginatively into the thick of the task their students face in learning to write for diverse audiences.

II

Experience with the new students so far suggests that at least some of the premises that governed the teaching of writing in the past, premises that most English teachers inherited from their own training, are problematic in the basic writing class. I have mentioned the problem, for example, of mistrust which results when students define their situations in the classroom very differently from the way teachers define them. Whether a teacher uses games or computers or a grammar book to teach standard inflections, whether the need for evidence in academic discourse is illustrated by slides or dialogues or rules, the student who experiences the grammars and logics of academia as competitive with those he has acquired on his own is certain to have difficulty mastering his lessons unless his teacher is prepared to mediate between the two worlds.

This is a problem college teachers rarely thought about in the past. Criticized individually, perhaps, for being tough or easy or boring or unapproachable, they rarely felt called upon to justify their subject matter as well. They taught "the King's English," not a standard dialect, the universals of sound reasoning, not "linear causality." They assumed a cultural trust, a vast body of unspoken but shared routines and information, which freed them from the need to explain what they were up to.

But once having discovered that he and his students do not share a universe of discourse but must discover one another's, the teacher begins to look with different eyes at his subject matter, much as a traveler begins to discover the assumptions and features of his *own* culture by observing someone else's. This transforms his task, which is no longer simply to make the old lessons clearer and simpler nor yet to abandon the goal of teaching students the national language and its uses but to try to understand why the conventions and routines that seem so simple to him are not simple to his

153

students. Thus he does not so much simplify as go deeper into his subject. It is no longer enough, for example, to ask, "How do I teach students to write correctly?" He must first ask, "What is correctness?" Not "How do I get students to be logical?" but "What is the context within which the logic and modes of academic discourse have developed?" Not "How do I get more adverbs or embedded clauses or free modifiers?" but "What are the conditions that give rise to greater sentence complexity?"

Such questions lead the teacher far beyond the immediate problem he is attempting to solve, even beyond the territory of his expertise. Thus the "simple" *s* inflection upon which so many hours are spent in remediation may involve the teacher in larger considerations than he might expect if he views himself as only a sentence mechanic. The teacher must know more about language and learning than English teachers have had to know in the past — more about how people acquire languages, how language functions in different social settings, what writing is as a product and a process, and what theories of learning might inform his pedagogy. The teacher faces, in short, the formidable task of extrapolating from a number of complex, even turbulent, fields whatever insights and information will serve him in his work with his students.

In what remains of this essay, I will suggest readings I would expect to be helpful to teachers as they attempt to close the gap between Monday morning and the large themes of inquiry that now dominate the study of language.

Classic Studies of Language. While the documents of science are always superseded, the outstanding documents continue to be worth reading. Not only does much of what the scientist said continue to be valid, but the way he observed and thought is communicated in his work, and the reader is thus apprenticed to him through what he wrote. Among the outstanding documents in the study of language are four which seem of special value to the writing teacher.

Leonard Bloomfield's *Language* (New York: Holt, 1933) was the handbook for American linguists for at least twenty years. Historically it is the link between the "old" and the "new" grammars, but beyond that, an example of a brilliant linguistic intelligence at work. Edward Sapir's *Language* (New York: Harcourt, 1921) is a philosophical effort to get at the nature of language by describing its variability, its elements and processes, and its relation to thought and culture. With its combination of grammatical and cultural insights and its non-technical discussion of the relation of sound to the development of language it is still perhaps the most stimulating and re-orienting book a writing teacher can find. Benjamin Lee Whorf's reflections on the influence of native languages upon thought in *Language, Thought and Reality*, ed. John B. Carroll (New York: Wiley, 1956) have been argued over for years, but his sensitivity to the ways in which particular languages order and shape our perceptions along culturally important lines is of importance to a basic writing teacher. Finally, Otto Jespersen's attempt in *The Philosophy of Grammar* (New York: Norton, 1965) to explore the ideas underlying grammatical concepts such as tense or number and, beyond that, to suggest the outlines of a universal grammar, remains a tremendously invigorating work for the English teacher.

Readings in Grammar. The objectives of linguists and teachers are of course quite different. The linguist, seeking to describe the neutral possibilities in language, develops an ideal model of the language that serves as his instrument of analysis; the teacher, seeking to control certain features of a student's language in the interest of clarity, style, and correctness, develops an ad hoc grammar that draws from whatever grammatical models serve him in particular situations. Thus the linguist is committed to *a* system and the teacher to whatever works, which at one point may be traditional grammar or just plain drill and at another some aspect of transformational or structural grammar.

155

With the stormy allegiances that have developed among linguists, however, and the great complexity of their theories, teachers have tended either to become discipled to one grammatical system, whatever its inefficiencies in certain areas, or to piece together their classroom grammars on the sly, somewhat embarrassed about their eclecticism, even when it appears to be working. The wisest and clearest statement on the uses of grammatical theories in the English class is James Deese's "The Psychology of Learning and the Study of English," in *The Learning of Language*, ed. Carroll E. Reed (New York: Appleton-Century-Crofts, 1971), 157-185. This should be read before a teacher ventures into current linguistic theory. Following Deese's essay, I recommend a general guide to theoretical linguistics such as John Lyons' *Introduction to Theoretical Linguistics* (Cambridge: Oxford Univ. Press, 1969), which is comprehensive and assumes no previous knowledge of the field. Then the teacher might turn to two individual works that have been of value to basic writing teachers. Charles Fries' *The Structure of English* (New York: Harcourt, 1952) demonstrates the difference between a normative and a descriptive approach to language, specifically to the sentence, and proposes a break-up of old grammatical categories, thereby refreshing one's response to the sentence even where it does not produce a conversion to Fries' terminology. Noam Chomsky's *Syntactic Structures* (The Hague: Mouton, 1957) is the key to understanding all subsequent interpretations and applications of his grammatical theories. Because of the conceptual density of this work, the reader may also want to consult John Lyons' explication of Chomsky's theories in *Noam Chomsky* (New York: Viking, 1971). I would add two works on semantics: Stephen Ullman's *Semantics: An Introduction to the Science of Meaning* (Oxford: Basil Blackwell, 1970), particularly chapter 4 on transparent and opaque words, which illuminates many of the vocabulary difficulties that arise in basic writing; Geoffrey Leech's *Semantics* (Middlesex, England: Pelican, 1974), which is also an introduction to the science but one that devotes more time to theoretical semantics.

Attempts to study the relationship of traditional grammar study to writing go back at least to 1906 and suggest with unusual consistency that traditional grammar has not made a difference. J. Stephen Sherman has summarized this long history of research in *Four Problems in Teaching English: A Critique of Research* (Scranton, Penn.: International Textbook, 1969), 116-135. Studies of the effect of the study of more recent grammars, namely structural and transformational grammars, upon writing are somewhat more encouraging. Jean McColley reports some positive results for structural grammar in "Effects of a Method of Teaching Sentence Structure upon Sentence Structure Used in Writing," in *RTE*, 8 (Spring, 1967), 95-97, as does Eva Klauser in her comparison of structural and traditional methods in "A Comparison of a Structural Approach and a Traditional Approach to the Teaching of Grammar in an Illinois Junior High School," (Diss. Univ. of Colorado, 1964). The history of experiments in sentence-combining has been well summarized by Sandra L. Stotsky in "Sentence-Combining as a Curricular Activity: Its Effect on Written Language Development and Reading Comprehension," *RTE*, 9 (Spring, 1975), 30-71. Among the works she mentions, John C. Mellon's *Transformational Sentence Combining*, Research Report No. 6 (Champaign, Ill.: NCTE, 1966), and Frank O'Hare's *Sentence Combining*, Research Report No. 15 (Champaign, Ill.: NCTE, 1971) are the most useful sources of information on sentence-combining as a method of instruction. James Wesley Howell has studied transformational approaches among remedial writers and reports postively on the results in "A Comparison of Achievement of Students in Remedial English Using a Linguistic and a Traditional Approach" (Diss. New York Univ., 1973).

Many teachers claim impressive results among remedial students from grammar study of all kinds. Unfortunately their claims are seldom supported by reliable research descriptions, but the special constraints within which they teach and the special uses to which they would put grammar suggest that yet another study of the relation between grammar study and writing may be in order. At this point, one can simply report a remarkable kind of eclecticism among basic writing teachers. Some hold to the effectiveness of traditional grammar drill; others subscribe to the total course designs developed by linguists such as Paul Roberts and Robert L. Allen; still others report various applications and adaptations of more recent grammars to remedial-level instruction. Elaine Chaika's description of how she leads her students to a discovery of grammatical principles through the close observation of sentences, reported in "Who Can Be Taught?" *CE*, 35 (Feb., 1974), 575-583, is sensitive and linguistically enlightened. Jacqueline Griffin's description of her eclectic grammar, combining insights from Robert Allen's sector analysis, Chomsky's transformations, and Francis Christensen's multi-level sentences, demonstrates well how the ways of teachers must depart from the ways of linguists. ("Remedial Composition at an Open Door College," *CCC*, 20 [Dec., 1967], 360-363.)

Both structural and transformational grammars have offered teachers more open, more potentially productive ways of viewing student sentences. They have affirmed, as prescriptive grammar did not, the resourcefulness of speakers, whose intuitions about their native languages provide the linguistic data from which grammatical rules are derived. "A speaker of a language," writes Wayne O'Neill in his foreword to N. R. Cattell's excellent introduction to present-day grammar, *The New English Grammar* (Cambridge, Mass.: MIT Press, 1969), xiv, "has a knowledge of it in a way that he has knowledge of few other things. The knowledge . . . can be tapped in ways that his knowledge of American history, say, cannot be until he is filled full of the facts of American history. Moreover, in grammar there are no unchallenged or unchallengeable explanations; the teacher does not and cannot hold the secret in his back pocket."

Readings on Language in Various Social Settings. Many recent events have turned our attention to the fact of diversity in language and to the controversies that arise when the social and political hierarchies that have held languages and dialects in their "places" begin to give way. The basic writing classroom is simply one of the places where the fact of diversity has become not merely an "academic" topic but a complex and troubling issue affecting what English teachers teach and how they teach it. The literature on diversity can be divided into works that attempt to analyze the problems that arise out of diversity and works that describe the languages that are the sources of this diversity, but the borderlines tend at times to be obscure.

Among the first group are three collections of essays on aspects of diversity I would recommend for basic writing teachers. *Language and Poverty*, ed. Frederick Williams, Institute for Research on Poverty Monograph Series (Chicago: Markham Pub. Co., 1970) is valuable for the variety of views and issues it explores through the papers of linguists, sociolinguists, and educators who disagree among themselves about the ways in which poverty affects language. Three essays in particular serve to articulate basic differences: William Labov's much anthologized essay "The Logic of Nonstandard English" (Chapter 9); Siegfried Engelmann's behavioristic proposal for teaching standard English, "How to Construct Effective Language Programs for the Poverty Child" (Chapter 6); and Basil Bernstein's attempt to define the differences in language styles according to class styles of socialization, in "A Sociolinguistic Approach to Socialization: With Some Reference to Educability" (Chapter 3).

The Summer 1973 issue of *Daedalus*, entitled *Language as a Human Problem*, gathers the views of leading anthropologists, educators, and linguists on the phenomenon of linguistic diversity. It is a much broader treatment of language than the *Language and Poverty* collection, with several essays on language variations in other countries. The

159

collection includes Dell Hymes' powerful essay "On the Origins and Foundations of Inequality among Speakers" (59-86), with its appeal for a shift from the study of languages in the interest of cultural hegemony to the study of languages in contexts of inequality for the purpose of transforming these inequities "through knowledge of the ways in which language is actually organized as a human problem and resource."

A third collection, *Functions of Language in the Classroom*, eds. Courtney B. Cazden, Vera P. John, and Dell Hymes (New York: Teachers College Press, 1972), attempts to promote an anthropological perspective on the language problems that arise in the classroom. Directed largely toward elementary-school situations, the essays nonetheless pierce many of the myths that follow students to college.

The literature on social dialects has not concerned itself directly with the college-enrolled adult so much as with children or with youths who for social reasons have resisted the assimilation of standard forms of English. What research we have on second-language and dialect interference suggests that college-level remedial students, whatever their native dialects or languages, end up with a common stock of difficulties with standard English. Marilyn S. Sternglass reported in "Similarities and Differences in Nonstandard Syntactic Features in the Compositions of Black and White College Students in Freshman Remedial Writing Classes" (Diss. Univ. of Pittsburgh, 1973) that the differences in frequency of nonstandard linguistic patterns between the two groups of freshmen were not significant enough to require separate language materials for each group. Samuel A. Kirschner and Howard G. Poteet's study, "Non-Standard English Usage in the Writing of Black, White, and Hispanic Remedial English Students in an Urban Community College," *RTE*, 7 (Winter, 1973), 351-355, also found similar types of non-standard English usages, generally with the same frequency.

To what extent more subtle problems in syntax, vocabulary, and organization are related to dialect at this level we do not know and probably will not until teachers become their own ethnographers. The most useful model for this kind of study remains William Labov's *Language in the Inner City* (Philadelphia: Univ. of Pennsylvania Press, 1972), particularly the final chapter of that study where Labov examines across a range of ages the devices in the vernacular for indicating the main point in a narrative. Through such insights it should be possible to help students see analogies between what they know and do and what academic tasks demand.

Valuable facts about specific dialects can be found in the collection *Culture, Class, and Language Variety* (Urbana, Ill.: NCTE, 1972), particularly William Card and Virginia McDavid's listing of the main problem areas in grammar (Chapter 6) and Al Davis's "English Problems of Spanish Speakers" (Chapter 9). The Spring 1975 issue of the *Basic Writing Journal* contains three useful articles on dialect interference in the writing of remedial-level students of college age: Barbara Quint Gray's "Dialect Interference in Writing: A Tripartite Analysis," 14-22, which proposes three categories of interference that call for different types of instruction; Betty Rizzo and Santiago Villafane's "Spanish Influence on Written English," 62-71; and Nancy Lay's "Chinese Language Interference in Written English," 50-61. John Joseph Collins has measured deviations from standard written English among 66 disadvantaged college freshmen, 90 per cent Black, and presents a useful list of the most frequent deviations in "Deviations from Standard English in Written Compositions of Disadvantaged College Freshmen and Regular Admissions Students at Glassboro State College" (Diss. Temple Univ., 1971). A convenient list of Black English features appears in Ralph W. Fasold and Walter A. Wolfram's "Some Linguistic Features of Negro Dialect," in *Contemporary English*, ed. David Shores (Philadelphia: Lippincott, 1972), 53-85. Mary Jane Cook and Amy Sharp have described specific interference problems among

Navajo students in "Problems of Navajo Speakers in Learning English," *Language Learning*, 16 (nos. 1 and 2, 1966), 21-29.

Because of the quasi-foreign nature of the difficulties basic writing students have with formal English, many of the techniques developed in foreign-language teaching seem to be applicable to basic writing. Among these techniques, contrastive analysis, a method that uses a common analytic frame to describe the mother tongue and the target language at those points where differences between the languages produce errors, has been much discussed but not well researched. A full curriculum using contrastive materials has been under development for several years at Brooklyn College, New York, under the direction of Carol E. Reed and Milton Baxter. In a project conducted at Clafin College in the early sixties the techniques of oral-aural pattern practice proved effective in teaching standard forms to speakers of Black dialect. San-Su C. Lin has reported on the project in "An Experiment in Changing Dialect Patterns," *CE*, 24 (May, 1963), 644-647. For a wider perspective on the possibilities and problems with ESL approaches in the teaching of English to natives, I recommend two essays: Peter Strevens' "Second Language Learning," *Daedalus* (Summer, 1973), 149-160, and J. C. Catford's "The Teaching of English as a Foreign Language," in *The Teaching of English*, ed. Randolph Quirk and A. H. Smith (London: Oxford Univ. Press, 1964), 137-159.

Readings on Writing. In his excellent table of specifications for writing in "Evaluation of Learning in Writing," in *Handbook on Formative and Summative Evaluations of Student Learning*, eds. Benjamin S. Bloom, J. Thomas Hastings, and George F. Madaus (New York: McGraw-Hill, 1971), 770, Joseph J. Foley lists 18 items under "content" and 18 under "behavior." Each item could in turn be elaborately subdivided. But even with such refinements, the complexity of the writing act would barely be suggested. Somehow people of ordinary abilities nonetheless learn to write. Most of them acquire the skill over such a long period and in such a variety of contexts that we can't claim to know how they learned. But the question of training becomes crucial when we face the basic writing student, who must acquire through explicit instruction what others absorbed unconsciously over many years. One seeks therefore to know more precisely how writing differs from the other language skills the student has already acquired as a speaker and reader and how the skills he has support or interfere with his attempts to write.

Some stress the continuity between speaking and writing and encourage easy transitions between the two forms of language. John Hawkes' Voice Project, described in "An Experiment in Teaching Writing to College Freshmen" (Stanford University, California, 1967), was one of the early efforts to develop writing skills among unprepared students though a talk-write method. Where orality and literacy are perceived as vastly different forms of expression that have in the past given rise to different cultures, there is a more deliberate attempt to build careful transitions between talk and formal writing. Thomas J. Farrell, pursuing the distinctions that Walter J. Ong has developed in his broad cultural histories, has proposed a curriculum that uses such techniques as glossing and oral reading to prepare students to comprehend and produce academic literature in "Open Admissions, Orality, and Literacy," *Journal of Youth and Adolescence* (3:3, 1974), 247-260.

There is a sense in which writing is itself a special dialect, with not only its own syntax and vocabulary but even its own cognitive style, as Lev Vygotsky suggests in *Thought and Language* (Cambridge, Mass.: MIT Press, 1962), 98-101. This means that while the student's competence as a speaker serves as a bridge to writing, his real models for written language are probably absorbed through reading. Thus reading is inextricably linked to writing, much as the talk of adults is linked to the infant's acquisition of speech. The influence is doubtless subtle and pervasive. John M.

Broderick's analysis of formal and informal texts by proficient and non-proficient writers, reported in "Usage Varieties and Writing Competencies" (Diss. Georgetown Univ., 1972), not only finds that the vocabularies of proficient writers are larger and include verbs that increase the syntactical options of the writers but also suggests that the sense of how to use these words is acquired through careful readings of formal texts. I. A. Richards has written both practically and philosophically on the interrelatedness of reading and writing and on writing as a distinctive instrument with which the learner "can examine at another tempo and in another form and for the first time the miracles he has been accomplishing fleetingly in speech." ("Instructional Engineering," in *The Written Word* by Sheridan Baker, Jacques Barzun, and I. A. Richards [Rowley, Mass.: Newbury House, 1971], 67).

The writer is also engaged as a peculiar sort of reader in relation to his own text, shifting from the persona of the writer to that of the reader as he writes and then becoming his own copy editor after he has finished composing. Many of the students' writing problems are reading problems: inflectional and mechanical errors, syntactical snarls, and many misspellings. We need to know more about the perceptions and coordinations involved in such reading. Kenneth Goodman's *Miscue Analysis* (Urbana, Ill.: NCTE, 1973) suggests techniques of diagnosis that might be applied to the good proofreader as well as the good reader. Frank Smith's *Understanding Reading* (New York: Holt, 1971) analyzes the reading process in the light of recent research in such areas as cognition, perception, and linguistics. There exists as yet no analysis of the spelling problems of basic writers and therefore no adequate way of tending to a difficulty that seriously handicaps students both as readers and writers.

Little attention has yet been given also to the kind of writing students are expected to produce and read while they are in college and afterwards in most professions. Yet only by understanding the situation of the writer in an academic community can the student grasp the purpose behind those features of academic writing that give him difficulty. The attention to examples and evidence, the well-marked routes of reasoning, the tone of "fairness," the predictable formats of essays and research papers — all arise from the nature of the task: namely, to present to an anonymous, critical audience ideas that are both new and possibly unsound. (Again, unless the student has played the role of critical reader, the conventions of academic writing can but appear arbitrary.) As I have mentioned, teachers disagree about which sequence of lessons leads most efficiently to the mastery of academic writing. Some would even abandon the goal. It is an old argument, but the issues that underlie it might be clarified by a closer look at the literature on discourse analysis and the writing process.

James L. Kinneavy's *A Theory of Discourse* (Englewood Cliffs, New Jersey: Prentice-Hall, 1971) helps sort out the differences between the aims and modes of discourse, the first referring to what he calls referential, literary, persuasive, and expressive forms of discourse and the second to ways of thinking about reality (narrating, describing, classifying, etc.) that are used in all types of discourse. This useful distinction suggests a sequence in which each mode might be taught across a range of discourse, from expressive to referential so that the student is repeatedly exposed to the critical stance and analytical methods of academic writing and yet not cut off from the resources he brings to the classroom, the experience of having classified, compared, and described features of the world he has lived in for eighteen or more years.

A better understanding of the writing process might similarly save us from false dichotomies between content and correctness or creativity and convention, for what little we understand about the process suggests that writing includes both generative and administrative actions, the proliferation of subordinate levels of generality and the control of these powers in the interest of making a point. Janet Emig's pioneering study *The Composing Processes of Twelfth*

Graders, Research Report 13 (Urbana, Ill.: NCTE, 1971) reveals that students do not compose the way they or their teachers think they do, that in fact schools have failed to create the conditions that encourage both the impulse and ability to write. If the composing processes of competent writers are little known, we can be certain that even less is known about the ways incompetent writers set about writing their papers. We can observe that the characteristic behaviors of good writers which Charles K. Stollard lists in his study "An Analysis of the Writing Behavior of Good Student Writers," *RTE*, 8 (Summer, 1974), 206-218, are foreign to basic writers and often to the circumstances in which they must write — spending time contemplating the assignment, extensive revising, contemplating the work at intervals, and having a clear purpose for writing.

We know little about how student writers typically behave or how they ought to behave, however. Among the works on language learning, three should be mentioned, and with these I will conclude my recommendations. Jean Piaget's *The Language and Thought of the Child* (New York: World, 1955) has already influenced many writing teachers but no effort has as yet been made to determine how accurately the developmental model Piaget describes for children fits the experience of the young adult learning to write for college. Robert Selman has pointed up the difficulties that arise when Piaget's theory is applied to education in his review of Hans Furth and Harry Wach's *Thinking Goes to School* in the *Harvard Educational Review*, 45 (Feb., 1975), 127-134. Robert Zoellner's monograph, "A Behavioral Pedagogy for Composition," *CE*, 30 (Jan., 1969), 267-320, is a model of the kind of rigorous and informed thinking that must take place before there is any substantial yield for writing from current learning theory. The pedagogy he proposes is in many ways supported by the experience in basic writing classrooms. Finally, James Britton's *Language and Learning* (Middlesex, England: Penguin, 1970) is a sensitive attempt to trace the development of language in the child and to distinguish the different functions of language that develop as the child matures. Many of the strands of research we have touched upon here are brought together in Britton's work in a way that makes them seem close to the concerns of the teacher.

I began by saying that the teaching of writing to unprepared college-age students is but the frontier of a profession. The readings I have cited in this essay must suggest that this is so. For basic writing teachers, the world is indeed all before them. The skill they have contracted to teach is itself among the most complex of human activities and the students who sit in their classrooms, young, intelligent, and miseducated men and women, depend as students have never depended before upon having good teachers. The "remediation" of their teachers may, in fact, be the most important education going on today.

THE USES OF MEDIA IN TEACHING COMPOSITION

JOSEPH J. COMPRONE

University of Cincinnati

THIS ESSAY IS BASED on the study of some two hundred and sixty-eight articles in ten professional journals and on the analysis of some thirty books. In its final form, the essay refers to sixty items, all chosen by application of the following general criteria:

1. how thoroughly the article or book discussed the theory and practice of the media
2. how thoroughly the article or book discussed the theory and practice of composition, including rhetorical theory, approaches to the writing process, and evaluation
3. how effectively the article or book related theory and practice
4. how well the article or book fit into the general categories which I devised for the entire essay.

In devising categories, I have assumed that teachers and researchers into the composing process would prefer articles and books in both theoretical and practical areas. The first three categories provide general, theoretical background for teachers who wish to understand clearly why they ultimately decide to use a particular methodology, exercise or classroom structure.

The items that are mentioned in Section One, "Theories of Media as They Apply to Writing," cover the *why* questions, primarily by articulating why composition courses should include media, by explaining the general differences among the media as modes of communication, and by explaining how general theories about the media can be adapted to teaching writing, to theories of rhetoric, language, and editing as they are currently used in composition classrooms.

Section Two, "The Language of Media and Writing," describes theories of language in visual media, especially as they apply to the teaching of writing. The grammar, punctuation and syntax of film, for example, are analyzed and compared to similar elements in writing. Section Two also develops a few essential comparisons between the semantic qualities of media and writing.

The items mentioned in Section Three, "The Rhetoric of Persuasive Media and Writing," define and describe general theories behind the classroom uses of advertising, propaganda in films and newspapers, and the rhetorical and semantic qualities of political discourse. Many of the items in this section do not explicitly discuss writing, but all provide theories of analysis which might easily be adapted to the composition classroom. In fact, several of the theories that are outlined in this section are later applied specifically in the section "Practical Uses of Media in Teaching Writing."

Sections Four and Five include more practical and specific references; different media are discussed in particular terms to show how essential forms can be meaningfully applied to writing. Section Four, "Different Kinds of Media and Writing," discusses the essential forms and characteristics of visual, print, and listening media in order to illustrate, in relatively specific terms, how these media can be adapted to the teaching of writing. General similarities and differences between particular mass media and writing become the foundations for general classroom plans and methods.

Section Five, "Practical Uses of Media in the Classroom," refers to articles that describe or outline specific, media-based classroom activities. Many of these articles are scientifically supported by experiments and tests, but most have been written by creative teachers who wish to share a media/composition idea with other teachers. The articles and books in this section have also been selected because they follow logically from and build upon the media theories which have already been developed in the first three sections.

Obviously the conventional apology for the idiosyncracies of the author must be mentioned here. Readers should treat this bibliographical chapter as a first-step; much more work — research, analysis and concept-formation — remains to be done. Although I suspect that I have left out, ignored, or not even read an article or book somewhere that would have greatly improved one of my sections, I do believe that my general categories, when they finally become complete, will accurately reflect what effective writing teachers are currently thinking and doing with media.

I. Theories of Media as They Apply to Writing

Generally my research in this area indicated three major areas of experimentation and speculation: articles that argue for the inclusion of media in English courses in general and composition courses in particular; general theories of media interrelationships as they apply to the teaching of writing; general theories about how film differs from writing as a mode of communication, with some attention to how similarities and differences between film and writing can lead to improved methods of teaching writing.

Numerous articles fit into these three categories; I have, however, referred only to those articles and books that go beyond the conventional, sometimes even tiresome tendency to claim a place for media in the writing course merely because students are exposed to a great deal of media in their everyday lives. These conventional defenses of media, which are often combined with diatribes against the traditional teaching of rhetoric and composition, are perhaps best summed up in Jesse Hise's "In Defense of Popular Culture in the Classroom," *EJ*, 61 (September, 1972), 902-907, in which the author argues that popular culture and the media will enable the composition teacher to teach basic rhetorical and analytical skills within a context familiar to most students. Hise also argues that students can be taught to observe more fully and accurately, to develop ideas and plans for writing with more interest and care, and to "read" the media with more critical acumen through carefully planned treatment of media in English courses.

In an earlier article, Jerry L. Walker ("Bach, Rembrandt, Milton, and Those Other Cats," *EJ*, 42 [May, 1968], 631-636) foreshadows most of Hise's general arguments and includes a list of specific reasons for including media in writing classes. Walker argues that sensitivity to media will produce students who (1) are better able to adapt to change and the explosion of information throughout our society and who (2) are better prepared to reconcile methods of communication in scientific and technological areas with traditional attitudes toward rhetoric. Like Jesse Hise, however, Jerry Walker needlessly pits the media against more traditional approaches to composition, thereby constructing an oversimplified stereotype of the traditional English teacher as well as a false dichotomy between media and rhetoric.

Those who oppose the use of media in teaching writing will find their arguments succinctly stated in John H. Clarke's "One Minute of Hate: Multi-Media Misuse Pre-1984," *EJ*, 63 (October, 1974), 50-51. Clarke fears that media are too often used as mere entertaining fillers in writing classes and create, as a result of this misuse, passive students and teachers who, rather than learning to criticize what they see and hear, become passive receivers, completely under the control of the media-makers: "Relieved of the responsibility to respond by the media, the students return to the teacher his payoff in the form of docility, order and acceptance."

Two seminal articles nicely sum up the arguments for and against using mass media to teach writing: Thelma Altschuler's "Using Popular Media to Achieve Traditional Goals," *CCC*, 19 (December, 1968), 340-347, and James Morrow and Murray Suid's "Media in the English Classroom: Some Pedagogical Issues," *EJ*, 63 (October, 1974), 37-44. Altschuler's moderate position is that the use of media in teaching writing need not deny the use of classics, of printed literature in general, or the analytical and rhetorical skills that are taught through the classics. Morrow and Suid complement Altschuler's argument by providing both theoretical explanations and practical hints on how media can be used to reinforce traditional rhetorical, analytical and expressive skills. Both Altschuler and Morrow and Suid contend that media components in a writing course should be as carefully planned and directed as the traditional principles of rhetoric and language; they also argue that accurate observation and perception, effective planning and organization and the ability to relate particularities to generalities are best taught by contrastive analyses of media and print.

Two articles and a book carry the arguments for including media in the teaching of writing into more substantive areas of discussion. Richard Coe, in a recent article in *Freshman English News* ("Rhetoric 2001," 3 [Spring, 1974], 1-13), contrasts cybernetic theories of communication with the traditional, primarily Aristotelian study of rhetoric. In a new theory of rhetoric, Coe contends that writing teachers will need to confront *overdetermination*, a concept taken from Freudian dream theory, by developing strategies for analyzing and expressing multiple causation. Strictly linear and logical modes of analysis and expression, Coe argues, will need to be complemented by holistic, non-rational modes so that students will learn to communicate in a world where clearly defined categories of discourse are being replaced by the mass media's explosion of information and the crossing of traditional rhetorical categories. Coe specifically mentions the study of visual media as providing ample opportunity to analyze forms of communication in which the whole is apprehended before the discrete parts, in contrast to print media, where a subject is usually apprehended part by part, line by line and sentence by sentence.

Father Walter J. Ong, S. J., provides a fast-moving and witty account of how the "talked book" represents the inter-relationships of electronic media and their effects on writing ("Media Transformation: The Talked Book," *CE*, 34 [December, 1972], 405-410). The "talked book" strives to maintain the immediacy and voice-play of real people talking, most often through the use of taped interviews, films, and photographs. The result, as Ong suggests, is that more voice-play than ever before has appeared in print: "Our public speaking is private speaking now." In sum, Ong's thesis is that newer media never simply replace older media; rather they naturally interrelate with the old in ways that profoundly alter both.

The pioneering work in the experiential approach to composition — Walker Gibson's *Seeing and Writing*, 2nd ed. (New York: David McKay Company, 1974) — also makes theoretical contributions to the study of media in writing classes. Gibson's text includes fifteen composing exercises based upon careful visual analysis. Each exercise develops in progressively greater detail the idea that writing begins with perceiving — that we actually compose the world as we perceive it. Moving from considerations of objective, concrete reality to analyses of more abstract, language-based reality, *Seeing and Writing* can provide the writing teacher with background theory as well as useful classroom exercises for the study of media.

In recent years, much attention has been given to film's place in the writing class. Numerous articles and books have theoretical contributions to make to the media-based writing class. In this essay, I will mention only those articles and books which make explicit connections between film and writing. This first section mentions items whose primary purpose is to develop theory; a later section will describe more practical, classroom-oriented articles and books.

Two articles provide useful general discussions of how film should be studied in the writing class, although the authors of each article do not explicitly mention writing.

174

Joyce Gould Boyum and Gordon Morrell Pradl ("The Necessary Balance in the Teaching of Film," *EJ*, 63 [October, 1974], 52-57) develop a transactional analysis approach to film as communication, illustrated by a viewer/film-as-perceived/film-itself diagram. This diagram becomes the illustrative support in an argument that concludes by contending that formal considerations — specific film techniques, as well as overall considerations of structure and imagery — must be studied along with analysis and content. Too many teachers, Boyum and Pradl argue, are either totally involved in technique or completely ignore technique and form and use film merely to involve their students in content.

William Kuhns' "The Instructional Film Is Dead," *MM*, 4 (October, 1967), 21-23, makes the same point as Boyum and Pradl by arguing against the use of instructional or solely content-oriented films in English classes: "Quality short films," Kuhns states, are far more effective than traditional educational films in involving students in considerations of form and technique in relation to content.

Two brief articles examine the similarities and differences between film and writing and suggest specific ways in which film can be meaningfully compared and contrasted to writing. Joseph Comprone argues that film can be used to involve students in a process of self-discovery; he also lists basic similarities and differences between film and writing ("Counterstatement: Response to Richard Williamson, 'The Case for Filmmaking as English Composition," *CCC*, May, 1971, 131-136, and to C. F. Angell, 'Counterstatement,' *CCC*, October, 1971, 256-259." This article appears in *CCC*, 23 [February, 1972], 55-58). C. F. Angell, in responding to an earlier article contending that filmmaking should replace or, at best, complement writing in English composition classes, argues that the differences between film and writing are more' important than the similarities and that these differences might prove instructive in analyzing film as a dramatic medium, but they can only confuse and disorient the student

175

when writing is the primary objective of a class. These three articles, read in succession, can provide useful summary arguments of how film might be used in teaching writing.

John Stuart Katz, in "An Integrated Approach to the Teaching of Film and Literature," *EQ* (Winter, 1969), 25-29, carries the arguments on how films should be used in the English class into the more specific category of film/literature comparison. Katz defines four ways of approaching film in the classroom: as supplementary audio-visual aid, as an example of mass media in the McLuhan tradition, as a technical medium, and as a literary medium used to develop critical and expressive skills. In supporting the latter approach, Katz contends that film as a supplementary aid is inferior to reading or doing the original as well as an ineffective way to motivate student discussion, that the McLuhanesque approach, because of its almost totally affective emphasis, often confuses the student rather than providing him with the analytical and expressive skills he or she will need to contend with the media's explosion of information. Finally, Katz argues that a narrowly technical approach to film causes the student to ignore the broader educational objectives of analysis, criticism and evaluation.

Katz then cites Joseph Conrad's and D. W. Griffith's statements that both the novel and the film, considered as literature, have the primary intention of "enabling the reader or viewer to go beyond apprehending to comprehending, to go beyond visceral reactions to an understanding of the sense of the work." Katz concludes by mentioning an Ontario film program that organizes itself around a contemporary theme ("Man and the Machine"), includes some exposure to filmmaking merely to teach basic terms and techniques and encourages students to apply technical terms in writing general critical responses to novels and films.

No bibliographical discussion of film and literature is complete without some mention of the pioneering work in this area: George Bluestone's *Novels Into Film* (Berkeley: University of California Press, 1957). Bluestone begins with

176

a specific analysis of the similarities and differences between film and novel, including considerations of how metaphors and other tropes are treated differently in film and writing. He also provides a full analysis of concepts of space, time and consciousness in both media. Bluestone then applies his theory to six classic films and their novelistic counterparts: John Ford's *The Informer* and Liam O'Flaherty's novel, Samuel Goldwyn's *Wuthering Heights* and Emily Brönte's novel, Robert Z. Leonard's *Pride and Prejudice* and the novel by Jane Austen, John Ford's *Grapes of Wrath* and the John Steinbeck novel, William Wellman's *The Ox-Bow Incident* and the Walter Van Tillburg Clark novel, and Vincent Minelli's *Madame Bovary* and the Flaubert novel. *Novels Into Film* is crammed with intelligent theoretical distinctions between film and novel as well as clearly illustrated practical analyses of the creative and critical processes of film. Many of the film/literature texts which are mentioned in a later section of this essay are based upon Bluestone's book. *Novels Into Film* also includes an excellent early bibliography of film theory and criticism.

II. The Language of Visual Media and Writing

The six items in this section discuss structural and semantic theories of visual language in comparison to the linguistic characteristics of writing. Obviously, no attempt has been made to review all relevant studies of semantic theory or the new grammars (structural, generative or transformational, and tagmemic) as they apply to the analysis of visual media. This section also does not include any review of contemporary writing on style as it might apply to either visual, print, or listening media, since relevant stylistic studies are included in a later section on the different media themselves. The six items referred to provide background theory and linguistic speculation on general properties of language in visual media, most particularly as they apply to the kinds of rhetorical and linguistic study that would prove useful to writing teachers.

David B. Bronson's "Reading, Writing, and McLuhan," *EJ*, 42 (November, 1968), 1151-1162, provides the best and most pointed summary of how writing teachers should apply the theories of Marshall McLuhan to the teaching of writing. Bronson argues that teachers should understand the essentially paratactic structure of most media communication, where images are usually presented in simple juxtaposition rather than in hypotactic or subordinated structures — as in most writing. Although Bronson does not provide a great deal of evidence or illustration for his thesis, his position is intelligently presented in enough detail to serve as an excellent orienting theory for teachers who wish to include media in their writing courses.

Probably the most thorough book on the contrastive languages of film and writing is John Harrington's *Rhetoric of Film* (New York: Holt, Rinehart and Winston, 1973). Harrington's text includes opening chapters that elucidate the rhetoric and syntax of film in relation to writing, working from an application of Aristotle's triad (speaker, subject, and audience) to the general rhetoric of film on through to a specific comparison of film's basic syntactical units —*frame*, *shot*, *scene* and *sequence* — to the basic units in writing: sentences and paragraphs. The *Rhetoric of Film* also includes chapters on the larger rhetorical/aesthetic components of film — the development of themes and theses, the uses of aural and visual imagery, control over point of view, structure and rhythm — and closes with a chapter on the persuasive qualities of film rhetoric. Although Harrington's book often uses awkward or inaccurate descriptions of several basic film techniques, his approach provides an effective general base for the careful comparison and contrast of film and writing.

Moving from the structural to the semantic consideration of visual language, Robert E. Probst develops a general argument for using film and literature together to sharpen the critical language skills of students ("Visual to Verbal," *EJ*, 61 [January, 1972], 71-75.) Probst specifically relates the imagery of a film version of *Hamlet* to a study of the text of the play, with the general intention of relating screened imagery to the written interpretation of that imagery by students.

John Debes, in "Communications with Visuals," *Etc.*, 25 (March, 1968), 27-34, returns to structural analysis by relating some of linguist Charles Fries' approaches to syntax to the "reading" of photographs. Fries' subject, predicate, and object "utterances" are applied by Debes to similar elements in dramatic photography, always with the idea of showing students why and how they respond to what they see in a photograph.

Most of these general approaches to the language of visual media are nicely summed up and illustrated in two practical articles on how visual literacy can be developed in the classroom: Sister Robert Joseph Lalor's "Verbal and Filmic Language: *The Red Badge of Courage*," *MM*, 4 (February, 1968), 40-42, and Walter J. Engler's "A Project on 'Our Town' for Communication Classes," *CE*, 14 (December, 1952), 150-156. Lalor illustrates how John Huston's film version of Crane's novel objectifies the interior consciousness of Henry Fleming, the novel's main character, through careful placing and use of visual imagery. This article uses George Bluestone's theory that film can never imitate a novel; rather it must remake the elements of a novel in its own forms.

Engler strives to make his students aware of "signs and symbols" as they perceive them in everyday life, whether in visceral, print, or aural media. He asks his students to study pertinent semantic theory, to read and discuss explicit symbolism in Thornton Wilder's *Our Town*, to compare those symbols as they appear on the printed page to their appearance on film and to make a collage in which they express symbols relevant to an understanding of their own hometowns. Although Engler does not explicitly apply this process to writing, most writing teachers should easily be

179

able to adapt his composing sequences to writing.

III. The Rhetoric of Persuasive Media and Writing

Three general areas of persuasion in the media are represented here. The section begins with references to several items on the language of politics, especially as persuasive language is used to control, manipulate, or evade the truth. References to several articles on both the positive and negative aspects of advertising follow the material on the language of politics, while two articles on news reporting conclude the section.

The most general and inclusive source for articles on the semantic and rhetorical aspects of political discourse is Hugh Rank's collection of essays, *Language and Public Policy* (Urbana, Illinois: National Council of Teachers of English, 1974). This collection includes both popular and professional essays on "Watergate as Watershed," articles on how classroom teachers can use examples of political discourse in the classroom ("In and Out of the Classroom"), articles on "A Call to Action . . . and Some Responses," in which professional critics and teachers offer solutions to the rhetorical/linguistic morass created by Watergate and similar examples of public doublespeak, and finally, articles describing the National Council of Teachers of English's Committee on Doublespeak. The entire collection develops a primarily negative slant on public discourse in the past ten years, although the experienced teacher of rhetoric ought to be able to compare the wrongs of present-day public rhetoric with the anti-sophistic rhetorical ideals of Plato, Aristotle and the Roman rhetoricians. Most teachers will also enjoy and benefit from the mixture of critical commentary from teachers, rhetoricians, journalists, political columnists, psychologists, theologians and politicians themselves — all offering useful models for applying rhetoric to contemporary public discourse.

Teachers seeking a general orientation toward contemporary rhetorical theory as it applies to the language of politics should first consult a series of four articles by Terence P. Moran in *CE*. The first article in this series, "Public Doublespeak: On Communication and Pseudocommunication," *CE*, 36 (September, 1974), 112-118, provides a working definition of *doublespeak*. In doublespeak, the communicator completely controls the materials and ideas; the reader or listener is never let in on the process of communication. Also, doublespeak tends to rely on abstractions that are never supported by concrete details, resulting in an evasive rhetoric. Moran also argues that doublespeak is often marked by a lack of specific authorship; groups and committees do the composing and the rhetorical evading. Moran concludes this first article by accepting William Safire's challenge to English teachers to clear up their own doublespeak — before attacking others — by scrutinizing the doublespeak of many basic English texts.

The following three articles in Moran's series examine particular aspects of Watergate, its doublespeak and the evidence Watergate gives us of the general deterioration of language in our culture. In "Public Doublespeak: On Politics and Pardons," *CE*, 36 (January, 1975), 605-609, Moran develops essential similarities between George Orwell's newspeak and Richard Nixon's public pronouncements before, during, and immediately after his resignation. Moran concludes by relating Nixonian rhetoric to Turkish Prime Minister Bulit Ecevit's "We regard this not as a waging of war but a waging of peace."

In "Public Doublespeak: On Expletives Deleted and Characterizations Omitted," *CE*, 36 (February, 1975), 689-693, Moran applies his rhetorical probe to the Watergate tapes, asking whether the English textbooks' emphases on learning standard English because the leaders of our political and economic systems use it is at all justified now that we have the Watergate tapes before us. Nixon's linguistic bluntness, his complete reversal of linguistic form as he moved

181

from private to public discourse and his complete disregard for linguistic decorum argue for a much more honest and sweeping treatment of rhetoric in the composition class-room, recognizing how our ideas of linguistic decorum can and have been abused by some public leaders.

The final article in Terence Moran's series on doublespeak ("Public Doublespeak: On Mistakes and Misjudgments," *CE*, 36 [March, 1975], 837-842) goes back over the tentative conclusions of previous articles in the series and concludes by relating Nixon's use of rhetoric to obfuscate rather than clarify to the idea that language obfuscation is coterminous with moral obfuscation; to save one's moral face at any cost becomes the primary function of language. Language abuse, Moran contends, is a general cultural malady that causes us to delude ourselves as well as others as we attempt to control rather than communicate.

As far as the language of advertising is concerned, Walker Gibson's chapter on "Sweet Talk: The Rhetoric of Advertis-ing," from his book *Tough, Sweet and Stuffy* (Bloomington, Indiana: Indiana University Press, 1966), pp. 71-89, remains the most thorough stylistic analysis of advertising, including an itemized account of the techniques of the adwriter — repeated use of noun adjuncts, overuse of the article *the*, manipulations of an intimate tone through use of the second person, numerous honorific modifiers and simplicity in dic-tion. Gibson also presents a witty analysis of the adwriter's creation of the voice he pitches in an advertisement through considerations of audience, product and language. Gibson rightfully finds the adwriter, for all his explicit chicanery, less offensive than the omniscient newswriter we often find in news magazines such as *Time* and *Newsweek*, who really does speak as if he or she knew what actually had transpired in a complex news event. The knowledgeable or aware reader surmises, Gibson argues, that the professional news writer often speaks omnisciently without having the facts or truth under his control.

182

The best general article on how advertising can be generally adapted to the needs of a composition course, surpassing numerous earlier, partial studies of the problem, is D. G. Kehl's "The Electric Carrot: The Rhetoric of Advertisement," *CCC*, 26 (May, 1975), 134-140. This article summarizes methods for teaching voice, tone, general aspects of style, using imagery and figurative language, developing and controlling theses, improving invention, and developing reasoning abilities. Kehl, in agreement with Walker Gibson, argues for both positive and negative approaches to ads, depending on whether the teacher wishes to emphasize the adwriter's creativity, or whether he or she wishes to develop the critical skills of students to encourage them to analyze the rhetoric of advertising.

Two articles supplement these articles on advertising with imaginative and thorough explanations of how the persuasive rhetoric of visual media can be used in the writing class. Mark Phillips' "The Propaganda Film," *MM*, 6 (March, 1970), 47-50, develops a complete course plan using the visual symbols and signs of propaganda films to teach general language awareness as well as basic critical and expressive skills. Leni Reifenstahl's Nazi propaganda film *The Triumph of the Will* serves as Phillips' illustrative material as he suggests methods of studying the symbolic structures as they operate within a closed communications system, where viewers are treated as passive receivers of contrived messages, rather than as individuals capable of free and open response. The article includes examples of specific teaching questions, exercises and assignments, as well as an annotated filmography of propaganda films.

Joe Michaels, a television news commentator, provides the best general commentary on how visual media influence the news they present ("News Reporting by Pictures," *CCC*, 9 [December, 1958], 226-230). Concentrating on television news programs, Michaels illustrates how newsmen invariably alter the news as they select, edit, and organize their reports for twenty-minute television presentations.

Michaels also argues that television reporters must learn to be exceedingly wary of the emotional impact that is created when words are matched with pictures, even to the point of deleting or adapting film footage when it contributes to a false general impression of a news event. This article will give writing teachers who wish to study the media's treatment of contemporary events a professional perspective. Simultaneously, it reviews the pertinent general issues that are related to the censorship and control of the news.

IV. Different Kinds of Media and Writing

1. Visual Media

As far as the general use of film to teach writing is concerned, two practical books, both of which clearly relate rhetorical, critical, aesthetic, and semantic theories of film to writing, can provide the composition teacher with useful introductions.

G. Howard Poteet's *The Compleat Guide to Film Study* (Champaign, Illinois: National Council of Teachers of English, 1972) provides a solid collection of articles defining a variety of classroom approaches to film. Working from a general rationale for using mass media in liberal education to specific and practical articles on how film can be used in the classroom, Poteet's book includes sections on rationale, history, language, literature, composition, curriculum and future potential. All the articles are intelligent and useful assessments of theory and practice; special attention ought to be given to Roy Huss and Norman Silverstein's "Film Study: Shot Orientation for the Literary Minded" (pp. 29-35), Ernest Callenbach's "Seeing Style in Film" (pp. 37-44), and Eileen Wall's "How to See a Film" (pp. 45-52), all of which do an excellent job of clarifying particular methods of approaching the language and structure of film.

Huss and Silverstein argue that films must be analyzed shot by shot, thus providing the viewer/critic with a clear perspective on how spatial relationships, point of view and imagery are progressively controlled by the director. Ernest Callenbach defines film *style* as primarily a result of visual arrangement; as we come to see that "it is possible to photograph and edit even a simple scene in an astonishing variety of ways." Eileen Wall, primarily a teacher rather than a critic of film, applies the visual emphasis of Huss, Silverstein and Callenbach to the English class, contending that teachers should always begin with careful visual/perceptual analyses of film.

In *Films Deliver: Teaching Creatively with Film* (New York: Citation Press, 1970), John M. Culkin collects a much more basic and practical group of essays, focusing on film as an example of mass communication, always gearing theory to classroom practice. Although most of the essays in the book deal with secondary schools, *Films Deliver* can provide a practical introduction to the theories behind film study as well as a few useful hints about how writing can be taught through film. The book's section on the technology of filmmaking ("The Nitty-Gritty of Films in Education") is indispensable for teachers who wish to employ filmmaking in the writing class. Culkin has also included useful filmographies on feature and short films and a bibliography on film study.

Television has resulted in very little pedagogical research and writing, at least in comparison to film. James Steel Smith, "Popular Culture and the Freshman: Three Questions," *CCC*, 10 (December, 1959), 253-259, begins by asserting that very few of the English teacher's responses to television have been supported by research, or even by careful observation of television itself. Smith then lists, in detail, many of the general characteristics of television programming: the pace of television action and information is either very fast or very slow, often forcing viewers into bored, passive responses to what they see; the audio portions of television are consistently loud, of consistent high intensity, often resulting in the almost hypnotic and mechanical attention that viewers give to television. Television also often represents, in its dramatic presentations, a small and stereotyped range of character types, attitudes, and values; the language used on television is most often simple, cliché, and extremely consistent in its representation of a stereotyped and oversimplified idea of how language works in everyday life. In closing, Smith argues that the television industry could, with teachers' and viewers' assistance and prodding, alter these simplistic patterns and encourage more informative and aesthetically-complex programming.

James Steel Smith does not discuss composition directly, but many of his criticisms of television could easily be turned to good use in the writing classroom. C. David Mortensen also provides only indirect help to the teacher of writing, but his study of the major networks' coverage of the national political conventions in 1960 and 1964 produced results interesting to teachers of communications in general ("The Influence of Television on Policy Discussion," *QJS*, 54 [October, 1968], 277-282). Mortensen concludes that presidential candidates communicated much more specifically and directly when they were asked questions by and engaged in dialogue with political experts or television commentators than they did when they were presented in more traditional campaign circumstances. Television, then, might become the composition teacher's laboratory for the study of the particularly contemporary forms of electronic communication, including the study of interviews, debates, talk shows, and documentaries on public issues, rather than the medium for bringing soap operas and simplistic forms of dramatic entertainment into the writing class.

In contrast to the minimal treatment television has received, many English teachers have been captivated by film. So far I have emphasized mostly those articles which discuss analytical approaches to the aesthetic and rhetorical aspects of film as they apply to writing. Numerous articles have also been written on filmmaking, most with at least some commentary on how the maker of films also learns to write. Most

THE USES OF MEDIA IN TEACHING COMPOSITION

of these articles, however, repeat similar learning transfers: students learn to compose by selecting and narrowing a topic, by developing and arranging detail to fit a thesis or general impression, and by editing and revising filmstock — all in manners similar to the writer's process as he or she controls words, sentences, and paragraphs. Jeannette J. Hanke ("Filmmaking — Some Experiences with the Gifted," *EJ*, 60 [January, 1971], 121-124) and Richard Williamson ("The Case for Filmmaking as English Composition," *CCC*, 22 [May, 1971], 131-136) have written the best articles in this area; both describe the composing process as it applies to filmmaking and writing, while Hanke simultaneously shows how students can adapt filmmaking techniques to the needs of both literary/dramatic and experiential themes.

Composition teachers interested in film, aside from discussing formal qualities and filmmaking as they apply to writing, have also written a good deal on how contrastive studies of film and written literature can be used to teach writing. Most of the articles and books in this area are based upon the pioneering work of George Bluestone, *Novels Into Film*, which has been described in the first section of this essay.

Gerald R. Barrett and Thomas L. Erkine's *From Fiction to Film* series, published by Dickenson Publishing Company, Encino, California, offers the writing teacher useful theoretical and practical materials in the film/literature area. Three books have been published in this series: *D. H. Lawrence's "The Rocking-Horse Winner,"* 1974; *Ambrose Bierce's "An Occurrence at Owl Creek Bridge,"* 1973; *Conrad Aiken's "Silent Snow, Secret Snow,"* 1972. Each book contains a somewhat discursive but generally informative introductory essay on the history and main aesthetic theories of film as well as a complete analysis of how literary terminology can be applied to film. Each text also includes shot analyses of the films, texts of the stories, and selections of criticism that are based on both the story and the film. Any teacher who wishes to develop a sound general background and useful pedagogical materials for a unit on writing about film and literature should at least consult these books.

Fred Marcus' "A Modern Modest Proposal: Read the Movie First," *EJ*, 63 (November, 1974), 94-96, argues that movies of novels and stories should be viewed *before* the reading of the story because movies often stimulate closer and more imaginative readings. Marcus' article is also useful because it specifically discusses Saki's "The Open Window," Shirley Jackson's "The Lottery," and Anton Chekhov's "The Bet," showing how these films and stories are particularly useful in teaching composition and literary analysis.

2. *Print Media*

Numerous articles and books on general journalistic theory and practice have been written, but few of these items discuss the writing process as it would apply to the general composition class. Ronald E. Dehnke and Ann W. Ely have produced the best article on using newspapers in the writing class ("The Newspaper: Medium Rare," *EJ*, 64 [May, 1975], 39-45). "The Newspaper: Medium Rare" begins by providing background information on mass newspaper publication in this country, proving that the industry is thriving. Dehnke and Ely then argue that teachers should encourage students to apply a process of inquiry derived from both the techniques of journalism and from general rhetorical theory to their newspaper reading. The article concludes by outlining specific units on reader attitudes and abilities, the voices and styles of newspapers, how readers choose what they read and the role of advertising in the newspaper industry. The general approaches that Dehnke and Ely apply to newspapers are equally applicable to most forms of public discourse as well as useful in generating student writing.

Ken Macrorie focuses on honesty in journalistic writings, even in that traditional butt of faculty humor, the campus newspaper ("Spitting on the Campus Newspaper," *CCC*, 14 [February, 1964], 28-31). Macrorie examines several examples of lively student editorials and news stories, all of which include friction, tension, and clarity because the writers are interested and involved in the issues they are discussing.

Robert Bain ("Journalism and Composition," *FEN*, 4 [Spring, 1975], 1-3), in contrast to Dehnke and Ely, who encourage the reading and analysis of journalism, argues that writing teachers should treat their students as potential journalists, suggesting that they ask the essential journalistic questions — *who, what, when, where* and *why*; Bain also suggests that students develop essays by asking how these factual questions might lead naturally to particular forms and patterns of discourse. For example, Bain contends, the traditional patterns of development might be applied as students write journalistic reports and essays on local events, issues, and architecture. In Bain's course, close observation, careful research, organization, and clear writing become the primary goals of the young writer.

3. *Listening Media*

Most articles in this section refer to the semanticist's division of communication into speaking, reading, listening and writing. Many of the articles that might have been included here, however, do not discuss the possible interrelationships between listening and writing skills. Those articles that do focus upon that relationship can be divided into those that discuss song lyrics and writing and those that analyze radio newscasting as a mode of communication and composition.

Dan Donlan's "Music and the Language Arts Curriculum," *EJ*, 63 (October, 1974), 86-88, provides intelligent background theory for using song lyrics to teach writing. He explains that (1) music can serve as an artificial environment within which students can write freely and associatively, that (2) music can be studied as literature — primarily as poetry — with song lyrics being examined for denotation, connotation, imagery, rhythm, allusion, and dramatic qualities and that (3) music can serve as a personal medium for self-expression, with students selecting music to complement literary pieces.

Steven Carter's "The Beatles and Freshman English," *CCC*, 20 (October, 1969), 228-232, is a much more specific and complete illustration of how song lyrics can add relevance and material of high quality to the writing class. The article begins by explaining why the Beatles' music serves well in the writing class: their lyrics and music are geared to popular issues and ideas, yet they are also of high musical quality. Carter then describes a rhetorical approach to three Beatles' albums, with specific attention to narrative personae in the various songs, to the satiric qualities of the songs as well as to their use of imagery in defining character.

Like Steven Carter, Nancy B. Wetherell ("Leonard Cohen: Poems Set to Music," *EJ*, 62 [April, 1973], 551-555) develops a primarily literary approach to song lyrics — those of Leonard Cohen — showing why his lyrics appeal to adolescents because of their emphases on loss of innocence and the desire to maintain individuality. Wetherell analyzes image patterns and clusters as they work together to create thematic statements and emotional appeals.

Turning to other forms of listening as they relate to writing, Florence M. Lumsden's "The School Newscast as a Project in Language Arts," *EJ*, 40 (September, 1951), 395-396, does the best job of relating general communications theory to composition. In Lumsden's article, students are asked to listen to a news broadcast, take notes, work in groups to criticize what they have heard, and to write, edit, and make news presentations.

V. *Practical Uses of Media in Teaching Writing*

While all the articles and books I have discussed so far introduce theoretical approaches to composing with only passing references to how these approaches work in class, the references cited in this section represent the best, most imaginative and rhetorically sound descriptions of the classroom use of media.

1. Media and the General Principles of Composition

Michael Paull and Jack Kligerman's "Invention, Composition, and the Urban College," *CE*, 33 (March, 1972), 651-659, supplies the best overall summary of how media can be used to help basically underprepared, urban students find and develop ideas for writing. Paull and Kligerman's article describes a series of "happenings and meditations" in which students sharpen their perceptual and conceptual skills before they actually begin writing, using media artifacts as the bases of carefully controlled rhetorical analyses. Their approach to composition moves from concrete descriptive and narrative writing to more abstract, expository contexts; they also describe an approach to journal-keeping in the writing course.

Harvey S. Wiener ("Media Compositions: Preludes to Writing," *CE*, 35 [February, 1974], 566-574) and Virginia M. Burke ("Why Not Try Collage?" *CCC*, 10 [December, 1959], 231-234) both specifically explain methods of using nonwritten media — student-composed collages, photographic essays and cassette and slide/tape presentations — to teach principles of composition. Both Wiener and Burke emphasize the student's developing ability to use specifics, to relate specifics clearly to generalities and to the basics of organization; these student media presentations are then used as pre-writing activities.

Two books provide numerous practical examples of how media can be used as the bases of writing exercises. Anthony Garcia and Robert Myers' *Analogies: A Visual Approach to Writing* (New York: McGraw-Hill, 1974) works from considerations of signs and symbols in the general process of communication through a series of creative composing exercises, all of which are based upon visual media. The second half of *Analogies* then applies the general composing principles learned in the creative, media experiments to writing.

191

While Garcia and Myers' book is directed to the less sophisticated and verbal student, Joseph Comprone's *From Experience to Expression* (Dubuque, Iowa: William C. Brown, 1974) develops a more formal, rhetorical approach to visual and verbal expressions. Working from narrative and descriptive modes to more abstract, analytical approaches to composition, Comprone asks students to discover forms in a variety of media and then to express those forms in their own writing.

2. *Practical Uses of Visual Media*

Films can be approached in at least three general ways in a writing course. The teacher can use film to sharpen the student's analytical and critical abilities; students can be asked to compare film and written literature to develop general critical and expressive skills and, finally, teachers can have students compose in the medium itself in order to teach general composition skills. In earlier sections of this essay, I have discussed articles and books that developed both the theory and practice of filmmaking as it applied to writing; in this section, I will limit my discussion to practical methods for developing the critical, analytical and creative skills of students through film study.

Gerard T. Hurley's pamphlet, *Writing For and About Film* (New York: Harper and Row, 1975), explains a very practical series of activities which would, inductively, give students the tools they would need to understand how prose imagery, actions, and ideas are transferred to the screen, how television and movie scripts are produced, analyzed, and revised, and how critics develop their written reviews and evaluations of movies. This book can function as an excellent background text in almost any kind of film/writing course.

The best basic, background text for the nuts and bolts analysis of printed and filmed literature is Margaret B. Bryan and Boyd H. Davis' *Writing about Literature and Film* (New York: Harcourt Brace Jovanovich, 1975). Divided by genre, Bryan and Davis' book provides a step-by-step, somewhat cookbookish introduction to basic film and literary terms as well as a thorough discussion of writing principles as they apply to critical essays in general. The section on film does not supply a complete list of terms or a complete analysis of what happens when movies are made from literature, but it does give students a useful way of seeing movies as art forms that can be criticized much in the same way that stories, poems, and plays are criticized.

In "A Dual-Media Look at 'An Occurrence at Owl Creek Bridge'," *EE*, 17 (Fall, 1972), 14-17, Joseph Comprone describes classroom exercises that put the comparative study of fiction and film into more specific pedagogical terms. This article includes a general account of where a unit on film as literature might fit into the composition course and a specific list of formal discussion questions and exercises which are based on the narrative elements of an Ambrose Bierce short story and a Robert Enrico film.

An excellent article on how the process of reading and writing movie reviews can contribute to the learning of writing in general completes our treatment of critical perspectives on film. Ralph Alan Cohen's "Reading and Writing Movie Reviews in Freshman English," *FEN*, 4 (Spring, 1975), 3-11, illustrates how the selective, critical reading of the best movie reviewers (the article specifically mentions James Agee, Dwight Macdonald, Pauline Kael, Andrew Sarris, Stanley Kauffmann and John Simon) can fit nicely into the process of learning to criticize films. Students learn the basics of research; they come to understand how the biases of particular popular magazines are reflected in their critics' work, and they learn to develop their own critical reactions to films without ignoring the insights of the experts.

Several articles suggest using various visual media as models for student writing. Joseph Comprone's "Using Painting, Photography, and Film to Teach Narration," *CE*, 35 (November, 1973), 174-178, describes a series of writing exercises as well as the theory behind them. All the exercises work toward an understanding of how point of view, spatial

193

arrangement, and time sequencing combine in narrative writing. Specific discussions of a nationally syndicated news photograph and the short film *Bang Head Go Bang Bang* are used to teach students how they can control narrative structure.

Donald Noble ("Television Script Book Reports," *EJ*, 49 [April, 1960], 259-261) and Joseph Comprone ("Role-Playing and the Short Film: A Creative Approach to Composition," *JETT*, 4 [Fall, 1971], 1-7) both develop creative writing exercises based on visual media. Noble specifically outlines an exercise in which students select a scene from a novel they have read and discussed, write a script (hopefully following some study of scriptwriting itself) for a brief television drama based on the scene, and present a version of the script to students through a report which is then supplemented by dramatic performances of scenes from the script. Comprone takes some basic principles of role-playing and applies them to the process of understanding, evaluating, and writing about short films. Specific discussion questions and writing exercises, all based on role-playing theory, are developed. The short film *The Game* provides the foundation for most of the discussion questions and exercises that are explained.

3. Practical Uses of Advertising

Bruce Reeves' "Ad-Man, Business-Man, Teacher-Man," *EJ*, 61 (May, 1972), 685-689, develops the most specific and best discussion of a composition unit based on advertising. Students analyze numerous advertisements and, with the teacher's help, select one for further analysis. They then define the advertisement's claim, set up a test to evaluate whether or not the claim can be substantiated, and conclude with a report on the results of their analysis — both to the class and, in writing, to the sponsor of the advertisement. This article is especially useful because it includes some emphasis on critical analysis of the structure, the language, and the psychology of advertising. Also, students use a scientific method to test an advertisement's rhetoric and they conclude by organizing and writing for a specific audience.

Hugh Rank's "Audience-Directed Writing: The Market Place," *CCC*, 21 (May, 1970), 194-196, suggests incorporating the study of mass print media in the writing class by using *Writer's Market* (Polking, Kirk and Natalie Hagen, Cincinnati: *Writer's Digest*, 1968) as the basis for studying the intended audiences of particular magazines. Numerous examples of brief editorial directives to potential writers — all taken from *Writer's Market* — are used to illustrate how a magazine's readership affects what it prints. This approach would, as does Reeves' article, help create for the student the sense that he or she is writing for a definite audience.

Acknowledgements

I wish to thank the English Department at the University of Cincinnati for supporting the basic research behind this essay. I also received indispensable research assistance from Alfred Rosa and the editorial staff of *Exercise Exchange* at the University of Vermont.

LINGUISTICS
AND COMPOSITION

W. ROSS WINTEROWD

University of Southern California

IT HAS BEEN EIGHTEEN YEARS since Chomsky's *Syntactic Structures* set off the revolution in linguistics which currently goes under the name of "transformational generative grammar." In those eighteen years, composition teachers have been dazzled by the elegance of the notational system of the new grammar, with its branching trees, arrows, brackets, and so forth; have been numbed by the seemingly impenetrable jargon of the field; have been intrigued by the complexity and ingenuity of grammatical arguments; and, in less guarded moments, have allowed themselves to hope that from the new field would emerge *the* panacea for the ills of teaching composition.

If we are now less dazzled and befuddled by the field than we were, say, fifteen years ago, we are also more realistic about the *uses* of modern linguistics, particularly transformational generative grammar, for teachers of composition. We are in a position to see where we stand and where we are likely to go from here.

The following essay will be an attempt to provide such an assessment. In the discussion, I will avoid the notational system that is so characteristic of TG grammar; I will use no branching tree diagrams, arrows, brackets, or other symbols. The works that I review will, in general, be non-technical enough to be understood by the reader who is not a professional linguist. In my discussion, I will attempt to give a coherent outline of linguistic theory, primarily but not exclusively as it bears on the teaching of composition. Most of the works that I deal with contain extensive bibliographies. Thus, in a sense, this essay will be a bibliography of bibliographies.

In other words, I hope that my essay will provide a general perspective on the field. Readers who are interested in "filling in" the details can go to the sources that I cite, and these sources generally contain bibliographic guidance for anyone who wants a specialist's knowledge concerning issues.

Syntax and Grammatical Theory

By and large, transformational generative grammarians are concerned with two related questions: the nature of deep structure, and the relationship between syntax and semantics. Whether or not the concept of deep structure has any psychological reality is a moot question. However, it is a fact that two of the following sentences are closely related, while a third seems not related to the other two:

(1) Man bites dog.
(2) Watermelons are expensive this year.
(3) Dog is bitten by man.

The weakest (and safest) claim that can be made about deep structure is that it consists in the sorts of properties that related sentences — like (1) and (3) — share. Thus, if we were to attempt to account for the similarities between (1) and (3), we would probably do so in the conventional manner, with a branching tree diagram, and we would say that the diagram represented the deep structure of the two sentences. It is futile to argue about whether or not (1) and (3) are exactly synonymous, but it is fatuous to claim that they are not nearly so.

From examples such as this, it can be seen that grammar must account for the relationship between semantics and syntax. Perhaps the best overview of the problem is to be found in a book which is, unfortunately, poorly edited and liberally salted with errors: John T. Grinder and Suzette Haden Elgin, *Guide to Transformational Grammar: History, Theory, Practice* (New York: Holt, Rinehart and Winston, 1973).

The problem — which Grinder and Elgin outline with admirable clarity and brevity — involves the relationship among the components of the grammar: syntax (including phrase structure and transformational rules) and semantics. Grinder and Elgin show the evolution of the question from *standard theory* through *extended standard theory* to *generative semantics.*

The problem of relating syntax and semantics is easily understood. Without attempting to recapitulate the history of TG grammar (which Grinder and Elgin do so well), one can say that the concern is with the nature of transformations. If we take the deep structure for (1) and (3) to be identical, then clearly we are positing that the grammar must have a transformational component. (In effect, we must argue that there is *at least* a passive transformation.) The next problem concerns the effects that transformations have on meaning.

The earliest theory posited a group of *kernel sentences* to which three sorts of transformations applied: *obligatory, optional meaning-changing* and *optional meaning-preserving.* A kernel sentence was one that was derived only from the application of phrase structure rules and obligatory transformational rules. (Phrase structure rules defined the components of, for instance, Noun Phrase.) Thus, *Man bites dog* is a kernel sentence, for the only transformations involved in its derivation are obligatory, such as the rule which makes the verb agree with its subject, but *Dog is bitten by man* is not a kernel sentence, for an optional transformation — the meaning-preserving passive — has been applied in the derivation. However, early theory also posited that the following are also derivations from the kernel *Man bites dog* through the application of optional meaning-changing transformations.

199

(4) Man doesn't bite dog. (negative)
(5) Does man bite dog? (yes/no question)
(6) Man, bite dog! (imperative)

In 1964, however, Klima, Katz, and Postal proposed that all transformations must be meaning-preserving or, conversely, that no transformation changes meaning. In that case, (1), (4), (5), and (6) all have different deep structures. This proposal is, after all, completely reasonable, for a deep structure representation is intended to capture the similarities among related sentences, not to obscure them.

The position that no transformation changes meaning brings about further difficult problems, however. We have seen that a grammar must include a passive transformation to account for the similarity between sentences such as (1) and (3). That being the case, how do we account for the following paradox?

(7) Many people don't like cabbage.
(8) Cabbage isn't liked by many people.

The application of the passive transformation seems to change the meaning in these two examples, as the following demonstrate:

(9) Many people don't like cabbage, do they?
(10) Cabbage isn't liked by many people, is it?
(11) *Cabbage isn't liked by many people, do they?

As Grinder and Elgin point out,

> The linguists who support the Extended Standard Theory ... typically respond to this dilemma [and others like it] by
>
> 1. giving up the hypothesis that transformations are meaning-preserving operations;
> 2. proposing an additional set of projection rules (often called rules of Surface Interpretation).

Generative semanticists argue that sentences such as (7) and (8) must have different deep structures.

This brief discussion has purposely avoided undue technicality. Grinder and Elgin provide sufficient detail to give readers a sense of the intricacy of the problems involved.

Which brings us to a necessary premise about the uses of TG grammar for teachers of composition. We need to understand the theory in general, but we are not obliged to remain at the cutting edge of the field or to follow the detailed arguments of linguists who are attempting to bring their instrument, the grammar, to perfection in any of its parts. For example, one of the more elegantly subtle arguments in grammatical theory was advanced by Emmon Bach ("Nouns and Noun Phrases," *Universals in Linguistic Theory*, ed. Emmon Bach and Robert T. Harms [New York: Holt, Rinehart and Winston, 1968]). In this essay, Bach attempts to account for the introduction of noun phrases into sentences. Sentences such as the following are paradoxical:

(12) The log is ashes.
(13) My wife was born in Fairview.
(14) Finish designing the airplane.

Here is the paradox: if the log is ashes, it is no longer a log; when the woman who is now my wife was born, she was not my wife; if the airplane is not yet designed, it is not in existence. Bach accounts for these and similar facts of meaning by proposing that in the deep structure all nouns are predicate nominals in clauses modifying variables. This point is more easily illustrated than explained. In general, here is what Bach proposes:

(15) *Something which was THE LOG* is ashes. X X was the log. . . .
(16) *Someone who is MY WIFE* was born in Fairview. X X is my wife. . . .
(17) Finish designing something *which will be THE AIRPLANE*. . . . X X will be the airplane.

This kind of argument — and linguistics is full of them — is interesting, but hardly necessary for the teacher of composition. We are much more concerned with the surface structure of nominals and, often, with a general notion of their derivation.

Grinder and Elgin, then, provide an excellent and fairly general discussion of issues in the development of TG grammar.

In *Syntactic Theory* (New York: Holt, Rinehart and Winston, 1974), Emmon Bach presents a coherent account of theory from phrase structure grammars through universal grammar. Bach's concern is primarily with the theory underlying the form that an adequate grammar must take. One chapter, "The Mathematical Theory of Grammars," will probably be well beyond most readers, but the rest of the book, though difficult, is manageable.

Most teachers of composition, including myself, have picked their linguistics up in bits and pieces. *Syntactic Theory* puts these bits and pieces together. So far as my knowledge extends, it is the best coherent account of the rationale behind the development of transformational generative grammar from *Syntactic Structures* to the present.

Relating to TG grammar, but differing from it in significant ways, is *case grammar*, first explained in detail by Charles J. Fillmore in "The Case for Case," one of the essays in *Universals in Linguistic Theory*, cited above.

A typical derivation in transformational generative grammar starts with the assumption that Sentence (S) is rewritten as Noun Phrase (NP), Auxiliary (Aux), and Verb Phrase (VP). This assumption imposes a sequential linearity on the derivational tree, in effect, a left-to-right "reading" of the deep structure that corresponds to the inevitable left-to-right reading of the surface structure. But there is no particular reason for assuming that the deep structure must have this ordering. Specifically, here is Fillmore's proposal:

In the basic structure of sentences ... we find what might be called the 'proposition', a tenseless set of relationships involving verbs and nouns (and embedded sentences, if there are any), separated from what might be called the 'modality' constituent. This latter will include such modalities on the sentence-as-a-whole as negation, tense, mood, and aspect.

Going back to our old friend *Man bites dog*, traditional TG grammar would analyze it something like this:

(16) <u>NP</u>   <u>Aux</u>   <u>VP</u>
      Man   +   Present Tense´   +   bite dog.

Case grammar, however, would give an analysis like the following:

(17)   <u>Modality</u>   <u>Proposition</u>
                        <u>Predicate</u>   <u>Case$_1$</u>   <u>Case$_2$</u>
   Present Tense   +   bite: Man   dog

I have purposely avoided assigning names to the cases in the proposition. Clearly, case grammar forces us to recognize more cases (or "roles," as they are sometimes called) than the traditional four that we have inherited. For instance, the following sentences lead us to assume that there is an *instrumental* case.

(18) George broke the window with *a hammer*.
(19) *A hammer* broke the window.
(20) George broke the window [presumably with some instrument, since **George broke the window with himself*].

It should be noted that (17) very nicely captures important similarities between *Man bites dog* and *Dog is bitten by man* that could not be captured by a grammar that assumes as its first rule that S is rewritten as NP + Aux + VP. That is to say, both the active and passive versions of the sentence have the same predicate and the same cases relating to that predicate. Cases are independent of surface relationships such as subject and object. Thus, "man" is the subject of the active sentence and the object of a preposition in the passive, but in both versions, it is in what we have called $Case_1$. Its case does not change with its surface syntax. In relating structure to meaning, case grammar attempts to account for the fact that in understanding sentences, we must know "who did what, and with which, and to whom," etc.

I would suggest that a careful reading of Grinder and Elgin, Bach, and Fillmore will give composition teachers the background to deal with much work in linguistics intelligently. Though we have no need to advance theory, we must understand it sufficiently to follow what is going on in the field.

An excellent and fairly comprehensive (but difficult) reference source is Robert P. Stockwell, Paul Schachter, and Barbara Hall Partee, *The Major Syntactic Structures of English* (New York: Holt, Rinehart and Winston, 1973). The major thrust of the book is to integrate Fillmore's case hypothesis with theories outlined earlier in this discussion. The chapter-by-chapter bibliography is extremely valuable.

The most direct and beneficial effect of TG grammar in the teaching of composition has been in the area termed *syntactic fluency*. Syntactic fluency is nothing more than the ability to use the syntactic resources of the language to embed proposition within proposition within proposition. . . . For example, the propositional content of the following:

(21) Typing furiously, the secretary, a woman of about thirty, hurried to complete the job which her boss had assigned her.
    (a) [the secretary] typing furiously
    (b) [the secretary (be)] a woman of about thirty
    (c) the secretary hurried
    (d) [the secretary] to complete the job
    (e) her boss had assigned her [the job]

It is assumed that the bracketed elements are in the deep structure, for we must be able to supply their semantic value in order to interpret the sentence. That is, we must know *who is typing, who is a woman of about thirty, who will complete the job*, and *that "which" is the equivalent of "the job."* Now note:

    (22) The secretary was typing furiously. She was a woman of about thirty. She hurried. She was completing the job. Her boss had assigned her the job.

Examples (21) and (22) are intended to make the simple but dramatic point about the importance of syntactic fluency.

It is a fact, of course, that the number of devices afforded by the language for embedding is severely limited. One thinks, for instance, of *relatives*:

    (23) The man *who came to dinner* wore a tux.
verbals:
    (24) *To go to dinner at the Ritz*, you must wear a tux.
    (25) *Having gone to dinner at the Ritz*, I am now broke.
complements of various kinds:
    (26) The fact *that I went to dinner at the Ritz* proves *I'm foolish.*
    (27) It is foolish *to go to dinner at the Ritz.*
    (28) *That I went to dinner at the Ritz* proves (that) *I'm foolish.*

It happens that the concept of syntactic fluency lies precisely at the interface between TG grammar as a theory of language and as a tool in the teaching of composition.

It was inevitable that a language theory as powerful as that of TG grammar would engage the attention of rhetoricians. The question was simple enough: Would a knowledge of TG grammar have an effect on the writing ability of students? The first tentative answer came in D. R. Bateman and F. J. Zidonis, *The Effect of a Study of Transformational Grammar on the Writing of Ninth and Tenth Graders* ("Research Report no. 6"; Urbana, Ill.: NCTE, 1966). Bateman and Zidonis concluded that the study of TG grammar did, indeed, increase both the well-formedness and the complexity of sentences written by their experimental groups. This study has been severely questioned, but it was a landmark — in effect, a starting point for other studies which, building on the work of Bateman and Zidonis, are more securely founded.

In particular, John C. Mellon, *Transformational Sentence-Combining: A Method for Enhancing the Development of Syntactic Fluency in English Composition* ("Research Report no. 10"; Urbana, Ill.: NCTE, 1969) reported that the study of TG grammar, *combined with exercises in sentence combining*, enhanced the syntactic fluency of ninth-graders.

I have not discussed the Bateman and Zidonis or the Mellon studies in detail, for they are superseded by Frank O'Hare, *Sentence Combining: Improving Student Writing without Formal Grammar Instruction* ("Research Report no. 15"; Urbana, Ill.: NCTE, 1971). In his monograph, O'Hare gives a fair appraisal of the work that Bateman and Zidonis and Mellon did.

I would like to comment on the importance of syntactic fluency in general and on O'Hare's conclusions specifically. However, much of what I say will be my own interpretation of O'Hare, though I feel that he would not disagree with me in any essentials.

In a later section of this essay, I will discuss the importance of the psycholinguistic concept of competence. For the moment, a fairly weak statement about the nature of competence in language will suffice. Namely: most students have the ability to accomplish all basic language learning tasks. This means that most students can develop a degree of syntactic fluency. I have felt for some time that the lack of syntactic fluency amounts to a "scribal stutter." That is, students who are not syntactically fluent must concentrate on merely getting simple ideas into sentences, and this tortuous, singleminded concentration prevents them from achieving larger (though not necessarily more important) goals of composing, such as supporting theses, developing paragraphs, supplying detail, achieving coherent organization. Just as the stutterer finds it difficult to get beyond his or her own difficulties with the utterance of words, so lack of syntactic fluency blocks the writer from the logical, developmental, and organizational concerns that bring about satisfactory written expression.

O'Hare provides tangential evidence in support of this claim. The compositions of students who had gone through O'Hare's sentence-combining routines "were significantly better in overall quality than the control group's compositions."

It must be stressed that the students in O'Hare's control group had absolutely no training in TG grammar, a fact which differentiates O'Hare from Bateman and Zidonis and Mellon. On the other hand, O'Hare did use the theories and analyses of TG grammar in designing his routines.

The exercises that O'Hare designed took the form illustrated by the following example:

(29) Some really effective sentences can be constructed by changing a word to its -ing form. . . . Notice how the (ING) instruction works:
A. Joe *burst through the line*. (ING)
Joe forced the quarterback to eat the ball on the fourth down.
B. Bursting through the line, Joe forced the quarterback to eat the ball on the fourth down.
The (ING) instruction causes *burst* to become *bursting*, and the italics are a reminder to get rid of the *Joe* in that sentence. Now try one of your own:
A. The angry crowd fell on the assassin. (ING)
The angry crowd tore him limb from limb.

Notice that O'Hare scrupulously avoids jargon of any variety of grammar. He talks about -*ing* words rather than present participles, and one finds no arrows or trees in his routines.

A useful adjunct to the concept of syntactic fluency is Francis Christensen, "A Generative Rhetoric of the Sentence," *Notes Toward a New Rhetoric* (New York: Harper & Row, 1967). Christensen identifies a group of structures that are typically used to expand sentence bases. For instance,

(30) Noun phrases
   The cigar, *a twelve-cent stinko*, clouded the room.
(31) Absolutes
   Summer having arrived, we went to the beach every afternoon.
(32) Verb phrases
   Having gone to the beach, we were ready for our sherry.

And so on.

Christensen's work has the virtue of clarity and simplicity. Its main drawback is that it is not so penetrating or so wide in scope as the suggestions that both Mellon and O'Hare make.

Tagmemics, the grammatical theory identified with Kenneth Pike, has been less influential in linguistics than either TG grammar or case grammar, but it has had significant impact on the teaching of composition, primarily through an excellent textbook based on tagmemic theory: Richard E. Young, Alton L. Becker, and Kenneth L. Pike, *Rhetoric: Discovery and Change* (New York: Harcourt Brace Jovanovich, 1970). A layman's introduction to tagmemic theory is Walter A. Cook, S.J., *Introduction to Tagmemic Analysis* (New York: Holt, Rinehart and Winston, 1969).

With the coming of TG grammar, the study of style was radicalized. Before the '60's, stylistic studies in America tended to be impressionistic and unsystematic. Indeed, Croce had argued that matter and manner are inseparable, and this being the case, there could really be no such thing as the study of style.

If, however, as TG grammar claimed, sentences have both deep and surface structure, then style can be mapped very precisely as the operations that bring a deep structure to its surface realizations. Croceans would argue that the following pair are simply different ideas, while TG grammarians in general would argue that they are surface variants of the same deep structure:

(33) It is fun to terrify babies.

(34) To terrify babies is fun.

In fact, TG grammar even supplied a vocabulary to *name* the stylistic differences between the two. TG grammar would argue that the deep structure of both sentences is something like this:

(35) It (for someone to terrify babies) is fun.

In other words, the infinitive phrase or "infinitival sentence" is embedded in the NP that serves as the subject of the sentence. In (33), the *extraposition transformation* has been applied, to move the infinitive to the end of the sentence; in (34), *it-deletion* has been applied. (And, of course, one or the other is obligatory.)

What TG grammar did was to provide stylisticians, first, with a rationale for dealing with an entity called "style" and, second, with a whole plethora of "point-atables." Let me give a simple illustration of what I mean. TG grammar posits the following derivation (in general):

(36) The man gets a sunburn.
   The man is bald.

(37) The man who is bald gets a sunburn. [The result of the *relativization transformation*.]

(38) *The man bald gets a sunburn. [The result of the so-called *whiz deletion transformation*, which gets rid of BE and the relative pronoun, and which, in the illustrative sentence, makes the next transformation obligatory.]

(39) The bald man gets a sunburn. [The result of the *adjective placement transformation*.]

This hypothetical derivation obviously yields a great deal of data. In general, TG grammar — and the computer — made it possible to do magnificently imaginative quantitative studies of style.

To gain a perspective on where style studies have gone since the advent of the new linguistics, one can consult three volumes: *Style in Language*, ed. Thomas A. Sebeok (John Wiley & Sons and M.I.T. Press, 1960); *Essays on the Language of Literature*, ed. Seymour Chatman and Samuel R. Levin (Boston: Houghton, Mifflin, 1967); and *Literary Style: A Symposium*, ed. Seymour Chatman (New York: Oxford University Press, 1971). This last volume — actually the result of an international conference on style — is probably the bést single source for a view of the state-of-the-art at present.

In the brave new world of transformational generative grammar, it might well be disheartening to realize that the argument over exactly what makes up style still rages. On the one hand, Roland Barthes, in his essay in the last volume cited, tells us that style should be seen as "an onion, a construction of layers (or levels, or systems) whose body contains, finally, no heart, no kernel, no secret, no irreducible principles, nothing except the infinity of its own envelopes — which envelope nothing other than the unity of its [the text's] own surfaces." On the other hand, Louis Milic tells us that a writer exercises options in creating his or her style, and that these options are both conscious and unconscious.

The theory of style as a branch of esthetics or even as a subdiscipline of linguistics is probably of less interest to teachers of composition than is such a basic matter as syntactic fluency. Nonetheless, becoming aware of modern work in stylistics is well worth the time. For one thing, we are confronted with the questions, "What is good style, and what is bad style?" These questions, in fact, lead directly to the next consideration in the present essay.

Speech Act Theory

In regard to speech act theory, one thinks primarily of two books: J. L. Austin, *How to Do Things with Words* (Oxford:

Oxford University Press, 1962); and John R. Searle, *Speech Acts: An Essay in the Philosophy of Language* (Cambridge, Engl.: Cambridge University Press, 1969). Valuable for a general background in the philosophy of language is *Readings in the Philosophy of Language*, ed. Jay F. Rosenberg and Charles Travis (Englewood Cliffs: Prentice-Hall, 1971). That latter volume deals with the following topics: analyticity, reference, propositions, methodology, theories of meaning, semantics, and speech acts.

My reasons for choosing to deal with speech act theory in a bibliographic essay for teachers of composition are various. In the first place, speech act theory begins to systematize the exploration of the rhetorical transaction between speaker and hearer. Furthermore, speech act theory gives an important dimension to the study of style. Finally, linguists are drifting more and more from the formal precision of their early work and into the kinds of questions that concern ordinary language philosophers. Indeed, it is becoming difficult to determine where the linguist ends and the ordinary language philosopher begins.

I must be frank. This section of my essay will show my own bias, but, even more clearly it will reveal my limitations, for my work in the philosophy of language is extremely narrow, having been concerned almost exclusively with speech act theory. With that much said, I can state my purpose: I want merely to suggest directions in which I think linguistic theory is moving, and I want to explore the usefulness of speech act theory for composition teachers.

To begin with, certain concepts are fundamental. The first is that of *performative verbs*. As Austin and a great many others point out, performatives are verbs in which the saying is the doing. Thus,

(40) I (hereby) *pronounce* you man and wife.

when uttered by the proper person under the proper circumstances, is a performative sentence, for the saying is the doing. Conditions being right, the following are also performative sentences:

(41) I (hereby) *promise* to pay my bill.
(42) I (hereby) *state* that I am contented.
(43) I (hereby) *christen* you Murgatroyd.

Quite as clearly, the following are not performatives:

(44) I (*hereby) am running. ["Run" is not a performative verb.]
(45) You (*hereby) promise to pay my bill. [A performative sentence must have a first person subject.]
(46) I (*hereby) stated that I am contented. [A performative sentence must be in present tense.]
(47) Do I (*hereby) christen you Murgatroyd? [A performative sentence must be declarative.]
(48) I (*hereby) don't pronounce you man and wife. [A performative sentence must be positive.]

Furthermore, if I am not a clergyman and you are not getting married, etc., (40) will not be a performative sentence.

John Robert Ross ("On Declarative Sentences," *Readings in English Transformational Grammar*, ed. Roderick A. Jacobs and Peter S. Rosenbaum [Waltham, Mass.: Ginn, 1970]) argues that all non-performative declarative sentences are objects of deep structure performative verbs which are deleted in the surface. Ross's argument is far too intricate to trace here, but what it leads to is essentially this: in order to interpret a sentence, the listener must understand (supply?) its intention if that intention is not already stated. In order to illustrate the point, I will now adopt a simple convention. Bracketed elements in the following examples do not appear in the surface forms — either spoken or written — of the sentences, but are unuttered (or deep structure) intentive elements.

If I say to you,

(49) I'll be here tomorrow.

and you take this statement to be a promise, your interpretation can be represented somewhat in the following manner:

(50) [I (hereby) *promise* you] I'll be here tomorrow.

And here are further illustrations of the surface sentence with interpretation of intention in brackets:

(51) [I (hereby) *warn* you (to)] Stop smoking, or you'll die of lung cancer!

(52) [I (hereby) *state* to you that] It's a lovely morning.

(53) [I (hereby) *ask* you] Are you coming to the party?

And so forth.

The concept of performative verbs is, then, closely connected with the concept of intention in utterances, and intention is a part of total meaning. As the following ambiguous sentence demonstrates, meaning is not "consummated" until intention can be interpreted:

(54) Can you raise the window?

The ambiguity is clarified by the following:

(55) [I (hereby) *ask* you or *inquire of* you] Can you raise the window?

(56) [I (hereby) *request* of you] Can you raise the window?

In other words, performatives lead us to the concept of intention, and the concept of intention leads us to an analysis of the speech act.

Following, modifying, and arguing with Austin, Searle presents the following analysis of the speech act.

Any given sentence consists, first, of an *utterance act*: "Uttering words (morphemes, sentences)"; a *propositional act*: "Referring and predicating"; and an *illocutionary act*: "Stating, questioning, commanding, promising, etc." But, obviously, these three kinds of acts are not all that there are:

> To these three notions I now wish to add Austin's notion of the *perlocutionary act*. Correlated with the notion of illocutionary acts is the notion of the consequences or *effects* such acts have on the actions,

213

thoughts, or beliefs, etc., of hearers. For example, by arguing, I may *persuade* or *convince* someone, by warning him I may *scare* or *alarm* him, by making a request I may *get him to do something*, by informing him I may *convince him* (*enlighten, edify, inspire him, get him to realize*). The italicized expressions above denote perlocutionary acts.

The sentence

(57) The girl sings.

is an *utterance act*:
  a string of graphemes or phonemes;
a *propositional act*:
  in which the verb *sing* is predicated of the referring term *girl*;
an *illocutionary act*:
  in which the intention is to *state, inform*, etc.;
a *perlocutionary act*:
  in which the effect is to *inform, enlighten*, etc.

In a speech act that "works" (i.e., in the jargon, is "felicitous"), obviously there is a correspondence between the illocutionary act and the perlocutionary act.

Even the rapid and sketchy discussion so far should have made it apparent that linguistics and rhetoric meet precisely at the concept of speech act. Transformational generative grammar, during the first years of its history, was preoccupied with the structure of the sentence, and then with the relationship between meaning and syntax. (As we saw, a major question in grammar concerned the point at which the syntactic and the semantic components meet and begin to function together.) Speech act theory demonstrates that to account for the meaning of sentences, it is necessary to consider intention (whereby we can correlate illocution with the classical concept of *ethos* or the nature of the speaker) and with effect (whereby we can correlate perlocution with *pathos* or the nature of the audience). Speech act theory has "rhetoricized" the linguistic investigation of syntax and semantics. (Sociolinguistics is necessarily rhetorical.)

This essay is intended to be synoptic and suggestive, not exhaustive. However, I would like to make one more point about the usefulness of speech act theory.

As teachers of composition, we are inevitably concerned with style in a very general sense — that is, style as effective utterance. Speech act theory moves us away from the tendency — brought about by transformational generative grammar and computer technology — to view style as a quantitative property of texts. In studying and evaluating style, we need to find what I call, somewhat inelegantly, "point-ables." To be sure, there is the text itself, with its strings of morphemes, its structures, its figures, and so forth. (Drawing on Austin's terminology, we can term the text as artifact the "locutionary act.") But as Austin, Searle, and others demonstrate, we will not get very far with our investigation unless we take a more global view of style, as, simultaneously, locutionary act, illocutionary act, and perlocutionary act. Speech act theory, then, reintroduces the concept of speaker/writer with intentions and hearer/reader with idiosyncratic responses into the study of style. Style once more becomes the concern of rhetoric proper.

For a demonstration of the "uses" of speech act theory in the study of style, I refer the reader to Richard Ohmann, "Speech, Action, and Style," *Literary Style: A Symposium* (cited above).

Psycholinguistics

It is irresistible to conclude that a "psycho linguist" must be a "crazy grammarian." Nonetheless, in two fields at least, psycholinguistic work is crucial for teachers of composition. These are language acquisition and reading.

It seems to me that the best introduction to and survey of work in psycholinguistic theory is Dan I. Slobin, *Psycholinguistics* (Glenview, Ill.: Scott, Foresman, 1971).

215

Though this bibliographic essay is concluding with psycholinguistics, it might well have begun with that field, for psycholinguists are concerned with basic questions such as competence and performance, the psychological reality of grammatical rules, the relationship of language to cognition, and so on.

For instance, Slobin begins with a concise and lucid discussion of the nature of linguistic intuitions — that is, with the knowledge that a native speaker must have of his language. These intuitions are important enough to warrant brief outline here.

First, native speakers recognize sentences that are well-formed in terms of the language in question. That is to say, virtually every native speaker will be able to identify the asterisked sentences in the following as unlikely to be produced by other native speakers. In just that sense, *all of the un-asterisked sentences are perfectly grammatical.*

(58) Them guys don't know nothing.
(59) Those guys don't know anything.
(60) *Those guys know that dinner ready is.
(61) Daddy be here. (an urban black sentence)
(62) *Daddy being here.
(63) *Over the fence to the cow some hay I threw.

Second, native speakers intuitively recognize grammatical relations. In other words, they know that (65) is a paraphrase of (64) and that (67) is a paraphrase of (66):

(64) John is easy to please.
(65) It is easy for someone to please John.
(66) John is eager to please.
(67) John is eager to please someone.

Or

(68) John is easy [someone] to please [John].
(69) John is eager [John] to please [someone].

Third, native speakers intuitively grasp relationships among sentences — the following, for example:

216

(70) The President makes the decisions.
(71) The decisions are made by the President.

And fourth, native speakers recognize ambiguity, as in the following:

(72) Visiting relatives can be a nuisance.
(73) The lamb was too hot to eat.

Any theory of grammar must account for this intuitive knowledge. Or, to put the point another way: a theory of grammar is an attempt to account for what we already know about the language. (By implication, studying grammar can't really "teach" us anything that we don't already "know" about the language.)

A second important concern that Slobin deals with is *competence* and *performance*. Competence is the hypothetical global ability that "every" native speaker of a language possesses; performance is the actual outcome of this ideal in the real world of discourse. It is extremely important for teachers of composition to understand competence and performance, for these concepts imply that there is no absolute limit to the individual's ability to increase the level of his or her performance of basic language tasks. The composition student, for example, has a virtually limitless potential (competence), but *every* writer is limited in performance. The task of the language teacher is to activate basic competence so that it appears in the arena of performance. (In essence, the whole thrust of programs in syntactic fluency, such as that developed by O'Hare, is to activate competence.)

Of particular interest are Slobin's handlings of "Problems of Meaning" (Chapter 4) and "Language and Cognition" (Chapter 5). In general and throughout, the book puts the reader in touch with the central notions of linguistics as a theory of mind.

Moving from the general to the more specific, we find that much of the most exciting psycholinguistic work currently under way involves *language acquisition*.

217

Courtney B. Cazden, *Child, Language, and Education* (New York: Holt, Rinehart and Winston, 1972) is, in my opinion, the best single overview of work in language acquisition and its implications for teachers.

Cazden surveys the field in some detail. She deals with the acquisition of syntax, the acquisition of sounds and meaning, the developmental process and its dimensions, environmental assistance, dialect differences and bilingualism, communication styles, the roles of language in cognition, and language education.

Clearly, in work on language acquisition, there is a healthy overlap between psycholinguistics and sociolinguistics. (Work in sociolinguistics is covered by another essay in this volume.)

A more technical and narrowly focussed, but equally fascinating, book is Roger Brown, *A First Language: The Early Stages* (Cambridge, Mass.: Harvard University Press, 1973). Both Cazden and Brown base their books on work that a group did at Harvard, beginning in the fall of 1962. In this investigation, language development in three children was followed from ages 18 months through ages 48 months, resulting in a mass of detailed empirical data.

In discussing some of the implications of studies in language acquisition, I will not try to differentiate Brown's and Cazden's books, but will range over them briefly and freely.

Perhaps the most striking notion for teachers of composition concerns the principle of *imitation*. (After all, since antiquity, imitation in one form or another has been the principal means of teaching writing. The thousands of "readers" — essay collections — that are used are predicated on imitation.) It is clearly the case that a first language in its early stages is *not* learned primarily through imitation. That is, a child's language has its own grammar, its own regularities, which are not merely an imitation of adult forms. In fact, the process of acquiring mature grammar is one of simultaneous integration and differentiation. The child (intuitively) makes generalizations about language, uses those generalizations as productive principles, gradually differentiates the generalizations, and thus integrates his or her grammar with adult grammar. For instance, Cazden cites Carol Chomsky, who pointed out that younger children make Donald do the hopping in both of the following sentences:

(74) Bozo [*the clown*] *tells* Donald [*Duck*] to hop up and
down.
(75) Bozo promises Donald to hop up and down.

In effect, the child has generalized a subject-verb-object structure and has not differentiated between verbs like *tell* and verbs like *promise*. For the child, the deep structure subjects of the embedded sentences in both (74) and (75) is "Donald."

This, and other evidence, contradict behavioristic notions of language acquisition. In saying, "Mommy *singed* me to sleep," the child is not imitating a form that he or she has ever heard, but is demonstrating the natural propensity to generalize and then differentiate.

Restrictions on space here prevent me from following this notion as far as I would like to, but it seems to me that generalization and differentiation are rich concepts for teachers of writing at all levels. Somehow composition students must gain the data on which to base generalizations about rhetorical strategies, but just as surely, they will follow their own intuitions to integrate those strategies into their own mature rhetoric of the essay.

Studies in language acquisition also make the point that learning any language task results from a tension — or interaction — between a natural languaging capacity and an environment or culture. As Cazden says, " . . . ethnic background and social class have different effects. Ethnic background affects the pattern of mental abilities, while social-class affects the levels of scores across mental-ability scales." In other words, and most bluntly stated, ethnicity affects the way in which mental abilities manifest themselves, but social-class seems to affect *tests of* mental abilities in general. Here, again from Cazden, is a statement which should give all composition teachers nightmares: " . . . in all four ethnic groups [Jewish, Black, Chinese, Puerto Rican], and all scales and subtests, the middle-class children were significantly superior to the lower-class children."

For composition teachers, the great limitation of the language acquisition studies carried out by Brown and his group is that they deal with young children and touch the concerns of secondary and college teachers only by implication and tangentially. Their great virtue is that they apply the theories of modern linguistics to the understanding of how language learning takes place. In fact, the field has advanced light years in the last decade or so, and it seems to me that composition teachers are obliged to know all that they can about this vital area.

Finally, I would suggest that the first fifty-nine pages of Brown's book — "An Unbuttoned Introduction" — constitutes one of the best and most interesting available discussions of general concepts of grammar and language.

A composition teacher is inevitably a reading teacher, and reading theory is a field that has come to life in the past few years. Three books, taken together, present a more than adequate survey of the field: Frank Smith, *Understanding Reading* (New York: Holt, Rinehart and Winston, 1971); *Psycholinguistics and Reading*, ed. Frank Smith (New York: Holt, Rinehart and Winston, 1973); Yetta M. Goodman and Carolyn L. Burke, *Reading Miscue Inventory Manual: Procedure for Diagnosis and Evaluation* (New York: The Macmillan Co., 1972).

These works lay to rest, once and for all, the logomachy concerning phonics: one reads to derive meanings, not sounds. They define the reading process as the way in which a mind meets a page — and of the two elements, the mind is, of course, by all odds the more important.

Reading theory is rich with implications for the composition teacher-rhetorician and perhaps even more so for the literary critic.

Finally

This essay could be extended greatly. In it, I have tried to give a general outline of work in linguistics and of the implications of that work for teachers of composition. It is a fact, however, that every topic introduced could have been pursued at great length.

I have tried to demonstrate that linguistic theory ultimately leads to rhetorical theory. Sentences are not merely structures; they are speech acts; and speech act theory is a sort of formalized micro-rhetoric. But speech act theory itself leads to important implications for literary theory, and it turns out, literary theory also can be — should be — viewed as rhetorical theory.

The major concerns of English teachers have always been grammar, rhetoric, and literature, but these are not separate disciplines and not even distinct compartments in one discipline. They inter-relate in so intricate a fashion that they are inseparable. Or look at the matter another way. The English teacher can start with linguistics, literature, or rhetoric; following any one of these fields in all of its implications will inevitably lead to the other two. It seems to me that composition teachers who are unable to follow these implications and make the connections are shortchanging both themselves and their students.

RHETORICAL ANALYSIS
OF WRITING

JIM W. CORDER

Texas Christian University

I HAVE JUST BEEN READING the abstracts in a program for a forthcoming meeting of rhetoricians. In one of them, the author speaks of "a critic using the rhetorical method." The phrasing left me befuddled. I suppose the news has not yet reached me — I didn't know that negotiations had ended and that we had decided upon *the* rhetorical method. I had been thinking all along that there were several, which probably accounts for another befuddlement I suffer: I don't know what to exclude from a bibliographical essay that reports on the rhetorical analysis of writing. I don't know what to exclude because I believe that *all* analysis of writing is rhetorical. I believe that all discussion of writers and writing is rhetorical. I'm even inclined to believe that idle chitchat about writers and writing is rhetorical. All kinds of analysis are forms of rhetorical analysis.

The extraordinarily comprehensive nature of rhetoric as a subject matter and as a mode of organizing knowledge is, of course, one of the art's most compelling qualities. One may range widely or focus narrowly and still claim the pleasures of rhetoric. Biographical studies, explorations of literary influence, archetypal criticism, historical studies of the givens and resources of an age for a writer, politically-oriented criticism — these and a host of other analytical approaches, each having its own justification and end, belong to and are partial forms of the study of rhetorical *invention*. Form, design, and genre studies of various kinds are illustrations of the rhetorician's study of *disposition*. Grammatical analyses, linguistic studies, examinations of imagery and figurative language, explorations of public and private styles, and of available styles, are within the province of *style*. Sociometric analyses of reader responses, data on book sales, casually-exchanged impressions, even book-and-author gossip are fragmentary forms of the rhetorician's interest in *audience*. The list might go on. Anything that can be said about writers, writings, readers, and their coming together is rhetorical examination, though partial, and the sayer is a rhetorician, though unaware.

Such a view is contrary, of course, to that still commonly held of rhetoric, which only permits rhetoric to be about persuasion, mostly empty and usually dishonest, or public oratory, or (once in a while) a freshman theme or two. An example or two may help to illustrate the conception of rhetoric I want to work with. An issue of *Saturday Review* (that for September 6, 1975) is on my desk. It contains an extended review by John W. Aldridge of Saul Bellow's new novel, *Humboldt's Gift*. Aldridge, coming to this novel through all of Bellow's earlier novels, suggests that they all tell the same story: "They are all informed by what can only be called a desperately affirmative view of human experience and possibility, a view too complicated to be reducible to a philosophical proposition, too dialectical and contradictory to be taken as dogma, creed, or panacea." Aldridge, as I am able to understand matters, is exploring Bellow's *inventive world*, the complex geography out of which a new book emerges. He is to that extent a rhetorician. Several pages deeper into the same issue is a regular column by William Cole, "Trade Winds." It is full of talk about books just out, books soon to be published, books the author has enjoyed, and consequently is a rhetorical study: though light and entertaining, it is about the *occasions* in which writing occurs, and it connects books and *audiences*. I turn to the 1970 *MLA International Bibliography* (choosing it not for scholarly reasons, but because I could find it) and find every item listed there to be a rhetorical study of one kind or another. John W. Foster's article, "A Redefinition of Topographical

Poetry" (in *JEGP*), is, for example, an examination of the inventive world of certain seventeenth and eighteenth century writers and of structural and stylistic possibilities generated by that inventive world. Irving Ribner's book, *Patterns in Shakespearean Tragedy*, also listed there, is among other things a study of rhetorical *disposition*. Neither announces a rhetorical purpose or orientation, but both studies are rhetorical. I take particular pleasure in this. The MLA bibliography shows no heading or sub-heading for rhetoric. That error can be corrected and a wiser perspective can be gained by this simplest of means, the appropriation of the MLA bibliography as a partial record of rhetorical studies.

All kinds of analysis are forms of rhetorical analysis. Accordingly, nothing should be excluded from a bibliographical essay on the rhetorical analysis of writing. But most things must be excluded. In what follows, then, I have made no effort to rehearse "literary" bibliography, which is fully available, at any rate, in the annual *MLA International Bibliography* and in the annual field and period bibliographies that appear in various journals. In addition to these, E. P. J. Corbett's collection, *Rhetorical Analyses of Literary Works* (New York: Oxford University Press, 1969), with its splendid bibliography, is an indispensable guide to students of rhetoric and literature.

That much already excluded, I have in addition usually obeyed three conditions for inclusion. First, as nearly as possible I have included works that use the language of rhetoric. My own judgment, suggested above, is that all analyses of writing are rhetorical. Only a portion of them, however, actually use the language long associated with the field. Second, I have generally included only rhetorical analyses of non-fiction prose or works useful to the analysis of non-fiction prose. Other kinds of literary analysis, as I have suggested, are readily enough available, and studies of non-fiction prose, especially of essays, seem likely to be most directly useful to teachers in composition courses, where reading samples are commonly essays and where the student

225

writing is almost always in essay form. Third, I have used somewhere around 1965 as a beginning point, on the assumption that useful works published before that time have generally entered our consciousness through re-publication or frequent citations.

What remains after these various exclusions and inclusions is arranged in three groups: works that seem to provide good *bases* for rhetorical analysis, works that seem to provide *guides* for rhetorical analysis (the distinction between *base* and *guide* I'll come to a little later), and works that are themselves rhetorical analyses of writing.

Every rhetorical analysis of a piece of writing is an exemplification of some theoretical conception of rhetoric, whether or not the theoretical conception is expressed in the course of the analysis. One analyzes when one has a sense of what to look at, when one has a sense of what analysis is for. A rhetorical analysis of an essay, for example, useful and stimulating as it may be, is then more nearly an end than a beginning. A teacher in the classroom can of course use a rhetorical analysis to good effect, showing voice, structure, or other features of the essay's workings, but the rhetorical analysis often can only generate copies of itself. A rhetorical analysis is likely to work as a pattern; what is done with one essay can often be done with another, and another. But a rhetorical theory, a conception of rhetoric, is likely to work not as a pattern, but as a generator, raising many questions, making many different kinds of analysis possible. A conception of rhetoric is an enabling base for rhetorical analysis.

An example of what I mean is provided by James E. Kinneavy's paper, "The Basic Aims of Discourse," *CCC*, 20 (December, 1969), 297-304, the seed paper for his *A Theory of Discourse* (Englewood Cliffs: Prentice-Hall, Inc., 1971). Using the familiar triangle representation of communication, AUTHOR, SUBJECT, AND AUDIENCE as the points, MEDIUM as the sides, Kinneavy differentiates among different kinds of discourse. Author-oriented writing he calls *expressive*, subject-oriented writing he calls *referential*, audience-oriented writing he calls *persuasive*, and writing that is its own end he calls *literary*. This scheme of organization does not provide a rhetorical analysis; it does not tell how to do rhetorical analysis. It does, however, raise a number of questions and open a number of possibilities that generate rhetorical analysis. It invites a student to inquire where the speaker in an essay is and which way he or she is looking, at self, subject, audience, or literary need. It invites a student to consider the rhetorical occasion and its needs and to determine whether or not the orientation within the essay serves the occasion. For example, politicians in their speaking and writing often prefer to look the wrong way: just when we need them to know and speak to the subject, they choose to win us; just when we need them to make themselves clear to us, they choose to ruminate on their own past record. Kinneavy's scheme of organization is a vehicle that may enable a student to inquire into the whole inventive complex of an essay. It invites a student to examine the rhetorical distance set between author and subject, between author and audience, between subject and audience. It invites a student to consider the effects upon the structure and style of the positions and distances created.

These possibilities and others are opened up by the original conception of the author-subject-audience-medium triangle. The conception itself cannot be described as rhetorical analysis; it is a *base* for rhetorical analyses. A similar base, valuable both for itself and for the studies it generates, is Richard Ohmann's "In Lieu of a New Rhetoric," *CE*, 26 (October, 1964), 17-22. Ohmann's account of how contemporary ideas of rhetoric differ from older ideas provides a useful perspective from which both older and newer writing may be examined. The notion that older rhetoric is predicated upon the transmission of truth already known while modern rhetoric is predicated upon the pursuit of truth yet to be discovered calls for new scrutiny of invention, structure, and style.

S. M. Halloran provides further starting points in a recent essay that is both sad and intensely provocative, "On the End of Rhetoric, Classical and Modern," *CE*, 36 (February, 1975), 621-631. We once assumed, Halloran says, that the world is knowable, "that values are coherent, that wisdom is public and can be fully mastered by one man, who in turn can relate the accumulated wisdom of mankind to the particular case at hand in a clear and persuasive fashion." Now, "it is no longer valid to assume that speaker and audience live in the same world." Now, he says, rhetoric "is the means whereby the self and its world are constituted," and the speaker "must articulate his own world in such a way that his readers can enter it with him." Halloran's essay calls for new explorations of *ethos*, other modes of argument, inventive openness, structural and stylistic accessibility. Somewhat similar ground is searched in Thomas F. Mader's "On Presence in Rhetoric," *CCC*, 24 (December, 1973), 375-381. "For anything to have presence for us," Mader says, "we must be aware of it, and we will be aware of it only if it has meaning for us, and it will have meaning for us only if it satisfies one of our needs." Mader goes on to examine why presence is essential in argumentation and how presence is achieved. He takes his originating notion of presence from still another base for rhetorical analysis, Chaim Perelman and L. Olbrechts-Tyteca, *The New Rhetoric: A Treatise on Argumentation* (Notre Dame, Indiana: University of Notre Dame Press, 1969).

Another way of looking at prose is suggested in the classifications offered by George R. Bramer in "Like It Is: Discourse Analysis for a New Generation," *CCC*, 21 (December, 1970), 347-355. Beginning with the assumption that all language is persuasive, Bramer proposes an initial division between objective and subjective discourse, each subdivided into perceptual and conceptual forms. Particularly interested in detecting subjective discourse that wishes to pass for objective discourse, Bramer offers a vision of discourse that can generate many different kinds of rhetorical analysis.

The question of stance or position has also been examined in Wayne C. Booth's "The Rhetorical Stance," *CCC*, 14 (October, 1963), 139-145. More than just a study of *ethos* and *pathos* and the need for adjusting to an audience, though it is that, the essay is a beginning exploration of a whole conception of communication through study of position and distance.

From the many book-length works that can serve as bases in the sense I've mentioned, I'll cite six in particular.

Two books I'd wish to place side by side in first place by any measure. The first is E. P. J. Corbett's *Classical Rhetoric for the Modern Student* (New York: Oxford University Press, first edition, 1965, second edition, 1971). One of the key works in the revival of rhetoric, Corbett's book has been for many both the best and the most accessible accounting of the systems of classical rhetoric. Corbett's recovery of classical rhetoric is sufficiently thorough to serve as a base for many different kinds of rhetorical analysis. His own examples illustrate the uses of the theory he recounts and are particularly pertinent here. At the end of each of his chapters Corbett provides good readings, and he provides an analysis of at least one reading for each chapter. So, in addition to the rhetorical base given by the book, Corbett also provides nine separate rhetorical analyses of readings. The second book appeared much earlier than 1965, the beginning date I set.

Richard Weaver's *The Ethics of Rhetoric* (Chicago: Henry Regnery Company, 1953) is a pioneer work in modern rhetoric, opening territory for analysis that is still not fully mapped. Three of its chapters are particularly notable: "Some Rhetorical Aspects of Grammatical Categories," "The Spaciousness of Old Rhetoric," and "Ultimate Terms in Contemporary Rhetoric."

Four other recent books should be mentioned as what I have called bases for rhetorical analyses. W. Ross Winterowd's *Rhetoric, a Synthesis* (New York: Holt, Rinehart and Winston, Inc., 1968) seeks to accomplish three things: to bring various fragments of a new rhetoric together; to put theory into practice with extended analyses of style and form; and, as Winterowd puts it, "to synthesize the theory and practice of rhetoric in a way that will make the book a real introduction to the subject." Chapter Eight, which includes special discussion of rhetorical criticism, is important to practitioners of rhetorical analysis. Winterowd's anthology, *Contemporary Rhetoric, A Conceptual Background with Readings* (New York: Harcourt, Brace, Jovanovich, Inc., 1975), has an introductory essay on teaching rhetoric, introductory essays for the three sections (on invention, form, and style), each accompanied by a useful bibliography, and twenty-four essays by different authors on particular topics. Frank J. D'Angelo's *A Conceptual Theory of Rhetoric* (Cambridge, Mass.: Winthrop Publishers, Inc., 1975) "attempts to explore the relationships that exist between thinking and writing, within the framework of a coherent theoretical system of rhetoric." James Moffett's *Teaching the Universe of Discourse* (Boston: Houghton Mifflin, 1968) is an important book for pedagogical uses in the teaching of composition, and its visualization of various kinds of discourse opens possibilities for analysis.

A number of other works should be mentioned while I am still talking about bases for rhetorical analysis. I am thinking now about books and articles that, though some of them may not say anything about rhetorical analysis, *stimulate* analysis.

For example, W. Ross Winterowd's essay, "The Realms of Meaning: Text-Centered Criticism," *CCC*, 23 (December, 1972), 399-405, is an admonition and an exhortation. "I would argue," Winterowd says, "that the proper goal of *all* criticism is to find out how the text achieves its effects; that is, I would resist the separation of rhetorical and literary criticism." Urging students of rhetoric first to find out what the text means, Winterowd suggests that a text holds formal, referential, and extrinsic meanings. Another argument against the separation of literary criticism and rhetorical criticism is in Alexander Scharbach's "Rhetoric and Literary Criticism: Why Their Separation," *CCC*, 23 (May, 1972), 185-188. Therese B. Dykeman suggests a new way of looking at exposition, description, narration, and argumentation in "The Physics of Rhetoric," *CCC*, 25 (December, 1974), 382-387. Searching for the foundation for these distinctions among discursive types, Dykeman proposes "that description concerns space, exposition concerns matter, narration concerns time, and argument concerns motion." William Jovanovich's "A Tumult of Talk," *ASch*, 41 (Winter, 1971-1972), 40-49, sensitive to many of our discursive faults, calls for expression that is "plain in intent, consonant in tone, and explicit in meaning." "Everyman's innate competence to learn language is perhaps warranted to him with life," Jovanovich says, "but his very own, his particular use of language is neither promised nor foretold. His command of language is enlarged and freed by desire, by practice, and by reward." A related argument and a reminder of the perpetual need for analysis is in Douglas Bush's "Polluting Our Language," *ASch*, 41 (Spring, 1972), 238-247. Valuable for their views of rhetoric and for the kinds of analysis they can stimulate are Donald C. Bryant's "Rhetoric: Its Function and Scope," *QJS*, 39 (December, 1951), 401-424; Bryant's "Rhetorical Dimensions in Criticism," in his book, *Rhetorical Dimensions in Criticism*, (Baton Rouge: Louisiana State University Press, 1973); Robert D. Clark's "Literary and Rhetorical Criticism," in *Essays on Rhetorical Criticism*, edited by Thomas R. Nilsen (New York: Random House, 1968); and Richard Murphy's "Teaching Rhetorical Appreciation of Literature," *EJ*, 55 (May, 1966), 578-582.

Finally, among initiating works, I'll cite four books that are provocative and evocative, sometimes moving: Walter Ong, *The Presence of the Word* (New Haven: Yale University Press, 1967); Wayne C. Booth, *The Rhetoric of Fiction* (Chicago: University of Chicago Press, 1961); Marie Hochmuth Nichols, *Rhetoric and Criticism* (Baton Rouge:

Louisiana State University Press, 1963); and Walker Gibson, *Tough, Sweet, and Stuffy: An Essay on Modern American Prose Style* (Bloomington: University of Indiana Press, 1966).

I have been hoping, these last several pages, that when the time came I could remember the distinction I set out with between *bases* for rhetorical analysis and *guides* for rhetorical analysis. The distinction, I expect, is arbitrary, and many works, by my own definition, could go easily in either grouping. What I have meant by *bases* for rhetorical analysis is works that are initiators, prompters, vision-givers, works that lay out conceptions of rhetoric and communication. By *guides*, I mean works that begin to show us how to *do* rhetorical analysis, works that show us some of the possible ways of going about the work, works that indicate the range of analytical possibilities, even works that may be taken as models for rhetorical analysis.

Among these, first, are some primary references. Corbett's anthology already cited, *Rhetorical Analyses of Literary Works*, is especially helpful, both for the range of analytical essays it contains and for its bibliography. Richard A. Lanham's *A Handlist of Rhetorical Terms* is an indispensable reference. It offers a 105-page alphabetical list of terms, an eleven-page classification of the terms by type, a three-page classification of the terms as ornaments, and an eleven-page catalog of terms especially useful in literary criticism. James P. Bennett's "Contemporary Concepts of Literary Style," *A Symposium in Rhetoric*, edited by J. Dean Bishop, Turner S. Kobler, and William E. Tanner (Denton: Federation of North Texas Area Universities, 1975), includes a useful checklist of stylistic domains. *Speech Monographs* publishes regularly a bibliography in rhetoric, though it is naturally enough focused on oral discourse. The *Rhetoric Society Newsletter* is gradually developing its annual bibliography. *Style* publishes an annual bibliography on stylistics, and from time to time publishes specialized bibliographies, such as "Style in the Bible" in the Fall, 1973, issue and "Style in Biography" in the Spring, 1975, issue. A valuable resource for some kinds of analysis is the book edited by Louis T. Milic, *Style and Stylistics: An Analytical Bibliography* (New York: The Free Press, 1967). Extremely valuable as a reference, though in quite another way, is Marjorie Boulton's *The Anatomy of Prose* (London: Routledge and Kegan Paul, Ltd., 1954). Describing her studies, Boulton remarks, "I soon realized that even if I ignored my personal prejudices I could prescribe no simple book on the study of prose. I could find nothing. Perhaps I have merely been unobservant; but if such books are infrequent enough to elude my enquiries for some thirteen years a new one seems unlikely to be superfluous." Circumstances haven't changed much in the intervening years.

Historical studies of rhetoric are remarkably useful guides for rhetorical analysis. By showing what has been studied in the name of rhetoric in former times, they extend the range of inquiries in our own. A particularly good example is Donald L. Clark's *Rhetoric in Greco-Roman Education* (New York: Columbia University Press, 1957). A host of good historical studies could be cited, but I mention only seven in addition to Clark's. Three are by Charles S. Baldwin: *Ancient Rhetoric and Poetic* (New York: Crowell-Collier and Macmillan, Inc., 1924); *Medieval Rhetoric and Poetic* (New York: Crowell-Collier and Macmillan, Inc., 1928); and *Renaissance Literary Theory and Practice* (New York: Columbia University Press, 1939). Two are by W. S. Howell: *Logic and Rhetoric in England, 1500-1700* (Princeton: Princeton University Press, 1956); and *Eighteenth-Century British Logic and Rhetoric* (Princeton: Princeton University Press, 1971). Sister Miriam Joseph's book, *Shakespeare's Use of the Arts of Language* (New York: Hafner Publishing Co., 1947), is a valuable account of Renaissance rhetoric. A newer book, Aldo Scaglione's *The Classical Theory of Composition, From Its Origins to the Present, A Historical Survey* (Chapel Hill: The University of North Carolina Press, 1972), is helpful, though less well known, I think. Chiefly concerned with

233

theories of sentence structure and word order, Scaglione surveys antiquity, the Middle Ages, the Renaissance, the period of Baroque and Enlightenment, and concludes with a chapter on modern linguistic approaches to the problem of composition. There is an excellent bibliography.

Far too often overlooked — sometimes completely ignored — as guides to rhetorical analysis are composition and rhetoric textbooks primarily intended for use in first-year college writing classes. We're not accustomed to thinking of them as useful for analytical techniques — they're supposed to be guides for freshman writing, we're likely to think, and so we sometimes don't bother to consider their uses in exploring what others have already written. And besides that, too many of us are still not accustomed to taking them seriously — textbooks are something one does with one's left hand while with the right hand one goes on about one's serious scholarship. But ordinary textbooks can be useful guides, sometimes by providing entire schematic designs of the communicative process, sometimes by raising particular questions about particular features of the process.

I have no way of surveying all composition and rhetoric textbooks, and there is at any rate no need: a few examples will serve. Texts specifically intended as guides to writing about literature are useful. I am thinking about such books as B. Bernard Cohen's *Writing About Literature* (Glenview: Scott, Foresman and Company, 1963); Edgar V. Roberts' *Writing Themes About Literature*, 3rd. ed. (Englewood Cliffs: Prentice-Hall, Inc., 1973); and the text by Mary Rohrberger and Samuel H. Woods, Jr., *Reading and Writing About Literature* (New York: Random House, 1971). The opening pages of the discussion of argument and the three chapters on style are suggestive in Richard E. Hughes and P. Albert Duhamel, *Principles of Rhetoric* (Englewood Cliffs: Prentice-Hall, Inc., 1966). The heuristic system laid out in Richard E. Young, Alton L. Becker, and Kenneth L. Pike, *Rhetoric: Discovery and Change* (New York: Harcourt, Brace and World, Inc., 1970), intended as a guide to student writers in discovering what they can say, is also a guide for analyzing the inventive world of works already written. Maxine Hairston's exploration of Rogerian conflict analysis has implications for studies of ethical and other modes of argument. (*A Contemporary Rhetoric*, Boston: Houghton Mifflin Company, 1974.) Any number of writing texts could be cited, in whole or in part.

Important as guides to rhetorical analysis are various studies of the nature and form of the essay. Part One of Robert Scholes and Carl H. Klaus, *Elements of the Essay* (New York: Oxford University Press, 1969) is a valuable introduction. The essay, Scholes and Klaus note, "is the form most directly concerned with truth, most concerned with convincing us of the version of reality that it presents." Richard L. Larson's "Toward a Linear Rhetoric of the Essay," *CCC*, 22 (May, 1971), 140-146, offers provocative suggestions about how essays take their direction. Linear analysis, Larson says, "assumes that discourse is a series of moves, deliberately made, intended for achieving a particular purpose — usually to leave the reader satisfied about the reasonableness of the writer's way of viewing a particular subject or experience." Closely related is W. Ross Winterowd's "The Grammar of Coherence," *CE*, 31 (May, 1970), 828-835, which identifies seven kinds of "transitional relationships" that unite elements of discourse longer than the sentence. In "Aesthetic Form in Familiar Essays," *CCC*, 22 (May, 1971), 147-155, Howard C. Brashers proposes that "the principle of organization in the familiar essay is not arrangement for clarity of idea, nor for force of expression, but arrangement for aesthetic effect." He then suggests eight patterns of arrangement for aesthetic effect. Frank D'Angelo, in "A Generative Rhetoric of the Essay," *CCC*, 25 (December, 1974), 388-396, describes the essay as "a kind of macroparagraph. The first sentence of the essay (or extended discourse) is the organizing sentence. (I shall call it the *lead sentence* to distinguish it from the traditional concept of the thesis sentence.) The lead sentence is the top sentence of the

235

sequence; it is the sentence that gets the discourse going. Subsequent sentences in the discourse are related to it by coordination or subordination." Michael Grady proposes another way of understanding essay form in "A Conceptual Rhetoric of the Composition," *CCC*, 22 (December, 1971), 348-354, where he argues that the introductory sequence in a composition is roughly comparable to the topic sentence in a paragraph. A study that deserves close attention is Keith Fort's "Form, Authority, and the Critical Essay," *CE*, 32 (March, 1971), 629-639. Fort argues that our attitudes are determined by available forms: "in general, we cannot have attitudes toward reality that cannot be expressed in available forms. If, for example, we can only express our relation to literature in the form of the standard critical essay, we can only have an attitude that would result in the proper form." Emphasis on the critical essay, Fort says, is tyrannical and destructive, imprisoning the student and turning literature into a consumer product.

This should bring me to the largest and most immediately pertinent section of these notes. Given the title of this piece, it's reasonable to assume that the third and last section earlier forecast, a catalogue of rhetorical analyses of non-fiction prose works, would be both the largest and most important. Actually, the number of books and papers that can be cited is small. Most of us, when we are trying to be rhetoricians, work with theory, the pedagogy of rhetoric, large issues (for example, the classification of all forms of discourse), or with smaller elements of discourse (for example, sentence structure, paragraph relationships). When we are trying to be critics and analysts, we're likely to forget all of that and work not with essays and extended non-fiction prose works, but with poems, plays, stories, novels, schools, periods, or whatever we can conclude is *real* and *literary*. Mostly, when we are practicing our profession for publication, we just don't analyze non-fiction forms, and we don't expect our graduate students or those preparing to be teachers to do so — though we do often ask freshmen to examine essays in their freshman readers. Should we happen on a thoughtless day to be so unmindful of our duty and our tradition as to ask a doctoral student in his or her doctoral examinations some alien question about the essay as art form, we should first have to endure the stunned silence of our colleagues, then submit to the snipping of the tassels from our caps, finally surrender our subscription to *The Explicator*.

When we are trying to be composition teachers, however, we do talk about essays a lot. We assign them for reading, we expect students as well to talk about them, and we imagine that they are models for student writing. But our conception of the essay, or of non-fiction prose in general, limits what we do and may be responsible for our apparent failure to make non-fiction readings genuinely useful as models. It is not even accurate to speak of essays as being lower than various kinds of poetry, drama, and fiction in the scale of literary value. Essays never made it into any hierarchy of literary types. They are outside and otherwise. They are not *fictions*; hence, they are not *created*. They are chunks of actuality — reports, propositions, evidences, reminiscences — written out on paper. They are not *to be*, but *to be for*.

And so what we do with essays in the composition class is limited. We *use* essays. We use them to provide ideas for student writing. We use them to initiate class discussions. We use them for outlining. We use them to show students discursive tools, but only of certain types: transitional devices here, development by comparison there, a periodic sentence yonder. The more we do such things with essays, the more we reaffirm our limited conception of essays. One of the reasons students don't profit as much as they should from reading essays is that while we at least have these pragmatic uses for essays, students don't or think they don't. Since we inadvertently teach them that essays are *to be for*, rather than *to be*, essays don't register consequentially with students who have no use to make of them.

Even in the one place where we do consistently talk about essays — the composition classroom — we seem not to get at them in fruitful ways. Essays are, to be sure, sometimes *for* some purpose. But they are also created fictions, composings of experience, created orders. As such, they have only to be. Being, they have generative powers, and we can learn to talk about them in new ways. We could, for example, begin to face such central issues as that raised by Georges Gusdorf in *La Parole* (translated into English as *Speaking*):

> It seems then that the use of speech obliges us to choose between two opposite forms of alienation. On the one hand, like the madman or mystic, we can speak as no one else speaks. On the other hand, like the practitioner of a "basic" language, we can speak as every one else does. In both cases the very meaning of personality is done away with. The more I communicate, the less I express myself; the more I express myself, the less I communicate. It is necessary to choose between incomprehensibility and inauthenticity — between excommunication and self-denial.

Well, perhaps it's not really as bad as I have claimed. Still, essays are seldom the subject of our work outside the composition class, and inside, our study of essays is often misdirected. Rhetorical analyses are available, to be sure; the annual bibliography in Corbett's *Rhetorical Analyses of Literary Works* is an efficient guide to many.

One chief hunting ground for analyses of essays is in various kinds of texts intended for the freshman composition course. I've already mentioned, for example, the analyses contained in Corbett's *Classical Rhetoric for the Modern Student*. Rhetoric texts, anthologies, and teachers' guides for texts and anthologies frequently contain analyses, sometimes comprehensive, sometimes narrowly focused. For example, the third edition of Francis Connolly's *A Rhetoric Case Book*, done by Gerald Levin (New York: Harcourt, Brace and World, Inc., 1969) has two features following each essay, "Comment" and "Analysis and Composition," which, while they do not pretend to be thorough analyses, do direct attention usefully. The fifth edition of Paul Haines' *Problems in Prose* (New York: Harper and Row, 1963) has no formal analyses, but each reading selection is followed by so thorough and thoughtful a list of questions, suggestions, and directions (usually three to five pages for each selection) as to outline analyses for the reader. *Composition of the Essay* by Simeon Hyde, Jr., and William H. Brown (Palo Alto: Addison-Wesley Publishing Company, 1967) provides for each essay included a thorough marginal gloss. Many anthologies for freshman composition contain sample analyses; more have suggestions for study, comments, or questions. In *The Writer and the Worlds of Words*, edited by Robert Bain and Dennis G. Donovan (Englewood Cliffs: Prentice-Hall, Inc., 1975), to cite one example, each essay is accompanied by four sets of questions and suggestions, on "Words and Sentences," "Ideas and Implications," "Strategies," and "Suggestions for Writing."

Another source of rhetorical analyses, largely unused, I'm afraid, is in teachers' manuals prepared to accompany anthologies designed for composition courses. Most teachers' manuals have, at least, useful questions, suggestions, or directions for use in studying particular reading selections, and some include analyses, though the length, type, and complexity vary considerably. Probably the fullest, and easily one of the richest collections of essay analyses is Richard L. Larson's *Rhetorical Guide to The Borzoi College Reader* (New York: Alfred A. Knopf, 1967).

Other analyses are available. Part Two of Scholes and Klaus, *Elements of the Essay*, already cited, contains commentaries on four essays. Richard L. Larson, in "Invention Once More: A Role for Rhetorical Analysis," *CE*, 32 (March, 1971), 665-672, uses analyses of essays by Golding, Podhoretz, and Orwell to answer his own question: "What is there in finished essays that can guide us toward ways of inventing?" I'd also call attention to Richard Ohmann, "Modes of Order," in Donald C. Freeman, editor, *Linguistics and Literary Style* (New York: Holt, Rinehart and

Winston, Inc., 1970), 209-242; Mark Ashin, "The Argument of Madison's 'Federalist,' No. 10," *CE*, 15 (October, 1953), 37-45; Curtis W. Hayes, "A Study in Prose Styles: Edward Gibbon and Ernest Hemingway," *TSLL*, 7 (1966), 371-386; Francis D. Ross, "Rhetorical Procedure in Thoreau's 'Battle of the Ants,'" *CCC*, 16 (February, 1965), 14-17; Marshall M. Brice, "Lincoln and Rhetoric," *CCC*, 17 (February, 1966), 12-14; and F. C. Reidel, "A Classical Rhetorical Analysis of Some Elements of Stevenson's Essay Style," *Style*, 3 (Spring, 1969), 182-199. Karlyn Kohrs Campbell's *Critiques of Contemporary Rhetoric* (Belmont, Calif.: Wadsworth Publishing Company, 1972) contains five extended analyses of oral or written discourses by Nixon, Agnew, Ehrlich, Cleaver, and Wald. *The Rhetorical Dialogue: Contemporary Concepts and Cases*, by John J. Makay and William R. Brown (Dubuque: William C. Brown Company, 1972), contains analyses and commentaries of varying length on a large number of speeches and essays.

Other rhetorical analyses are no doubt available, but I'm led to think that few of us study essays, that still fewer study book-length works of non-fiction. Of course we talk about such things, often for the ideas they contain, but they remain second-class, somehow inferior, other than art. We can easily enough conceive a poem or a short story to be an imagined whole, emerging from an inventive world, finding itself in a form and style that are its content and being, but we can seldom nerve ourselves to come in this way to an essay or a non-fiction book. And what a sad loss there is for us in this, that we've not yet fully come to the loveliness and complexity of, say, John Graves' *Goodbye to a River* or Loren Eiseley's *The Immense Journey*.

COMPOSITION AND RELATED FIELDS

JAMES L. KINNEAVY AND C. ROBERT KLINE, JR.

The University of Texas at Austin

PROCLUS, THE FIFTH CENTURY NEOPLATONIST, attempting to divide poetry into its basic genres, ended up with a collection of exceptions, which for want of a better category, he called "all those others left standing around." This chapter will, of necessity, strike the reader as being similar to the last category of Proclus. When all of the important bibliographic entries immediately relevant to composition have been detailed, there still exist references which have (or should have) had considerable influence on composition theory and practice and which do not fit neatly into the obvious perimeters of the discipline. It is the function of this chapter to consider some of these.

The word *some* should be emphasized. Because discourse analysis in one sense is relevant to any discipline and because nearly all disciplines have introspective analyses of the language of their own discipline, in an important sense the *fields related* to discourse analysis become coterminous with the areas of scholarship itself. For example, the language of law, the language of politics, the language of advertising, the language of psychiatry, etc., have all been studied and are relevant to a theory of discourse analysis. Consequently, anyone venturing into the fields related to composition must arbitrarily make the choice of his wanderings. And the exclusion of areas will undoubtedly offend some.

Nonetheless, it seems to the authors of this chapter that philosophy, speech, and education at least ought to be given consideration. In many instances there have been direct applications of work in these disciplines to matters of composition. In other cases the application to composition has not yet been made. Sometimes the application is currently in process; in other cases, the application is not at all imminent, but seems urgently needed. Since the purpose of these essays is partly to take a backward look at past achievements but also partly to offer a forward look to future progress, it has been felt useful to incorporate all three viewpoints — applications already made, applications in progress, and applications yet to be achieved.

The relationships of speech and education to composition would seem to be almost self-evident. Ever since the formal break of speech teachers from English teachers in the historic confrontation in 1914, speech teachers even more than English teachers have been the bearers of the rhetorical standard passed on from the tradition of the liberal arts. It is probably true that more original investigation of rhetorical issues is going on in speech departments than in English departments at the present time. Similarly, colleges and departments of education have taken on much of the burden of training secondary and college teachers of English in important aspects of their preparation — pedagogical skills, supervision of apprenticeships, research into curriculum planning and effectiveness, etc.

The relationship of philosophy to composition may not be so obvious to many teachers. It has, however, preoccupied some of the best minds of history. Three crucial reasons might be advanced to establish the necessity of a philosophical background for a rhetorician and a composition teacher. In the first place, it can be readily established that the great rhetoricians of history have almost invariably also been great philosophers; names like Plato, Aristotle, Cicero, Augustine, Bacon, Whately, Bain, and at the present time Kenneth Burke, Kenneth Pike, Chaim Perelman, and many others are names found in both disciplines. Rhetoric seems to be generated by philosophical positions. It is also obvious historically that unless a teacher is aware of the fundamental philosophical foundations within which a rhetoric or composition theory is grounded, it is only too easy to misinterpret whole composition theories. For instance, teachers of speech aware only of Aristotle's *Rhetoric* and ignorant of his *Poetics* and his *Organon* have sometimes radically distorted the basic meaning of many of Aristotle's rhetorical positions. Similarly, teachers in English departments, aware only of Aristotle's *Poetics* and unaware of his treatment of other language functions in the remainder of his work have sometimes completely misunderstood the *Poetics*. This consideration leads to a third notion, also supported by historical examples. There have been some composition theories, especially recent ones, which have evolved without a generating philosophical matrix. Without the judicious perspective of a broad intellectual framework, such theories have often been fanatically proposed as panaceas, with the result that even the valuable components of the theory are lost. Examples of such disasters are the general semanticist applications to composition in the thirties and forties and the inordinate claims made by transformational grammarians in some of their early forays into composition theory. Rhetoric, even more than other disciplines, seems to require the balanced perspective of a grounding philosophy. Without philosophy composition can easily degenerate into a series of fragmented gimmicks. This was Plato's criticism of his own rhetorical predecessors (see *Phaedrus*, 268A ff.), and it is still true today.

PHILOSOPHY

The provinces of philosophy that impinge on composition theory and practice are numerous. At least here some attention ought to be given to philosophical work which relates to the structure of the discipline of rhetoric, to the traditional notion of invention or heuristic, to logic, to information theory, to the notion of self-expression, and to the concept of explanation and to value theory. (The prevalent interest in speech acts is covered elsewhere in these essays.) Because

243

of space limitations, information theory and theories of explanation are here omitted. For a brief survey of these areas and for references to original sources, see James L. Kinneavy, *A Theory of Discourse* (Englewood Cliffs, N.J.: Prentice-Hall, Inc., 1971), pp. 84-86, 89-96.

For bibliographic coverage of the relations between composition and philosophy as well as for many excellent articles, probably the single best source is the journal *Philosophy and Rhetoric*, published by The Pennsylvania State University Press. Many of the reviews are directly related to the intersection of the two disciplines. In addition, excellent bibliographic material is amassed by George E. Yoos in *Newsletter: Rhetoric Society of America*, published by St. Cloud State College, St. Cloud, Minnesota. Of particular interest in this regard are the superb reviews in the *Newsletter* by Frederick Trautmann.

Anyone attempting to understand writings about language in this century should be aware of the large semiotic framework within which even quite controversial theories still coexist today. Despite their differences, many logical positivists, natural language philosophers, transformational grammarians, and speech act theorists still accept the basic divisions of the study of a language as comprising the grammar or syntactics, the meaning or semantics, and the use or pragmatics of a language. These divisions were established by Charles W. Morris in "Foundations of the Social Sciences," *International Encyclopedia for Unified Science*, Vol. 1 (Chicago, Ill.: University of Chicago Press, 1938). Morris refined his theory in *Signs, Language and Behavior* (Englewood Cliffs, N. J.: Prentice-Hall, Inc., 1946), especially pp. 217-220. Following Morris, many logicians adopted this schema (Carnap, Martin, Kotarbînski, Grzegorczyk and others) and elaborated syntactic, semantic, and pragmatic theories. Linguists such as Chomsky, Ross, Katz, and Fodor also adopted the schema, as did information theorists. Some communication theorists as well as propaganda analysts and psycholinguists have adopted it.

The schema is useful for composition teachers because it permits a useful division of labor for the problems of composition analysis and production: there are grammatical problems, there are semantic problems, and there are discourse (pragmatic) problems. If one adds to these the issues inherent in the situational context and the cultural context (to be discussed below in the speech section), there is established a gamut of issues which, though interrelated, can be distinguished for analysis. Some of the applications of this schema to composition will be examined below.

Several other models for the study of our discipline have been imported from philosophical sources. Richard McKeon, the Chicago neo-Aristotelian, in several historical and critical works but especially in his essay "The Uses of Rhetoric in a Technological Age: Architectonic Productive Arts," in Lloyd F. Bitzer and Edwin Black, eds., *The Prospect of Rhetoric* (Englewood Cliffs, N. J.: Prentice-Hall, Inc., 1971), pp. 44-63, has suggested a novel framework, derivative of Aristotle, but given an interesting historical interpretation. He follows Aristotle's basic division of activities into practical (having to do with doing), poetic (having to do with making), and theoretic (having to do with knowing). The first are moral concerns, governed by the virtues of prudence, justice, fortitude, and temperance; the second are production concerns of fine and useful arts governed by the virtue of art; the third are intellectual concerns governed by the virtues of understanding, science and wisdom. McKeon contends that the Romans gave rhetoric a practical orientation, the Renaissance gave rhetoric a poetic orientation, and our times should give rhetoric a theoretic orientation. In each case, rhetoric is an architectonic art, that is, one which can regulate, subordinate, and order other arts. The distinct advantage of this framework lies in its historical roots; nevertheless, its application to composition remains to be made.

A third philosophy of language (one which has been applied to composition, though only to a limited extent), is

245

the view espoused by the so-called ordinary language and the "Oxford" philosophers. Reacting to the ideal and formalized models of language spawned by some of those logicians mentioned above, some philosophers contend that hypothetical mathematical models are too limited and unrealistic for language analysis. Instead they take meanings and structures found in examples of language as it is actually spoken or written and analyze this "ordinary language." Ludwig Wittgenstein, especially in his later work, *Philosophical Investigations* (New York: The Macmillan Company, 1953), was the leader of this group of thinkers. Preeminent among his followers are Gilbert Ryle, *The Concept of Mind* (New York: Barnes and Noble, 1949) and J. L. Austin, *Philosophical Papers*, eds. J. O. Urmson and G. J. Warnock (London: Oxford University Press, 1961).

Two applications of this philosophy to composition have been made though, of course, there may be others of which we are not aware. The first was made in the Nebraska Curriculum and Demonstration Center materials under the leadership of Frank Rice and Paul Olson: *A Curriculum in English* (Lincoln, Nebraska: University of Nebraska Press, 1970-1973). The second application is in a small volume written by a secondary school teacher in England, John Wilson, in *Thinking with Concepts* (Cambridge, England: At the University Press, 1969). He also incorporates the rhetorical issues approach (see below).

A fourth philosophical basis for composition can be seen in the work of the tagmemicists (covered fairly thoroughly in the chapter on invention in this book).

A fifth model which has been used by several writers is that initiated by Karl Bühler, a German psychologist, in "Die Axiomatik der Sprachwissenschaften," *Kant-Studien*, 38 (1933), 19-90. This was refined by Roman Jakobson in "Linguistics and Poetics," *Essays on the Language of Literature*, Seymour Chatman and Samuel R. Levin, eds. (Boston: Houghton Mifflin Company, 1967), pp. 296-322. Jakobson's structure has been adopted by a fair number of anthropologists. In this regard, one can consult John G. Gumperz and Dell Hymes, eds., *The Ethnography of Communications*, a special publication of *American Anthropologist*, LVI, 6 (1964). Jakobson's model was related to others similar to it by James L. Kinneavy and made the basis of his work on the aims of discourse: *A Theory of Discourse* (Englewood Cliffs, N. J.: Prentice-Hall, Inc., 1971). This work has been recast in a less scholarly form for upper-class undergraduate composition classes in *Aims and Audiences in Writing* (Dubuque, Iowa: Kendall/Hunt Publishing Company, 1976). Kinneavy's work also uses the semiotic framework of Morris. Ross Winterowd, in *The Contemporary Writer* (New York: Harcourt Brace Jovanovich, Inc., 1975), has also used the Jakobson schema as a partial organizing framework for his composition theory. Basic to all of these approaches is a concern for the various aims or purposes of language use and a consideration of the differences necessitated in invention, organization, and style by different aims such as self-expression, expository writing, persuasion (in the narrow Aristotelian sense) and literature.

Probably the most common philosophical source for composition theory is the Aristotelian set of scientific questions: Is it? What is it? What qualities does it have? Why? (*Posterior Analytics* 89^b, 21-31.) These questions are the origin of what came to be called the rhetorical issues or constitutions — the four kinds of matters that can be a concern in law and composition theory. Cicero and Quintilian applied the questions to rhetoric and evolved the traditional issues or matters — matters of fact, matters of definition, matters of value. These "matters" were extremely popular in Antiquity, in the Renaissance, and have remained so in our time as a structure for teaching composition. Alexander Bain, *English Composition and Rhetoric*, 2nd American edition (New York: D. Appleton and Company, 1867), united the rhetorical issues with the tradition of the liberal arts and proposed the forms (now often called the modes) of discourse: narration, description, argumentation, exposition, persuasion, and poetry. In our century the latter two are nearly always omitted and the remaining four (narration, description, exposition, and argumentation) are extensively used in both composition books and anthologies of essays. The relationship of these modes to the tradition of the rhetorical issues can be seen in James L. Kinneavy, John Q. Cope, and J. W. Campbell, *Writing – Basic Modes of Organization* (Dubuque, Iowa: Kendall/Hunt, 1976). Possibly the most recent popular text at the college level with this orientation has been Harold F. Graves and Bernard S. Oldsey, *From Fact to Judgment* (New York: The Macmillan Company, 1963).

The previous philosophical models used or proposed for composition have been systematic adaptations of philosophical theories to problems of composition. The larger and more abstract question of the validity of such adaptations is treated philosophically in model theory. The notion of a borrowed system and the advantages of such a borrowing are emphasized by several writers in model theory. Max Black in *Models and Metaphors* (Ithaca, New York: Cornell University Press, 1962); Richard B. Braithwaite in "Models in the Empirical Sciences," and Yuen Ren Chao in "Models in Linguistics and Models in General," in *Logic, Methodology and Philosophy of Science*, Ernest Nagel, Patrick Suppes, and Alfred Tarski, eds. (Stanford, Calif.: Stanford University Press, 1962), pp. 224-231 and 558-560; and Leo Apostel in "Formal Study of Models," in *The Concept and the Role of the Model in Mathematics and Natural and Social Sciences*, ed. Hans Freudenthal (Dordrecht, Holland: D. Reidel Publishing Company, 1961) have all emphasized the advantages of such borrowings. These treatments are fairly ad hoc; the systematic study of the application in different contexts of a basic model is seen in a logical treatise like Abraham Robinson, *Introduction to Model Theory and to the Metamathematics of Algebra* (Amsterdam: North-Holland Publishing Company, 1963).

The application of such a theory to any specific discipline, such as composition, has not yet been made.

Traditionally, logic has consistently been a concern of composition theory and practice. Invention, in classical rhetoric, involved various kinds of logic and today heuristics still involves some aspects of logic (see the chapter on invention).

In this century, in composition books, three different trends may be seen in the treatment of logic. The most traditional composition books, in college and occasionally in high school, still treat something like deductive proof with a coverage of some Aristotelian syllogistic arguments and sometimes with a discussion of the various ways of distributing a term (affirmative or negative, universal or particular). Often they include a coverage of fallacies. A few typical illustrations of this approach can be seen in Hulon Willis, *Logic, Language, and Composition* (Cambridge, Mass.: Winthrop Publishing Company, Inc., 1975); Jack Pitt and Russell Leavenworth, *Logic for Argument* (New York: Random House, 1968).

Despite the prevalence of such an approach for decades, many have denied that it is useful either for helping students analyze the deductive arguments of others or produce their own. Part of the reason for this deficiency can possibly be traced to the limited range of the traditional syllogistic deductions. Modern logic has decisively demonstrated that these syllogistic forms account for only a fairly limited number of the deductions used in regular argumentation. Consequently, a second trend in the teaching of deduction in this century can be seen in the attempt on the part of several writers to use the expanded range of deductions offered by modern logic. Occasionally the treatment is accompanied by an attempt to use the mathematical symbolism of modern logic. Harold Martin and Richard Ohmann, in the first edition of *The Logic and Rhetoric of Exposition* (New York: Holt, Rinehart and Winston, Inc., 1963), exemplified both of these trends. In addition they attempted to relate more closely the logical rules to actual discourse. At the high school level, the Nebraska Curriculum and Demonstration Center materials also have included some of the scope of modern logic in their handling of the deductive theme.

Nevertheless, the symbolic formulae disappeared in the second edition of Martin and Ohmann, and the Nebraska materials have never been made commercially available. Today's treatments of deduction in composition texts are usually quite traditional — see, for example, Maxine Hairston, *A Contemporary Rhetoric* (Boston: Houghton Mifflin Co., 1974).

A third rather different trend in the treatment of deduction can be seen in work from three different countries. Chaim Perelman and L. Olbrechts-Tyteca, in *The New Rhetoric: A Treatise on Argumentation*, tr. John Wilkinson and Purcell Weaver (Notre Dame, Indiana: University of Notre Dame Press, 1969), undertake a thorough revision of the notion of deductive reasoning by focusing on the premises of reasoning used in actual argumentation. They carefully distinguish between real and preferable premises, the first presumably acceptable to universal audiences, the second more limited in range. They then analyze in great detail the various kinds of real and preferable arguments. This is a radical departure from the formalistic treatment of deduction in logic books. As yet, it has not been systematically applied to composition teaching, as far as we know.

A second quite different treatment, one which integrates deduction and induction into a unified system of argumentation, is presented by Stephen E. Toulmin in *The Uses of Argument* (Cambridge: Cambridge University Press, 1958). Toulmin's system of argumentation has been frequently used in speech texts. Typical of such treatments is that used throughout Douglas Ehninger's *Influence, Belief, and Argument: An Introduction to Responsible Persuasion* (Glenview, Ill.: Scott, Foresman and Company, 1974). Occasionally Ehninger's text is used in composition classes in English departments.

A third different approach to the treatment of deduction, derivative of modern logic but emphasizing the general structure of a deductive or axiomatic theory, can be seen in James L. Kinneavy, John Q. Cope, and J. W. Campbell, *Aims and Audiences in Writing* (Dubuque, Ia.: Kendall/Hunt Publishing Company, 1976). Here the basic components of a deductive system are first established by examining several examples: the rules of meaning, the axioms, the rules of inference, and the conclusions. Instead of focusing on the rules of inference (as logicians and composition teachers have in the past), this treatment emphasizes the search for and the use of assumptions or axioms and the meanings of terms throughout the argument. All three of the treatments move away from a major concern for the rules of inference to a concern for the axioms.

Three other areas of philosophical influence ought to be treated here. Kenneth Burke's critical system has, up to the present at least, been more influential in literary criticism than in composition theory. Nonetheless, a few composition theorists have drawn on Burke. Thus W. Ross Winterowd, in *The Contemporary Writer: A Practical Rhetoric* (New York: Harcourt, Brace and World, 1975), uses Burke's pentad of act, agent, agency, scene, and purpose as a heuristic device. Burke's main works that would seem most relevant to composition theory are *A Grammar of Motives* (Berkeley, Calif.: University of California Press, 1962); *A Rhetoric of Motives* (Berkeley, Calif.: University of California Press, 1969); *Philosophy of Literary Form: Studies in Symbolic Action* (Berkeley, Calif.: University of California Press, 1968).

One area of philosophy which has made considerable progress in this century and has been almost universally ignored both by literary and rhetorical criticism is the field of axiology, the theory of value. Despite these advances there still remain entire disciplines in the academic world in which "value judgments" remain anathema. Some of the recognized giants of literary criticism at the present time eschew evaluation. W. K. Wimsatt, for instance, reduces evaluation to explication in *Explication as Criticism*, a collection he edited. He states explicitly, "The title of this volume, taken from my introductory essay, asserts that explication *is* criticism; it *is* the evaluative account of the poem" (*Explication as Criticism: Selected Papers from the English Institute, 1941-1952* [New York: Columbia University Press, 1969], p. xiii; the italics are Wimsatt's). Northrop Frye, in an essay intended to introduce graduate students in English to the basic branches of their discipline, reduces scholarly criticism to genre classification and descriptive analysis of structures ("Literary Criticism," in James E. Thorpe, ed., *The Aims and Methods of Scholarship in Modern Languages and Literatures* [New York: MLA, 1963], pp. 57-62). In philosophy there are still many who maintain, with the logical positivists, that value judgments are scientifically meaningless; at best they are indicative of our emotional attitude to an object. Alfred Ayer, in *Language, Truth and Logic* (London: Oxford University Press, 1936) and later in *Philosophical Essays* (London: Macmillan, 1954) was possibly the most strident advocate of this position. Rhetorical criticism, on the contrary, usually retains its right to evaluate.

Yet it should seem obvious enough that neither literary nor rhetorical criticism can calmly abdicate the responsibility to evaluate. Distinctions of quality among literary works must be given some rationale — otherwise Bob Dylan and Shakespeare are equally important. Evaluations must be made among literary works in various media as well as among rhetorical products in various media; the effectiveness of various persuasive techniques must be measured by some intelligent norm; the ethics of various types of advertising and propaganda must be discriminated, etc.

To meet these challenges rhetorical and literary criticism should use whatever other disciplines can offer. Some elementary introductions to value theory which the average English teacher might read with no prior background necessary are: Risieri Frondizi, *What is Value?, An Introduction to Axiology*, tr. Solomon Lipp (LaSalle, Illinois: Open Court,

1963); William K. Frankena, *Ethics* (Englewood Cliffs, N.J.: Prentice-Hall, Inc., 1963); and Phillipa Foot, ed., *Theories of Ethics* (New York: Oxford University Press, 1967). Somewhat more advanced treatments are: C. D. Broad, *Five Types of Ethical Theory* (Atlantic Highlands, N. J.: Humanities Press, Inc., 1962); and Mary Warnock, *Ethics Since 1900* (New York: Oxford University Press, 1966). Two classics specifically related to evaluation and language are: Charles L. Stevenson, *Ethics and Language* (New Haven: Yale University Press, 1954); and P. W. Taylor, *Normative Discourse* (Englewood Cliffs, N. J.: Prentice-Hall, Inc., 1961). The reader will probably have noticed that a good number of the above entries deal specifically with ethics, and not with general value theory. Many of the problems of value theory generally have often been first examined in an ethical context. Later extrapolations are made to other realms of value.

Finally, many existential and phenomenologists today, following the lead of Heidegger and Husserl, have turned their attention to the specific nature of the act of self-expression, often self-expression in language. This, of course, is basic to a theory of composition. Jean Paul Sartre, in *Being and Nothingness: An Essay on Phenomenological Ontology*, tr. Hazel E. Barnes (New York: Washington Square Press, 1953), developed a fairly full-blown theory of self-expression. His co-editor for many years, Maurice Merleau-Ponty, in *Phenomenology of Perception*, tr. Colin Smith (New York: Humanities Press, 1962) and *The Primacy of Perception*, tr. and ed. James M. Edie (Evanston, Ill.: Northwestern University Press, 1964) and *Sense and Non-Sense*, tr. Hubert L. Dreyfus and Patricia A. Dreyfus (Evanston, Ill.: Northwestern University Press, 1964), developed a parallel theory of self-expression and inspired one of his disciples, George Gusdorf, to write what may be the best concise introduction to the phenomenological notion of self-expression applied specifically to language, *Speaking (La Parole)*, tr. Paul T. Brockelman (Evanston, Ill.: Northwestern University Press, 1965). A very interesting linguistic analysis of the notion of "expression" has been made by Alan Tormey, *The Concept of Expression: A Study in Philosophical Aesthetics* (Princeton, N. J.: Princeton University Press, 1971).

SPEECH AND PROPAGANDA ANALYSES

The separation of speech — often now called speech communication — from English departments in the early part of this century undoubtedly fostered the autonomous development of the discipline of speech, but it resulted in a long drought in several areas of rhetorical analysis of written discourse. However, many of the techniques of speech and propaganda analysis, whether made in speech departments proper or in allied departments, are very applicable to the written medium.

Bibliographically, most of the relevant materials are covered in *Speech Monographs*, *The Quarterly Journal of Speech*, and *The Journal of Communication*. An excellent recent bibliographic survey of experimental research in the field of persuasion is H. I. Abelson and Marvin Karlins, eds., *Persuasion: How Opinions and Attitudes Are Changed* (New York: Springer Publishing Co., 1970). An earlier work is Wayne N. Thompson, *Quantitative Research in Public Address and Communication* (New York: Random House, Inc., 1967). Several classic bibliographic studies also exist. Bruce Lannes Smith, Harold D. Lasswell, and Ralph D. Casey, in *Propaganda, Communication and Public Opinion* (Princeton, N. J.: Princeton University Press, 1946), summarize much of the work of these scholars with both World War I and II propaganda.

Harold D. Lasswell also cooperated with several others in *The Language of Politics* (Cambridge, Mass.: M.I.T. Press, 1965) and with Daniel Lerner and I. de Sola Pool in *The Comparative Study of Symbols: An Introduction* (Stanford, Calif.: Stanford University Press, 1952). In these works Lasswell and his collaborators made comprehensive analyses of political myths. Lasswell viewed political myth as including three basic elements: doctrine, formulae, and miranda (ceremonial and ritual elements).

Another massive set of experiments was performed by Carl I. Hovland and his colleagues in psychology at Yale. With Irving L. Janis and Harold H. Kelley he studied the credibility of various communicators, the success of fear as an appeal, and the persuasibility index of different types of persons. These studies were reported in *Communication and Persuasion: Psychological Studies of Opinion Change* (New Haven, Conn.: Yale University Press, 1953). In *The Order of Presentation in Persuasion* (New Haven, Conn.: Yale University Press, 1957), Lasswell and others studied experimentally the effectiveness of various organizational techniques, the law of primacy (presenting strong arguments early), the law of recency (presenting strong arguments late) as well as other facets of organization.

Some important directions in rhetorical criticism and theory which could well be made relevant to the teaching of composition are developing in speech communication. Speech theorists have been much more critical of Aristotelian rhetoric than have their counterparts in English departments. Certainly the most comprehensive of these criticisms has been that of Edwin Black, *Rhetorical Criticism: A Study in Method* (New York: The Macmillan Company, 1965). Possibly the most severe stricture of Aristotelian rhetoric made by Black is his accusation that Aristotle makes persuasion entirely too intellectual and logical a process.

A second limitation of Aristotelian rhetoric, according to Black, is Aristotle's neglect of the audience and of the entire rhetorical situation in which the act of persuasion occurs. Probably the seminal article on this topic is Lloyd Bitzer's "The Rhetorical Situation," in the journal *Philosophy and Rhetoric*, 2 (1968), 1-14. This tendency leads to an interest in larger entities of "persuasion," such as political and advertising campaigns rather than individual speeches or ads, or movements rather than isolated events. These concerns can

255

be seen recurring in the various reports and essays anthologized in Lloyd F. Bitzer and Edwin Black, eds., *The Prospect of Rhetoric* (Englewood Cliffs, N. J.: Prentice-Hall, Inc., 1971).

Given an interest in different types of audiences and in persuasion movements, it is not surprising that scholars in speech have done some excellent work in the rhetoric of Blacks and in the rhetoric of violence. Typical of the first is Arthur L. Smith, *Language, Communication, and Rhetoric in Black America* (New York: Harper & Row, Publishers, 1972) and of the second, John Waite Bowers and Donovan J. Ochs, *The Rhetoric of Agitation and Control* (Reading, Mass.: Addison-Wesley Publishing Co., Inc., 1971).

Anyone seriously interested in the full range of rhetoric as it is treated by modern scholars in speech might consult William Norwood Brigance, *Speech Composition* (New York: Appleton-Century-Crofts, Inc., 1953), for a work which has worn well in speech communication departments for two decades. A seminal article of considerable importance is Donald C. Bryant, "Rhetoric: Its Functions and Its Scope," *The Quarterly Journal of Speech*, 39 (December, 1953), 401-424. More modern treatments can be seen in A. Craig Baird, Franklin H. Knower, and Samuel L. Becker, *General Speech Communication* (New York: McGraw-Hill Company, 1971) and in Robert L. Scott and Bernard L. Brock, *Methods of Rhetorical Criticism: A Twentieth Century Perspective* (New York: Harper & Row, Publishers, 1972).

EDUCATION

In any essay attempting to present ideas which inform the teaching of writing, the necessity of looking at the *act of teaching* is paramount. In this section of the essay the authors will review some of the major works and ideas which they feel inform the teaching of composition, especially with reference to actual classroom teaching strategies. Several topics merit special attention: the teaching of reading and the relationship between the teaching of reading and the teaching of writing; the use of so-called "behaviorally-stated objectives"; curriculum design; and evaluation.

The journals in which information helpful to the teacher of writing can most often be found include *Research in the Teaching of English*, *College English*, *College Composition and Communication* (all of which are organs of the National Council of Teachers of English, 1111 Kenyon Road, Urbana, Ill., 61801), *Journal of Reading* and *Reading Research Quarterly* (both of which are organs of the International Reading Association, Barksdale Road, Newark, Del., 19711). The research reports and monographs of the National Council of Teachers of English cover major trends, important findings in research, and instructional guidelines.

The Teaching of Reading

Persons involved in the study of the teaching of reading have in recent years focused upon a few, very specific questions. While it is beyond the scope of this essay to discuss all these questions and their answers, it is important for us to focus upon two: How can a teacher determine the level of difficulty of reading material in order to give students materials they can adequately master? What strategies are common to the teaching of reading and the teaching of writing?

There are several formulas available for computing the difficulty level of textual material. Recent journal articles have included the use of the Dale-Chall formula, the Flesch formula, the SMOG Index, the FOG Index, the Fry formula, and so on. Perhaps the easiest for teachers to employ is the SMOG formula. McLaughlin, in "SMOG Grading — A New Readability Formula," *Journal of Reading*, 12 (May, 1969), 639-646, says that his formula is based upon manipulation of a count of polysyllabic words. The calculation is done by adding three to the square root of the polysyllable count, which is derived from counting the number of words of three or more syllables in a selection of thirty sentences. For example, there are approximately 190 words of three or more syllables in the first thirty sentences of this essay; the readability of this selection is, then, about seventeenth grade level (first year of graduate school), since $3 + 14 = 17$, with 14 being the approximate square root of 190. It should be noted that use of the formula requires no mathematical sophistication; key numbers are 144 (square root is 12, plus 3 equals junior college level; 81 (square root is 9, plus 3 equals senior year high school); and 196 (square root is 14, plus 3 equals graduate level).

Another frequently used formula is the Fry readability formula-graph; the actual calculations involved are minimal since Fry has plotted on a page-sized graph the variables involved. The user simply plots the intersection of the line representing the number of syllables (in the one hundred word selection under study) and the line representing the number of sentences in the selection; the point of intersection will be at or near a grade level. A complete discussion of the Fry graph and its use is in "A Readability Formula That Saves Time," *Journal of Reading*, 11 (April, 1968), 513-516 and 575-578.

Both the SMOG grading and the Fry graph techniques have been tested and validated against other readability formulas and the results have indicated that these formulas are as reliable and accurate as the older, more complex formulas. A thorough analysis of the problem of assessing readability is available in George Klare's "Assessing Readability," *Reading Research Quarterly*, 10 (Fall, 1974), 62-102.

Reading teachers have devised a test of reading ability based upon a collection of passages arranged from easiest to hardest readability. This test, usually called the Informal Reading Inventory (IRI), involves oral reading and may involve silent reading; in the oral and silent sections, the reader reads the material and then is asked comprehension questions by the teacher, who has listened carefully to the reading of the student (in silent reading, the teacher watches for signs of fatigue or frustration on the reader's face —

watery eyes, grimaces, etc.). Based upon observations of the reading given and the answers to the comprehension questions, the teacher determines the three reading levels of the student, which are usually termed Frustrational, Instructional, and Independent; these represent levels at which the student is totally frustrated, at which the student can read with assistance, and at which the student can read without assistance and without frustration. Class reading may be done at the instructional level, but work to be done on the student's own should be only at the independent level. The IRI is not usually given to groups, although it is possible to do so. The best introduction to the construction and use of the Informal Reading Inventory is a monograph entitled *Informal Reading Inventories* by M. S. Johnson and R. A. Kress (Newark, Delaware: International Reading Association, 1965).

In *Improving Reading in Every Class* (Boston: Allyn and Bacon, Inc., 1972) by E. L. Thomas and H. A. Robinson; in *The Improvement of Reading* (New York: McGraw-Hill Book Company, 1967) by R. Strang, C. M. McCullough and A. E. Traxler; in *Teaching Reading and Study Strategies: The Content Areas* (Boston: Allyn and Bacon, Inc., 1975) by H. A. Robinson; and in *Comprehensive High School Reading Methods* (Columbus, Ohio: Charles E. Merrill Publishing Company, 1973) by D. L. Shepherd, substantial segments of each book are devoted to a discussion of the importance of the readers' understanding of the nature of structures available to the writers of textbook materials. Teachers of writing will recognize that the discussions in these books focus directly on the ideas usually called by teachers of writing "structures and forms in expository writing."

In developing a reader's comprehension skills one of the most common tacks taken by educators is the teaching of the various ways in which materials can be organized for a given effect. Since the purpose of most prose textbook materials is to convey information, most of the work in the area of reading is directed towards teaching what are essentially the formats of expository prose. In these books, as well as in virtually every other source book for teachers of reading, the teacher is presented ways in which the following items can be taught to students: the relationship of the paragraph to the whole chapter, the placement of topic sentences and thesis statements, developmental patterns within a paragraph (i.e., coordinate and subordinate), structural versus substantive paragraph forms and purposes, and so on. One of the basic strategies, then, useful in the teaching of both reading and writing is to focus upon the basic structural principles which dictate to the writer the final form of the written presentation. It seems apparent that a teacher of writing could then move from a discussion of these principles to applications in both reading and writing lessons. Indeed, such a relationship is involved in what has been termed the "traditional deductive approach" to the teaching of writing: see, for example, J. L. Kinneavy, "Theories of Composition and Actual Writing," *Kansas English*, 59 (December, 1973), 3-17.

Many people have characterized an "essay" as discourse directed toward the answering of one specific question. Many textbooks used in composition courses characterize the essay as an answer to a specific question, in which each paragraph is an answer to a smaller question subsumed within the larger question. In the last several years reading educators have devoted a considerable amount of attention to the role of "pre-questioning strategies." The focus of this work has been on the idea that a reader will get the most out of materials read only when he is reading to answer questions; many teachers have provided students with study guides or study questions to be completed while reading through assigned materials, and, in fact, the research in reading shows that retention of the material read will be greater and last for a longer period when the student is reading to answer questions. While providing the student with a series of study questions is a good idea and a worthwhile strategy, it is important that students begin to generate their own questions and thus begin to rely upon themselves as questioners instead of on the teacher as the poser of questions. Perhaps the most popular method involving the idea of pre-questions is the SQRRR formula; the letters of the acronym stand for Survey, Question, Read, Recite, Review.

The student using the SQRRR method first quickly surveys the material (chapter, essay, article), paying particular attention to the title, any subheads or sideheads, any charts, graphs or figures, and words or phrases in italics or boldface type; he then takes these words or phrases and poses questions about how they relate to the idea conveyed in the title. The third step involves the student's reading of the passage and then (fourth step) answering the questions posed in step two. Immediately upon completion of this procedure the student reviews the questions and answers; if an examination is scheduled over the material the student will likely review several times the questions and answers. The essential factor is that the posing of questions informs both the act of reading and the act of writing and is, therefore, an essential strategy in reading and writing.

For additional discussion of the SQRRR procedure see D. L. Shepherd's *Comprehensive High School Reading Methods*, cited above, and *Reading Strategies for Secondary School Teachers* by L. Burmeister (Reading, Mass.: Addison-Wesley Publishing Company, Inc., 1974). These books also discuss the nature and variety of questions which both teachers and students can ask about materials read. There are also other materials available in the area of questioning. Perhaps the best general book dealing with the activity of questioning is *Involving Students in Questioning* by Francis P. Hunkins (Boston, Mass.: Allyn and Bacon, Inc., 1975). An earlier book by Hunkins, *Questioning Strategies and Techniques* (Boston: Allyn and Bacon, Inc., 1972), contains very helpful, specific guidelines in the planning, formulating, and evaluating of questions used in the classroom.

In Donald Spearitt's "Identification of Subskills of Reading Comprehension by Maximum Likelihood Factor Analysis," *Reading Research Quarterly*, 8 (Fall, 1972), 92-

111, Spearitt reports on a study to determine to what extent various subskills of reading comprehension are all measures of the same phenomenon. The purpose of such a study is to assist the teacher in helping students who have trouble understanding what they have read by pinpointing the source of the trouble. Spearitt found that the most distinguishable variable in his list of eight was word meanings; this means that the factor in testing comprehension which best discriminates the poorer readers from better readers is knowledge of word meanings. Three other factors were slightly less discriminating: drawing inferences from the content; recognizing a writer's purpose, attitude, tone, and mood; and following the structure of a passage. A fifth factor, finding answers to questions derived from explicit or paraphrased wording of the reading passage, correlated highly with the four factors enumerated above. It is therefore not unreasonable to continue to postulate the importance of: (a) understanding the structure of a passage, and (b) answering questions in the act of reading; since the relationship of these two factors to writing is obvious, the two factors provide the two most basic interrelationships between reading and writing.

Behaviorally-Stated Objectives

In recent years the use of and even the requirement of the use of behaviorally-stated objectives, more commonly called "behavioral objectives," has become a fact. Objectives written with statements of acceptable behavior on the part of the student are called behaviorally-stated objectives: or, interchangeably, "behavioral objectives." Instrumental in the movement towards behaviorally-stated objectives have been curriculum designers and teachers who see that a concise and specific statement of all activities to be required of the student is essential in: (a) designing goals and materials to teach ideas, concepts, or skills and (b) the evaluation of the student's progress through the materials. The upsurge in diagnostic-prescriptive based programs — in writing, in reading, and language arts in general — has pushed the consideration of behaviorally-stated objectives into every part of the field of English, from the elementary school through the university.

Advocates of behaviorally-stated objectives believe that the two aspects of instruction discussed above (designing instructional goals and evaluation of progress toward or to them) are possible only when the specific details of the student's behavior have been presented. *Mutatis mutandis*, the preparation of behaviorally-stated objectives by the teacher does assist the teacher in deciding exactly: (a) what is expected of the student, (b) in exactly what way achieving this expectation is to be verified, (c) and what level of performance is necessary to verify. These three aspects are the essential elements of an educational objective.

The movement toward behaviorally-stated objectives does not derive entirely from the considerations of the so-called behaviorist psychologists. Although the work of these psychologists has been instrumental in such widespread use of behaviorally-stated objectives, the most important influence has been the professional literature in education and educational psychology. People who teach English have been very slow to accept the use of behaviorally-stated objectives, because they feel that the use of such objectives does not allow for the incorporation and evaluation of the total range of possible human responses, especially those responses which are found in or are a result of reading and writing in the English language. The most concise statement of this position by an organization of English teachers is the one presented under the aegis of the National Council of Teachers of English by J. Maxwell and A. Tovatt, *On Writing Behavioral Objectives for English* (Champaign, Ill.: National Council of Teachers of English, 1970):

On.the Need for Caution in the Use of Behavioral Objectives in the Teaching of English

BACKGROUND: The Commission on the English Curriculum has recognized that the growing practice of proposing that behavioral objectives be defined for the language arts, and that these objectives be employed in testing, leads to a complex, demanding, and possibly educationally dangerous activity. Expert witnesses on the goals of English, in conference with the Commission, have echoed the Commission's concern that real damage to English instruction may result from definitions of English in the behavioral mode, and advise that the methods of measuring the attainment of behavioral objectives are still too imperfect to justify the extensive use of comprehensive behavioral definitions of English.

While the Commission advocates that all teachers be open-minded about possible alternatives for defining and structuring the English curriculum — including the use of behavioral objectives — at the same time it urges caution and accordingly presents the following resolution:

Resolved, That those who propose to employ behavioral objectives be urged to engage in a careful appraisal of the possible benefits and the present limitation of behavioral definitions of English with reference to the humanistic aims which have traditionally been valued in this discipline.

And be it further Resolved, That those in the profession who do undertake to write behavioral objectives (a) make specific plans to account for the total English curriculum; (b) make an intention to preserve (and, if need be, fight for) the retention of important humanistic goals of education; and (c) insist on these goals regardless of whether or not there exist instruments at the present time for measuring the desired changes in pupil behavior.

Members of the Commission on the English Curriculum, the group which formulated the resolution presented above, present in "Part II (Statements at Issue)" of *On Writing Behavioral Objectives for English* individual statements about the importance of essential issues involved in, and specific programs incorporating, behaviorally-stated objectives — notably the 'Tri-University Behavioral Objectives for English Project.'

While not directly related to behaviorally-stated objectives, the incorporation of a more behaviorally-based system of instruction in writing was the focus of Robert Zoellner's "Talk-Write: A Behavioral Pedagogy for Composition," *CE*, 30 (January, 1969), 267-320. In addition to Zoellner's article, the discussion about the article and Zoellner's replies to the comments and criticisms advanced in the six articles included under the title "On Zoellnerism" in *CE*, 30 (May, 1969), 645-668 are important reading for teachers of writing.

Two basic works in the area of objectives are *Preparing Instructional Objectives* by Robert Mager (Palo Alto, Calif.: Fearon Publishers, Inc. 1965) and *Taxonomy of Educational Objectives: Handbook Two, the Affective Domain* by D. R. Krathwohl, B. S. Bloom, and B. B. Masita (New York: David McKay Company, Inc., 1964); the latter contains a presentation of both the affective and cognitive domains, the second of which is often called "Bloom's taxonomy." There are many other issues involved in the use and formulation of behaviorally-stated objectives but a comprehension of these issues would be based upon a thorough understanding of the following questions, which are offered in summary of this subsection:

1. To what extent can a taxonomy, a hierarchy of levels, be imposed upon the teaching of writing?

2. To what extent can the specific aspects of the writing act be delineated?

3. To what extent can a teacher of writing predetermine acceptable levels of performance for each separate skill involved in the "process of writing"?

4. What changes in instructional strategies would be forthcoming as a result of a closer analysis of questions 1, 2, and 3 above?

Curriculum Design

The purpose of this short section is to present key figures and works in the area of the design of instruction, especially as it relates to the teacher of writing. It is not the purpose of this section to discuss thoroughly all aspects of curriculum planning or curriculum design, nor is it the purpose of this section to present thoroughly all the ideas of the individuals mentioned.

Several short volumes are very helpful for the teacher of writing who is attempting to get a general overview of trends and practices in the last decade. Frank M. Rice, in *English and Its Teaching* (Lincoln, Nebraska: Professional Educators Publications, Inc., 1972), presents an analysis of traditional programs, new developments in literature curricula, language curricula, and composition curricula (in each of these three sections specific attention is devoted to teaching methodologies) and a brief summary of important factors in the development of the field of English teaching, including the influence of the National Council of Teachers of English, the recent increase in the use of instructional media, the move towards individualized curricula, standards advanced for preparation of teachers, and the Dartmouth Conference. This brief book, while not attempting to be thorough in its discussion of every subject presented, is a fine overview of the teaching of English.

While the publications of the National Council of Teachers of English, including *Language Arts, English Journal, College English, College Composition and Com-*

munication, *Research in the Teaching of English*, as well as others, detail from year to year the various fashions, fads, and emerging concepts within the field of English and the teaching of English, it is perhaps the special publications of the Council, the research monographs, which best detail important facets of the teaching of English. For the composition teacher, curriculum design will involve consideration, among others, of the specific points addressed in the following: Paul B. Diederich, *Measuring Growth in English* (NCTE, 1974); William Labov, *The Study of Nonstandard English* (NCTE, 1970); Janet Emig, *The Composing Process of Twelfth Graders* (NCTE, 1971); Alan Purves, *Elements of Writing About a Literary Work: A Study of Response to Literature* (NCTE, 1968); and Frank O'Hare, *Sentence Combining: Improving Student Writing Without Formal Grammar Instruction* (NCTE, 1971).

An understanding of the bases of curriculum planning and design can be discovered from a study of J. M. Gwynn and J. B. Chase's *Curriculum Principles and Social Trends* (London: Macmillan Company, 1969). This book begins with an historical overview, proceeds into a discussion of the most salient of the research data over the last half century, presents in detail various trends and innovative techniques in both teaching and program design, and culminates with a discussion of the relationship between the curriculum and the greater society in which the school or college functions.

The National Society for the Study of Education Yearbook, 1964, *Theories of Learning and Instruction*, contains an interesting essay by N. L. Gage entitled "Theories of Teaching." In this essay Gage discusses the possibility and indeed the appropriateness of a movement towards a general theory of the act of teaching. Another author who has an article in the same yearbook is known for two books of importance to the designer of instructional materials: J. S. Bruner, in *Process of Education* (Cambridge: Harvard University Press, 1960) and *Toward A Theory of Instruction* (Cambridge: Belknap Press, 1966), advances concepts and theorems

267

which lead toward a general theory of the act of teaching. While many authors and researchers continue to study the possibility of deriving a general theory of teaching, it seems that whenever such a theory appears it will be complex. As P. F. Brandwein, *Notes Toward a General Theory of Teaching* (New York: Harcourt, Brace, and World, Inc., 1966), indicates:

> Further, as has been indicated, the teaching act embraces cognitive, psychomotor, conative, affective elements, or, if you will, enactive, iconic, and symbolic elements. A general theory of learning must account for them, as must a theory of teaching. Gage and Bruner emphasize this. Certainly students of teaching and learning (from the Greek philosophers through Comenius and Rosseau) before the time of experimental procedure per se . . . have given attention, with varying emphasis to these elements (p. 11).

In instructional design it is important to recognize the individual student and the evaluation procedures which will be used to assess the individual student's progress. While an analysis of evaluative techniques is beyond the scope of this essay, it is important to note that the discussion of behaviorally-stated objectives and the discussion of the interrelationship between the teaching of reading and the teaching of writing and the discussion of evaluative techniques present some ideas useful for the teacher attempting to arrive at a better understanding of the process of evaluation. The importance of the individual in the curriculum plan — while intuitively understandable — is emphasized in the Gwynn and Chase book, in Brandwein's monograph, as well as the various publications of the National Council of Teachers of English. It is also important to note that student evaluation of teachers is related to the total evaluation process. For more consideration of this latter point, see C. R. Kline, Jr., "Students Rate Profs in Accord with Grade Expectations," *Phi Delta Kappan*, 57 (September, 1975), 54, and Kenneth E. Eble, *The Recognition and Evaluation of Teaching* (Washington, D.C.: American Association of University Professors, 1971).

Evaluation

Perhaps no other single issue so pervades the mind of the teacher of writing as the issue of evaluation of the student's work. For the teacher of writing wishing to study the problems attendant upon this issue, three monographs are basic: Richard Braddock, Richard Lloyd-Jones, and Lowell Schoer, *Research in Written Composition*; F. I. Godshålk, F. Swineford, and W. E. Coffman, *The Measurement of Writing Ability*; and P. B. Diederich, *Measuring Growth in English*. This section of the essay will be focused upon a discussion of each of these publications followed by a summary of relevant, recent findings.

In 1963, Braddock, Lloyd-Jones, and Schoer's *Research in Written Composition* (Champaign: National Council of Teachers of English) was published. The methods advocated by the authors in section two, "Suggested Methods of Research," became the standards for both empirical and quasi-empirical studies. After a discussion of the importance of the variables in evaluating student writing (writer, assignment, rater and colleague) the authors state (pp. 15-16):

> Typically, frequency counts have been a most frustrating type of composition research to read, yet perhaps they are to become one of the most important types.... The importance of the frequency count (in contrast to rating procedures) lies in its potential for describing a composition in fairly objective terms which *can* mean the same things to most teachers and investigators and which are subject to more statistical analyses than are ratings.

After a discussion of problems in frequency counts as measures of specific writing errors, the authors advocate use of frequency counts according to several factors: errors of certain types, errors in specific situations (e.g., apostrophe), rank ordering of frequency of types of errors, error quotient (number of errors of a certain type over the number of possible errors of the same type), and number of errors of a certain type per set length (as 100 or 1000 words).

Section three, "The State of Knowledge About Composition," surveys the available knowledge about factors influencing composition (environmental and instructional), about rhetorical considerations in studies of composition, about objective tests versus actual samples of student writing, and about other concerns, such as size of class, typewriting, use of media. The questions listed by the authors on pages 52 and 53 became the basis for much of the research conducted in the past decade.

After a discussion of research techniques and statistical terms, the authors in section four, "Summaries of Selected Research," discuss five studies. The presentation of these studies and the discussion of the results found in each are essential reading for the teacher of writing. Notable, also, is the detailed concluding section, "References for Further Research," including over five hundred entries.

In *The Measurement of Writing Ability* (New York: College Entrance Examination Board, 1966) the use of certain aspects of paper and pencil tests to predict writing ability are discussed. Particularly interesting to the teacher of writing is the discussion in section four, in which the authors present research data involving the correlation of the English Composition Tests and selected combinations of subtest scores. The authors note that their data indicate that one of the most important factors in the reader's impression of an essay is the sentence, or more precisely different kinds of sentences and their characteristics. Indeed, section four of this book is a discussion of the possible use of measures of writing involving an essay and of measures not involving an essay. In the introduction to the monograph E. S. Noyes states (p. iv):

270

The measurement of a student's ability to write has been a perplexing problem to the College Board ever since 1901, when its first examinations were offered. The importance of this monograph ... lies in the fact that it presents evidence that this problem has at long last been solved, insofar as the current English composition tests are concerned.

The authors, in summarizing the results of their investigations (which involved 646 students in the eleventh and twelfth grades writing on five different topics, taking six objective tests, and completing two interlinear exercises over a three-month period), present three generalizations (pp. 39-41):

1. The reliability of essay scores is primarily a function of the number of different essays and the number of different readings included.
2. When objective questions specifically designed to measure writing skills are evaluated against a reliable criterion of writing skills, they prove to be highly valid.
3. The most efficient predictor of a reliable direct measure of writing ability is one which includes essay questions or interlinear exercises in combination with objective questions.

In *Measuring Growth in English* (Champaign, Ill.: National Council of Teachers of English, 1974), Diederich presents a fairly complete discussion of various facets of the problem of evaluating student performance in writing. From the discussion emerge two important considerations for the teacher of writing. First, evaluation of student writing should be based on improvement; Diederich advocates collecting student writings in a folder and evaluating one paper as compared to another by the same student. In this way the discussion of the student writing is based on considerations of what is better in one paper than in another, of how what

271

was done in one could have been done in the other. Second, evaluation of student writing should be done by a "staff grading procedure." By this Diederich means that grading is done by all members of the composition staff; the grades are impersonal since the graders do not know which student author wrote which paper (the only identifying mark is a six digit number picked at random by the student). The student writings evaluated in the system are ones done on the same day using the same topic. Diederich states (p. 14):

> Moreover, since each student's writing will be judged by at least four different readers in the course of a year, any bias toward liberal or conservative views, plain or fancy writings, and the like will almost certainly be cancelled out. Four readers are not necessarily better than one, but it is unlikely that all four will err in the same direction.

The balance of the volume is a discussion of the terms used in reporting the results of research and discussions of methods useful in testing the results of specific programs and exercises in writing.

In the second section of the volume (called "Appendices") Diederich presents topics for essays, objective test items, sample paper descriptions, and a list of ninety-six objectives for students in writing classes.

R. M. Jewell, J. Cowley, and G. Rhum, in *Final Report: The Effectiveness of College Level Instruction in Freshman Composition, Project 2188 – Amended* (Cedar Falls, Iowa: University of Northern Iowa, 1969) ERIC No. ED037467, discuss the results of a project which involved researchers at the University of Northern Iowa and four cooperating institutions; the purpose of the project was to test the assumption that students write better as a result of completing freshman composition. Students who were excused from taking freshman composition were compared to students enrolled in freshman composition courses; data were collected over a three year period (year one was the pilot study). The evidence which emerged from an analysis of the data tended to support the hypothesis that there would be no significant difference between the two groups. The question then becomes, "Why have students study composition if that study makes no difference in their later writing?"

The most recent, and thorough, response to the question comes in an article by S. A. Sanders and J. H. Littlefield. In "Perhaps Test Essays Can Reflect Significant Improvement in Freshman Composition: Report of a Successful Attempt," *Research in the Teaching of English*, 9 (Fall, 1975), 145-153, the authors report that while the differences over the semester due to instruction were not significant on impromptu essays, there was a significant difference between the pre- and the posttest essays which involved research. All students wrote both types of papers for the pretest and the posttest; all classes were instructed in the persuasive aim of discourse. The results, then, show that there are differences between pre- and posttest essays when the class members are focusing upon a specific aim and are free to choose topics (a factor likely to produce more motivation to write than assigned topics).

DIALECTS AND COMPOSITION

JENEFER M. GIANNASI

Northern Illinois University

THE STUDY OF DIALECTS FOCUSES attention on the social, geographical, and temporal conventions and constraints of language varieties as they are rendered by the members of their respective sociolinguistic communities. Such study (a) distinguishes pronunciations, vocabularies, and syntax available to various habit pattern sets (i.e., *dialects* or varieties), (b) emphasizes the primacy of speech, and (c) draws attention to the differences between spoken and written language varieties. As a result, dialect study is intimately involved with the rhetorical problems of speaker-audience contact *in situation* — a problem of first importance to the researcher and teacher of composition.

The speaker of broadcast English utters a language code accepted for general, public reportage and consultation. The writer of technical English composes in a language code used to convey the data of a referent-oriented world. The speaker of Black English Vernacular renders a language code which reflects a distinct cultural orientation to time, space, and people involved in social contact. The writer of Edited American English records through a language code which seeks to render the thoughts of people involved in the conduct of behavior in the public world. Each is concerned about using a variety of language which will most accurately reflect speaker intention, respond to audience expectation, and reinforce social and cultural attitudes. Each is concerned about appropriate and effective choice of the usage

275

options available within the habit patterns allowed for each code. And each is involved in exhibiting communicative competence—performance in situation which exhibits practical control of the grammar of a variety.

No less involved in this process is the teacher of written composition. For example, the teacher who commits a group of students to the writing of a business letter is involving both student and teacher in a complex set of sociocultural and linguistic concerns. The student must take into account an audience's attitudes and expectations. The teacher and the student must answer many questions before each letter is ready for "publication."

Which dialect usually informs such writing?
What are the written conventions of that dialect?
Which dialect mix would the audience consider acceptable?
Which usage options of the speaker's dialect and the audience's dialect can be drawn into the more neutral written pattern?
What social distance should be maintained through the choice of appropriate code markers?

Suppose that a student, using text materials and class directives, begins his orientation paragraph with this sentence:

In answer to your request for names of witnesses to the accident, didn't nobody see it.

As a statement which conveys mutually intelligible information, it succeeds. But as a statement which exhibits competence in showing speaker intention and in answering to expected behavior patterns and social sensibilities, it works against itself. The pre-comma prepositional phrases increase the formality of this written style of Edited American English, while the post-comma statement suggests the informal oral style of Black English Vernacular. This particular mix of oral and written code markers and dialect habit patterns would probably interfere in the consultation process. The audience would react to the mix of patterns rather than receive the message. Effective consultation depends on a careful balance of linguistic and extra-linguistic components, all of which must be considered by teacher and student and by speaker and audience.

Thus, all are involved in a process which encourages them to accept or seek multi-varietal proficiency. As listeners and speakers or as readers and writers, they are faced with the need to understand inter-dialectal (e.g., standard versus nonstandard; middle class versus lower class; Middle Atlantic versus Appalachian) and intra-dialectal (e.g., spoken versus written; formal versus informal; consultative style versus intimate style) differences and similarities. And it is for this reason that the researcher and teacher of written composition must be aware of the scope, influence, and uses of the various dialects (more accurately, *varieties*) of the language. Questions about dialect status, code switching, mutual intelligibility, and social attitudes may be answered only if the researcher, teacher, and composer can differentiate varieties by their situational and contextual categories. Decisions about availability and extensiveness of usage options can be made only if the researcher, teacher, and composer differentiate varieties and institute adequate controls to avoid cross-cultural interference. Projections about changing social and linguistic conventions and constraints can be provided only if the history and values of the users and uses of the many varieties are understood. Thomas Kochman demonstrates this in "Cross-cultural Communication: Contrasting Perspectives, Conflicting Sensibilities," *Florida FL Reporter*, 9 (Fall/Spring, 1971), 3-16, 53-54. "Cross-cultural interference occurs when communicants who operate from different codes interpret the same behavior according to respectively different, and often conflicting, code perspectives." As he discusses some types of interference and communication failure which result specifically from Black and white Americans' cultural differences, Kochman shows that these problems result from lack of understanding of the ramifications of dialect as a manifestation of both linguistic and social habits and expectations. Cultural codes determine the value to be given to linguistic habit patterns in situational context.

The study of dialects, of their users and uses, and of their importance in written composition may be considered most appropriately at the present time from the perspective of sociolinguistic studies. This new field attempts to focus attention on the study of language as a part of culture and society; it embraces contributions from linguistics, dialectology, ethnography, sociology, psychology, anthropology, communications theory, componential analysis, ethnoscience, ethnomethodology, paralinguistics, kinesics, folklore, and stylistics. As this body of literature has grown within the past three decades, it has taken the study of dialects far beyond the development and publication of linguistic atlases and has expanded the study of usage beyond the listing of rules and etiquette options.

The scope and influence of these studies are summarized by Pride and Labov. J. B. Pride's "Sociolinguistics," in *New Horizons in Linguistics*, edited by John Lyons (Baltimore: Penguin Books, 1970), surveys the field through a review of some of the major contributors and their contributions. Pride concludes that sociolinguistics (a) encourages "reciprocal validation" through interdisciplinary work; (b) recognizes the "interpenetration of language . . . with almost all walks of life and varieties of experience"; (c) seeks "criteria for the demarcation of boundaries (or recognition of irrelevance of boundaries) among languages, dialects, and styles"; (d) produces studies of code-switching between languages and between dialects; (e) establishes methodologies for observation of private and public verbal behavior; and (f) characterizes cultural values which determine verbal transactions. William Labov's "The Place of Linguistic Research in American Society," in *Linguistics in the 1970's* (Washington, D.C.: Center for Applied Linguistics, 1970), outlines the major results and new theoretical questions which sociolinguistic study has encouraged. He explains that "within the past fifteen years, there has been a noticeable movement away from the extreme asocial position in theoretical work towards a view of linguistic structure and evolution which includes the evidence of every-day speech outside of the university community." He sees five major research areas which warrant development: (a) field studies of linguistic diversity in urban communities, (b) investigations of the social implications of dialectology, (c) identification of co-existent systems and bilingualism, (d) attitudinal studies of the social evaluation of language, and (e) reconsideration of the relation of language and thought.

By focusing on the structures and uses of language as they relate to social and cultural functions, this theoretical, pedagogical, and research literature has begun to provide the researcher and teacher of composition with a new framework for viewing spoken and written discourse, with new techniques for eliciting discourse, and with new information about those options available to the speaker and writer. As a result of the development and refinement of data-gathering methodologies, this literature has demonstrated the need to (1) assume sociolinguistic orientations and consider the social attitudes and realities which determine whether and how varieties are manifested as speech events or as written acts, (2) develop varieties differentiation and view dialects as functional varieties of language, and (3) emphasize communicative competence and identify the cultural values, situational constraints, and usage options which affect the relationship of speaker and audience.

Toward Sociolinguistic Orientations

That there is a need to understand and respond to the influence of dialects in written composition has been pointed out by those involved in the teaching of composition. Wallace Douglas's "On the Crisis in Composition," *ADE Bulletin*, No. 40 (March, 1974), 3-11, surveys generally some past and present attitudes and approaches to the teaching of composition. At the same time, Douglas points out that the present school-composition rationale encourages teaching techniques and textbooks which assume that students' speech is similar to, or the result of, familiarity with written texts. He advocates a move toward the use of contrastive analysis and the development of the ability to see a dialect system or dialect interference at work. Turning to the needs of minority students, he states that "our first task is to teach ourselves the need and possibility of learning how to read the writing codes developed by minority students."

R. W. Bailey's "Write Off versus Write On: Dialects and the Teaching of Composition," in *Varieties of Present-Day English*, edited by Richard W. Bailey and Jay L. Robinson (New York: Macmillan, 1973), suggests how the teacher of composition can establish a set of priorities which will build toward concentration on writing. The teacher must help the student draw distinctions between written and spoken varieties of language, extend his linguistic resources, and recognize that he is involved in translation from speech act conventions to writing act conventions. "The primary task that the composition teacher should set for himself is the development of skills in controlling the large patterns that unify discourses. Such study must acknowledge the important differences between the organization appropriate to a piece of writing and that natural in speech, and it must come to terms with the role of the teacher as both participant and spectator."

Dennis E. Baron's "Non-Standard English, Composition, and the Academic Establishment," *CE*, 37 (October, 1975), 176-183, first concentrates on reviewing major distinctions between spoken and written language and the constraints which are basic to each. Baron then considers the problems of translating a nonstandard spoken dialect into writing. Finally, he argues that "The function of the composition teacher, then, should be to focus the student's attention on the intelligibility requirements of the written code, rather than to attack the student's use of language. The arbitrary standards of correctness must be ignored, the relative means of effectiveness must be stressed, the student must develop a self-confident attitude toward his language." Language etiquette is not the teaching goal.

Michael D. Linn, in "Black Rhetorical Patterns and the Teaching of Composition," *CCC*, 26 (May, 1975), 149-153, focuses on the ways Black English Vernacular and the oral culture in which it is used interact to create and reflect verbal contests (such as *shucking, rapping*, and *stylin' out*) which are constrained by their respective rhetorical devices. He suggests that an understanding of idiom and oral situational formats will enable the composition teacher to develop a program of "high context" and "low context" writing situations. In such a setting the student can learn to translate the "styles" (see Joos) appropriate to various oral contexts into those appropriate to written situational formats.

Walt Wolfram and Marcia Whiteman, in "The Role of Dialect Interference in Composition," *Florida FL Reporter*, 9 (Spring/Fall, 1971), 34-38, 59, discuss interference problems which arise in written composition because of dialectal differences in grammatical and pronunciation features. The features are inventoried, and manifestations of hypercorrection are illustrated through Black English writing samples. The authors stress that writing Standard English is a productive skill which must be taught as a separate communicative skill and that the deliberative style of writing is quite different from spoken style.

Carol E. Reed's "Adapting TESL Approaches to the Teaching of Written Standard English as a Second Dialect to Speakers of American Black English Vernacular," *TESOL Quarterly*, 7 (September, 1973), 289-307, describes a bidialectal teaching program intended to develop functional productive competence in Standard English. Through extensive contrastive analysis (adapted from second-language teaching procedures) and dialogue exercises, speakers of Black English Vernacular are encouraged to identify vernacular features and cross-dialectal interferences in their

281

writing. Directions for the teaching of such a curriculum unit are provided. The intention is to verify understanding of the second dialect through appeals to the students' own cultural tradition and acknowledgment of the legitimacy of the BEV system.

Mary Newton Bruder and Luddy Hayden, in "Teaching Composition: A Report on a Bidialectal Approach" (Paper presented at the Sixth Annual TESOL Convention, Washington, D.C., 28 February 1972), describe a bidialectal approach designed to teach formal composition style to students whose repertoires lack a formal standard speaking style. The objectives of the approach are to teach how Black dialect and Standard English differ, how to recognize situational appropriateness, how to distinguish register features (especially the formal written register), how to recognize the functional interrelationship between registers and dialects and the speech community, how to write compositions in the standard dialect using standard rhetorical techniques, and how to carry out research in acceptable academic form.

Marilyn S. Sternglass, in "Close Similarities in Dialect Features of Black and White College Students in Remedial Composition Classes," *TESOL Quarterly*, 8 (September, 1974), 271-283, and in "Dialect Features in the Compositions of Black and White College Students: The Same or Different?" *CCC*, 25 (October, 1974), 259-263, reports the results of a study of the writing of students in remedial classes. Papers were analyzed for the presence of seventeen nonstandard grammatical features. All but one of the nonstandard features appeared in the papers of both Black and white students, though it was found that Black students employed all the nonstandard features more often. This study indicates that separate language materials are not needed for white and Black students in college level remedial writing classes.

Samuel A. Kirschner and G. Howard Poteet, in "Non-Standard English Usage in the Writing of Black, White, and Hispanic Remedial English Students in an Urban Community College," *RTE*, 7 (Winter, 1973), 351-355, also report the results of a study of the writing of students in remedial classes. Papers were analyzed for the presence of thirteen nonstandard grammatical and mechanics features. The authors' conclusion is that "up to now, instructors of remedial English composition have believed that there were significant differences between the writing of blacks, Hispanics, and whites, even though their socio-economic backgrounds were similar. This study suggests that in the main there are no significant differences in the type and frequencies of non-standard English usage between black, white, and Hispanic students."

The views, positions, and research results presented in the sources mentioned above are representative of the major concerns expressed most recently by teachers of composition. All demonstrate that greater understanding of varieties differentiation is crucial to the teacher of composition in a pluralistic society.

Varieties Differentiation

The researcher and teacher seeking an outline of the interconnections between dialects and composition can find a focus for study in Michael Gregory's "Aspects of Varieties Differentiation," *JL*, 3 (October, 1967), 177-198. This article summarizes the research which has led to our understanding of variety differentiation thus far. Gregory carefully delineates situational and contextual categories for *dialectal varieties*, which are "the linguistic reflection of reasonably permanent characteristics of the USER in language situations" and for *diatypic varieties*, which are "the linguistic reflection of recurrent characteristics of user's USE of language in situations." He demonstrates, for example, that *users* are characteristically governed by temporal, geographical, and social provenance and dialect while *use* is characteristically governed by role, relationship, and discourse requirements. He encourages more careful distinctions between spoken and written MODES. As he develops his

283

argument, he clarifies some of the "current terminological confusion in this area of study."

Dialectal varieties: Dialect definition, identification, and differentiation fit into a larger pattern of varieties differentiation. But the number of definitions place the term *dialect* within a series of shifting perspectives. From one perspective, it is treated as a non-judgmental linguist's term. Jean Malmstrom's "Dialects — Updated," *Florida FL Reporter*, 7 (Spring/Summer, 1969), 47-49, 168, considers the general nature of dialect, outlining and discussing its components and variables and its socio-economic and geographic determinants. Raven I. McDavid, Jr.'s "The Dialects of American English," in W. Nelson Francis' *The Structure of American English* (New York: Ronald Press, 1958), surveys the specific nature of American English dialects. He discusses dialect differences and causes, dialect geography, linguistic atlases, forces underlying dialect distribution, principal dialect areas (sample maps provided), foreign-language influences, class dialects, and literary dialect. Carroll E. Reed, in *Dialects of American English* (Amherst: U. of Massachusetts Press, 1967), provides an introduction to dialect study which concentrates on the geographical movements of American English across the country and points to the future of American dialect studies. Roger Shuy's *Discovering American Dialects* (Champaign, Ill.: NCTE, 1967) presents a simplified introduction to dialects as regional, social, and literary varieties. He considers how and why they differ and introduces the problem of foreign language influence.

Considering the term from the perspective of its misuse, Raven I. McDavid, Jr., in "A Theory of Dialect," *Linguistics and the Teaching of Standard English to Speakers of Other Languages or Dialects*, edited by James E. Alatis (Monograph Series on Languages and Linguistics, No. 22; Washington, D.C.: Georgetown U. Press, 1969), reviews the uses of the term "dialect" while pointing to misuses of the designation, redefining the functions and limitations of the dimensions of language varieties, and considering various standards. Joshua A. Fishman, in *Sociolinguistics* (Rowley, Mass.: Newbury House, 1970), also suggests that the term "variety," a non-judgmental designation, allows more objective consideration of dialect function. He distinguishes among dialect, variety, and language and considers all three within a sociolinguistic definition which considers attitude and behavior toward linguistic change, constraints, and repertoire range.

The problem of understanding and using the term when the definers attempt to distinguish standard and nonstandard dialects increases. In "Variations in Standard American English," *EE*, 45 (May, 1968), 561-64, 608, Raven I. McDavid, Jr., narrows his discussion to our "standard" variety, considering those historical and current variations in phonology, vocabulary, and syntax which reflect regional differences yet represent Standard American English. Albert H. Marckwardt's "The Concept of Standard English," in *The Discovery of English* (Urbana, Ill.: NCTE, 1971), considers the historical basis for the development of a standard dialect and the reasons for determining and defining one. Randolph Quirk, in *The Use of English* (New York: St. Martin's Press, 1968), points out that a standard variety may be viewed as "basically an ideal, a mode of expression that we seek when we wish to communicate beyond our immediate community with members of the wider community of the nation as a whole, or with members of the still wider community, English-speakers as a whole." But he cautions that members of different speech communities may produce different realizations. In contrast, William Labov, in "The Logic of Nonstandard English," *Linguistics and the Teaching of Standard English to Speakers of Other Languages or Dialects*, edited by James E. Alatis (Monograph Series on Languages and Linguistics, No. 22; Washington, D.C.: Georgetown U. Press, 1969), carefully illustrates the habit-pattern organization of nonstandard English and argues that nonstandard English is neither an illogical variety of speech nor a manifestation of verbal deprivation.

The difficulties of defining from the perspective of the standard versus the nonstandard are the central concern of *Contemporary English*, edited by David L. Shores (Philadelphia: Lippincott, 1972). In this reader, aimed at prospective and in-service teachers, the problems of establishing "accurate concepts and realistic attitudes toward standard and nonstandard varieties of English" are considered through the statements of twenty-one contributors. Temporal, regional, and social variations in standard and nonstandard English (Shuy, Bloomfield, Malmstrom, McDavid, Fasold and Wolfram, Stewart, and Davis), partial definitions of Standard English (Gove, Pyles, Kenyon, Kilburn, Joos, and DeCamp), and problems of learning and teaching standard and nonstandard English (Feigenbaum, Bloomfield, Hill, Allen, Shuy, Dillard, Goodman, Troike, and Sledd) are the major concerns of the collection.

Two introductory readers serve to establish the definitional perspective of the dialectologists. *Readings in American Dialectology*, edited by Harold B. Allen and Gary N. Underwood (New York: Appleton-Century-Crofts, 1971) presents forty-one articles about regional and social dialects. Regional dialects are defined through methodology and attitudinal overview (Atwood, McDavid), area studies (Thomas, Duckert, Marckwardt, Allen, Reed, Wood, and Norman), single feature studies (Hempl, Atwood, Ives, McDavid, Avis, Bloch, and Pace), comparative approaches (Orton, Francis, Kurath, Reed), and dialect theory (Bottiglioni, Weinreich, Stockwell, Troike, and Hill). Social dialects are defined in articles on interrelationships, structural differences, sociolinguistic factors, and social features (McDavid, Kurath, Sawyer, Pederson, Bailey, Loflin, Stewart, Labov, and Maurer and Vogel). *A Various Language*, edited by Juanita V. Williamson and Virginia M. Burke (New York: Holt, Rinehart and Winston, 1971) surveys the history and scope of dialect studies. Fifty contributors discuss origins and varieties (Scott, Kurath, Krapp, Kenyon, Currie, and McDavid), inherited features (Pyles, Hill,

Kurath, Francis, Turner, and Brooks), literary representations (Ives, Bowdrie, Harrison, Stockton, Rulon, and Blackburn), regional and social aspects (Kurath, Atwood, Morgan, Howren, Thomas, LaBan, Norman, Klipple, Davis, McDavid and McDavid, Allen, and Reed), sounds and forms (Avis, Wetmore, Kurath, Atwood, Williamson, Levine and Crockett, Sledd, and McMillan), and urban dialect studies (McDavid, Pederson, DeCamp, Sawyer, Williamson, Parslow, Bronstein, and Labov).

The work of William Labov places *dialect* within a clearly sociolinguistic perspective which reflects consistent treatment of the socio-economic and linguistic variables which affect social interaction. Intent on the development of methodology, field study, and accurate reportage, Labov focuses primarily on social dialects in the New York City area. *The Social Stratification of English in New York City* (Washington, D.C.: Center for Applied Linguistics, 1966) is an in-depth analysis of one multi-level speech community. Social context, social stratification, and contextual styles were surveyed through interviews; class and linguistic variables were differentiated; personal and public attitudes toward New York City speech were evaluated. The New York City vowel system was identified. The continuous social and stylistic variation of language influenced by socio-economic stratification and the transmission of prestige patterns is outlined. The nature of social control of language variety is considered; identification of linguistically discrete social dialect boundaries in New York City is shown to be impossible because of the influence of social variables.

Sociolinguistic Patterns (Conduct and Communication, No. 4; Philadelphia: U. of Pennsylvania Press, 1972) presents a nine-essay collection of Labov's research into social change and motivation in language and discusses contextual style and the subjective dimensions of change. His thesis is that "the basis of intersubjective knowledge in linguistics must be found in speech—language as it is used in everyday life by members of the social order." His chapter sequencing of now-classic articles reveals his key terms and demonstrates his concern for movement from particularity to synthesis: "The Social Motivation of a Sound Change," "The Social Stratification of (r) in New York City Department Stores," "The Isolation of Contextual Styles," "The Reflection of Social Processes in Linguistic Structures," "Hypercorrection by the Lower Middle Class as a Factor in Linguistic Change," "Subjective Dimensions of a Linguistic Change in Progress," "On the Mechanism of Linguistic Change," "The Study of Language in Its Social Context," and "The Social Setting of Linguistic Change."

Language in the Inner City: Studies in the Black English Vernacular (Conduct and Communication, No. 3; Philadelphia: U. of Pennsylvania Press, 1972) is a collection of nine essays in which Labov presents a reorganization and rewriting of several earlier statements into a sequenced study of the *structure* ("Some Sources of Reading Problems for Speakers of the Black English Vernacular," "Is the Black English Vernacular a Separate System?" "Contraction, Deletion, and Inherent Variability of the English Copula," and "Negative Attraction and Negative Concord"), *social setting* ("The Logic of Nonstandard English," "The Relation of Reading Failure to Peer-Group Status," "The Linguistic Consequences of Being a Lame"), and *uses of the Black English Vernacular* ("Rules for Ritual Insults" and "The Transformation of Experience in Narrative Syntax").

Still another in Labov's series of statements on dialects as conceptual systems is *The Study of Nonstandard English* (Champaign, Ill.: NCTE, 1970). This statement for teachers surveys the theoretical and educational issues surrounding the controversy about nonstandard English. Nonstandard English is considered within the context of the nature of language, sociolinguistic principles, educational implications, and needed in-school research. Reasons are given for studying nonstandard language; nonstandard dialects are viewed as self-contained systems; the relationship between standard and nonstandard English is described. Social stratification, linguistic rules and norms, sex differences, and acquisition stages are reviewed. The importance of socio-linguistic research to reading, speech, and vocabulary instruction and to classroom speech events is described. Consideration is given to informal and formal approaches to testing for presence of varieties of language in order to determine types of dialect differences and to testing students' perceptual competence, grammatical competence, and speech competence. Another statement for the classroom teacher, "Variation in Language," in *The Learning of Language*, edited by Carroll E. Reed (New York: Appleton-Century-Crofts, 1971), 187-221, presents Labov's organizational perspective through consideration of regional differences in language, urban language differences, language differences in age levels, learning of language differences, and the structure of linguistic variation. Labov discusses those language features which reflect the parameters of social mobility, demonstrate social stratification as it functions, and evidence those sub-cultural determinants which affect change in linguistic habit patterns.

The organized, integrated work of Labov raises the problem of identifying social *codes*, a concern which is taken up by Basil Bernstein. His largely theoretical studies serve to broaden the implications of Labov's field studies. *Class, Codes and Control*, Volume 1: *Theoretical Studies towards a Sociology of Language* (London: Routledge & Kegan Paul, 1971) is a collection of the British social psychologist's articles on the interaction of social class and language behavior. Spanning thirteen years of conceptualizing, these chronologically arranged statements demonstrate the development of Bernstein's theories and empirical studies. It is Bernstein's contention that "elaborated" and "restricted" language codes (i.e., those principles which regulate the selection and organization of speech events) are learned by the members of the middle and lower classes respectively, that each of these codes determines the linguistic and social competence of their speakers, and that speakers of restricted codes are confined to "public" language while speakers of elaborated codes have access to both "public" and "formal" language. The behavioral characteristics which result manifest themselves in the speaker's cognitive processes and in his responses to social and natural events and reflect his concept of reality. The linguistic and social characteristics of the codes are investigated throughout.

In a companion volume, *Class, Codes and Control*, Volume 2: *Applied Studies towards a Sociology of Language* (London: Routledge & Kegan Paul, 1973), Bernstein and others, working within the framework of his theories, investigate aspects of maternal orientations to communication and the speech of five-year-old children and seven-year-old children for contextual specificity, discretion, and cognitive socialization, for perceptual and verbal discriminations of code users, and for the influence of sex, social class, and pause-location in hesitation phenomena. Of special interest in this volume is R. Hasan's "Code, Register and Social Dialect" in which he investigates the three terms in an attempt to further define their meanings, interrelationships, and the correlation of the latter terms with Bernstein's category of *code*.

The defining of *dialect* from the perspective of Black English studies requires still another approach. The study of Black English dialects has been quite extensively developed in response to the needs of Black minority students in public school classrooms and in an effort to define total sociolinguistic contexts. *Language, Communication, and Rhetoric in Black America*, edited by Arthur L. Smith (New York: Harper & Row, 1972) is a collection of twenty-nine essays by communications specialists and educators who discuss the communication process in its totality, i.e., dialect, styles, tone, situational context, and rhetorical intention. Consideration is given to Black language (Baratz, Green, Erickson, Wolfram), ethnicity (Holt, Davis, Kochman, Mitchell), rhetorical case studies (Smith, Dick, Harris, and Kennicott, Campbell, Illo, Brockreide ånd Scott, and Bosmajian), criticism and social change (Smith, Epps, and Gregg, McCormack and Pedersen), and social-historical dimensions (Smith, Hannerz, Jones, Larson, Brooks, Richardson, and Garret). F. Erickson's comparison of white and Black college students in rap sessions is especially valuable.

Geneva Smitherman's "God Don't Never Change: Black English from a Black Perspective," *CE*, 34 (March, 1973), 828-834, argues for the uniqueness of Black expression as it lies in the situational context from which the style of the Black Idiom develops. The argument is placed in historical context. Thomas Kochman, in "Culture and Communication: Implications for Black English in the Classroom," *Florida FL Reporter*, 7 (Spring/Summer, 1969), 89-92, 172-174, makes cross-cultural comparisons between Black culture and white middle-class culture. In the process, he considers communication channels, prestige forms, mechanisms and networks, audience dynamics, speech styles, and the goals and assumptions for language programs. He states that increasing language skill in Black children is not dependent on teaching them the ability to perform in standard dialect. *Black-White Speech Relationships*, edited by Walt Wolfram and Nona H. Clarke (Washington, D.C.: Center for Applied Linguistics, 1971), presents eight viewpoints on the possible social and historical influences in the development of Black-white varieties of English. Considered are Gullah (Turner), Black-white speech relationships (McDavid and McDavid), Negro English dialectology (Bailey), historical continuity-change factors (Stewart), dialect research (Davis), Afro-American communication (Dalby), and Black-white speech differences (Wolfram).

Joan C. Baratz, in "Should Black Children Learn White Dialect?" *ASHA*, 12 (September, 1970), 415-417, argues that "standard English" is not "white dialect" but the LINGUA FRANCA of the "American mainstream" culture to which the Black student has a right. Standard English is defined as "that dialect which uses a set of grammatical patterns in oral production that are similar to those used in the written form of the language." She acknowledges the "mutual intelligibility" argument used to oppose teaching Standard English, defends the bidialectal teaching approach, and explains the interference problems which arise from imperfect understanding of the oral and written systems. *Teaching Standard English in the Inner City*, edited by Ralph W. Fasold and Roger W. Shuy (Washington, D.C.: Center for Applied Linguistics, 1970) assumes the biloquialist perspective and considers adaptation of foreign language teaching methods (Stewart), educational considerations (Baratz), linguistic features of Black dialect (Fasold and Wolfram), the use of nonstandard in teaching standard (Feigenbaum), educational sequencing (Wolfram), and teacher training for urban language problems (Shuy).

J. L. Dillard's *Black English: Its History and Usage in the United States* (New York: Random House, 1972) considers the ramifications of Black English, its historical development, and its cultural validity. Dillard discusses the implications of such information for teacher training and classroom practices. Chapter VII stresses the harm done Black students by failing them on the basis of dialect. Joan G. Fickett's "Tense and Aspect in Black English," *JEL*, 6 (March, 1972), 17-20, extends the concern for cultural validity into the identification of tense and aspect of the Black English verb system, showing how tense and aspect reflect cultural attitudes and values. Through representative illustrations, she demonstrates that "Black English has five aspects, four relative past tenses, two relative future tenses and a true present tense. It has combinations of tense and aspect, but only one tense may appear in a predicator. As many as three aspects are possible in the same phrase. It is clear that the system is present oriented." This work is expanded and fully documented in Fickett's *Aspects of Morphemics, Syntax and Semology of an Inner-City Dialect* (West Rush, N.Y.: Meadowood Publications, 1970). Still another approach to the Black English dialect system is described by Walter A. Wolfram in *A Sociolinguistic Description of Detroit Negro*

Speech (Washington, D.C.: Center for Applied Linguistics, 1969). This urban language field study reports on the interaction of social setting and linguistic (phonological and grammatical) variables which produce "nonstandard Negro English" specific to Detroit.

As can be seen, all attempts to define dialect for practical purposes are clouded by attitudes toward the nature of dialects, the users and uses of dialects, and the standard versus nonstandard argument. Concern for this has led to attitude studies which concentrate specifically on types of subjective reactions to language. In *Language Attitudes: Current Trends and Prospects*, edited by Roger W. Shuy and Ralph W. Fasold (Washington, D.C.: Georgetown U. Press, 1973), twelve research statements concerned with subjective reactions to language are presented. Attitudes, beliefs, and values held toward language varieties are investigated in studies dealing with such problems as dialect attitudes and stereotypes, teacher attitudes toward dialects, linguistic correlates of rater's subjective judgments, sociolinguistic correlates of speech style, subjective reactions toward accented speech, anatomical and cultural determinants of male and female speech, stereotyped attitudes and dialect communities, reactions to various American-English dialects, objective and subjective parameters of language assimilation, bilingual attitudes and learning, and a conceptual framework for dealing with language, speech and ideology. This collection serves the double purpose of (a) identifying the major directions being taken in attitude research and (b) displaying methodologies which are being developed and employed.

Single studies of special interest consider attitudes affecting education, business, and the community. Walt Wolfram's "Sociolinguistic Premises and the Nature of Nonstandard Dialects," *ST*, 19 (September, 1970), 177-184, presents sociolinguistic considerations which affect teacher evaluation of speech behavior and teacher attitudes toward nonstandard speech behavior. Verbal options as arbitrary and/or established by custom, adequacy of a dialect as a communicative system, and language as learned in a community context are discussed. Nancy Hewett's "Reactions of Prospective English Teachers Toward Speakers of a Non-Standard Dialect," *LL*, 21 (December, 1971), 205-212, tests "the hypothesis that prospective English teachers have unfavorable stereotypes of speakers of non-standard dialects." Standard and nonstandard pronunciation styles (taped) of Black and white speakers were judged for personality characteristics, race, and probable occupation of the speakers. Prospective teachers participating in this matched-guise experiment exhibited common, culturally-determined responses which produced the expected stereotyping. Raven I. McDavid, Jr., in "Dialect Differences and Social Differences in an Urban Society," *Sociolinguistics*, edited by William Bright (The Hague: Mouton, 1971), discusses the class markers by which speakers are tagged by their listeners and the resulting prestige or lack of it which is attributed to the speakers and their linguistic utterances. Charles Billiard, Arnold Lazarus, and Raven I. McDavid, Jr., in *Identification of Dialect Features Which Affect Both Social and Economic Opportunity Among the Urban Disadvantaged*, Final Report (Washington, D.C.: Office of Education, 1969), report the results of a study undertaken to determine (a) dialect features associated with three ethnic groups (Anglo, Black, Latin American) and four social classes which were unacceptable to a dominant, urban culture (Fort Wayne, Indiana), (b) social markers which might handicap such speakers socio-economically and culturally, and (c) the implications of this for teacher preparation and classroom teaching. The results offer specific illustrations of code markers which may affect socio-economic mobility. The authors suggest that "greater emphasis should be given to [the] nature of usage and study of social dialects, problems of motivating students to learn a second dialect, and the techniques of developing two dialectal skills."

Studies such as the above-listed encouraged the publication of "Students' Right to Their Own Language," *CCC*, 25 (Fall, 1974), which attempts to help teachers of composition and communication review present attitudinal problems and linguistic knowledge so that they may more effectively respond to the variety of dialects which they face in the English classroom. The focus of the text and the extended bibliography is on the development of rational teaching positions based on present knowledge of language and its cultural effects.

Diatypic varieties: In varieties differentiation, studies of "levels," "styles," "keys," and "register" are viewed as intra-dialectal studies and are of special importance to the teacher of composition who must teach how variations and options within a dialect are used to create social distance. Albert H. Marckwardt's chapter on "Usage: Varieties, Levels, and Styles," in *Linguistics and the Teaching of English* (Bloomington: Indiana U. Press, 1966), summarizes historically the many attempts to define and label hierarchies of usage, the confusion of terms which has resulted, and the shift in focus which each definer has encouraged. His summary, which ends with considerations of Kenyon, Joos, and *Webster's Third*, attempts to demonstrate the pedagogical problems which face the teacher who must deal with dialect variations and options. John Kenyon's "Cultural Levels and Functional Varieties of English," *CE*, 10 (October, 1948) was an early and incomplete attempt to draw a distinction between *cultural levels* and *functional varieties* — to establish the independence of style and class stratification of language. Unfortunately the article does not recognize that the same linguistic variables may mark social distance and stylistic functions. The statement serves, however, to demonstrate the problems involved in delineating dialectal and diatypic varieties.

In his now-classic *The Five Clocks* (New York: Harcourt, Brace & World, 1961), Martin Joos defines levels of functional style which he labels *frozen, formal, consultative, casual*, and *intimate*. He is careful to point out that in the case of the last four styles he is dealing with transcripts of speech. Through this set of five usage scales, which Joos matches against age, breadth, and responsibility scales, he attempts to direct concern toward the sets of linguistic features and constraints by which speakers establish degrees of intimacy in varieties of dyadic relationships. He also encourages a tolerant view of varying linguistic patterns by illustrating the complexities of usage. H. A. Gleason, Jr., adapts Joos' functional styles identification in his chapter on "Language Variation," in *Linguistics and English Grammar* (New York: Holt, Rinehart and Winston, 1965). He identifies speech "keys" (*consultative, casual, deliberative, oratorical*, and *intimate*) to which the speaker appeals for signals by which to control the amount and length of required interaction and the structure of utterances. He also presents hearer adjustment features (status, assumed knowledge, polish of language, socially approved grammatical norms) which affect the keys. He distinguishes dialects as systems of keys. He also identifies written keys which he labels "literary": *formal*, corresponding to deliberative; *semiformal*, corresponding to consultative; *informal*, corresponding to casual. He then considers how they approximate equivalent speech keys. M.A. K. Halliday, Angus McIntosh, and Peter Strevens' *The Linguistic Sciences and Language Teaching* (Bloomington: Indiana U. Press, 1964) approaches the problem of social distance and use through the term *register*. In the chapter "The Users and Uses of Language," *register* is defined as a category "needed when we want to account for what people do with their language. When we observe language activity in the various contexts in which it takes place, we find differences in the type of language selected as appropriate to different types of situation."

Out of this orientation have come style studies such as David Crystal and Derek Davy's *Investigating English Style* (Bloomington: Indiana U. Press, 1969). This text, geared to the university student, identifies features of language which characterize several major spoken and written varieties of the present-day English of every-day life. The authors' stylistic analyses isolate linguistic features of one variety from another. The concern is to identify linguistic features restricted to specific social contexts. To help the reader of this text identify spoken and written varieties by functional orientation, the authors encourage comparative linguistic analysis of language samples (i.e., of conversation, unscripted commentary, religion, newspaper reporting, legal documents) within the dimensions of situational context.

Cautionary studies have also resulted. Robbins Burling's "Standard Colloquial and Standard Written English: Some Implications for Teaching Literacy to Nonstandard Speakers," *Florida FL Reporter*, 8 (Spring/Fall, 1970), 9-15, 47, investigates differences between written and spoken varieties of English and considers some of the ways in which they interact. He balances this information against the cautionary advice that teacher attitudes toward, and knowledge of, nonstandard habit patterns is the important factor in teaching literacy. Problems in teaching language usage are clarified. Burling points out lexical, phonological, and grammatical variables (both constraints and options), considers what happens when standard, nonstandard, and literary styles are mixed, and advocates teaching for understanding of lexical variability, contraction and deletion, homonymity, the colloquial passive, and shifting negation. The teacher must know other dialects, but teaching Standard English as a second dialect will only exacerbate the problem. His is a plea for teaching varieties differentiation dialectally and diatypically.

Attempts to identify social distance "levels," "styles," "keys," and "registers" have refocused attitudes toward usage theories and studies. Also, the growing controversy about standard and nonstandard varieties has encouraged new approaches to the gathering of usage data. An important article which directs attention to the ever-shifting attitudes toward English usage is Charles V. Hartung's "Doctrines of

English Usage," *EJ*, 45 (December, 1956), 517-525. Hartung defines the four "propriety of language usage" doctrines (rules, general usage, appropriateness, and linguistic norm) which have informed statements on English usage. According to Hartung, the "rules" doctrine depends on an "assumed correspondence of the rules of grammar with basic principles of reason" and the "supposed correspondence of the rules with the usage of the best writers." The "general usage" doctrine takes its authority from those "language habits which have attained the most social acceptability." The "appropriateness" doctrine depends on "the satisfactory communication of thought and feeling" in social situations. It assumes knowledge of the community's language habits. The "linguistic norm" doctrine takes its authority from the need to "hold in balance intention of the speaker, the nature of the language itself, the probable effect on the audience." He concludes that the linguistic norm doctrine with its concern for "maximum expression" would seem suitable for the classroom. His statement establishes a perspective for viewing subsequent statements about usage.

Standard sources of usage information are the usage handbooks. *Current American Usage*, edited by Margaret M. Bryant (New York: Funk & Wagnalls, 1962) offers a carefully researched, alphabetical usage handbook which bases decisions about acceptability on data collected from such varied sources as linguistic atlases, specialist journals, newspapers, popular magazines, radio broadcasts, formal grammars, and dictionaries. The aim is always to distinguish what has been identified with "Standard English" and what deviates from it. Distinctions are often rendered with "variety" labels of *informal, colloquial,* or *formal.* Items which represent divided usage are marked. A handbook for teachers is provided by Robert C. Pooley in *The Teaching of English Usage* (Urbana, Ill.: NCTE, 1974). This directive statement discusses English usage through consideration of the "problem of correctness," historical backgrounds, standard and nonstandard varieties of English usage, and "the nature of communication." Sources of specific information about usage and problems related to inflections and word order and to propriety are considered. The teaching of standard usage at the elementary, junior/middle, and high school levels is considered and suggestions for types of items to be considered at each level are given. Procedures for evaluating what has been taught are offered.

The need to deal with usage *in situation*, however, has become crucial as varieties differentiation has expanded. Mary Vaiana Taylor's "The Folklore of Usage," *CE*, 35 (April, 1974), 756-768, describes an attempt to make teacher-training students "conscious of the multiplicity of factors involved in judgments about usage." Students conducted a "field" study using a usage survey questionnaire in an effort to determine usage acceptability and the ways in which informants determined ultimate sources of authority. An awareness of the sociolinguistic forces which affect usage variations and options resulted. James L. Funkhouser's "A Various Standard," *CE*, 34 (March, 1973), 806-827, presents a discussion of how nonsituational handbook rules were superseded in the actual classroom by the writing of situational rules for effective communication of the ideas being developed by the students involved. Rule consistency is illustrated through Black English writing samples.

As a result of new attitudes toward authority and acceptability, knowledge of data-gathering methodologies is needed. Randolph Quirk and Jan Svartvik, in *Investigating Linguistic Acceptability* (The Hague: Mouton, 1966), investigate "acceptability" and "grammaticality" and concentrate on "establishing degrees and kinds of acceptability in English sentences." Reasons are given for using "operation" and "selection" tests with informants. Problems of lexical and grammatical deviance and divided usage are discussed, and conclusions are presented. Sidney Greenbaum and Randolph Quirk, in *Elicitation Experiment in English* (Coral Gables, Fla.: U. of Miami Press, 1970), explore the methodological problems involved in designing adequate elicitation procedures for determining use (performance) and attitude (judgment) responses to types of sentence tasks. "Acceptability" of utterance with regard to the grammatical and semantic constraints an informant feels bound to is investigated. Kinds of tests and procedures are described. The implications of this work for the gathering of usage data and facts are great. Rodney D. Huddleston's *The Sentence in Written English* (Cambridge: Cambridge U. Press, 1971) is "a syntactic study based on an analysis of scientific texts." Comparison study with other written varieties is not attempted. Instead it is an intra-variety study which uses data samples from specialist journals, undergraduate textbooks, and popular works in the sciences. His intention is to investigate areas of the grammar of "common-core" English through his samples and to present a description of his findings, thereby producing a grammar on which to base further study.

Communicative Competence

The absorption of *dialect* into concern for *varieties differentiation* requires the composition teacher to understand the nature and demands of communicative competence. COMMUNICATIVE COMPETENCE is a concept arising from ethnographic studies which seek to determine the social significance of competence *and* performance in speech events (and by extension in writing events). Dell Hymes in the Preface to *Direction in Sociolinguistics* (see later discussion) has defined communicative competence as:

> what a speaker needs to know to communicate effectively in culturally significant settings. Like Chomsky's term on which it is patterned, communicative competence refers to the ability to perform. An attempt is made to distinguish between what the speaker knows — what his inherent capacities are — and how he behaves in particular instances. However, whereas students of linguistic competence seek to explain those aspects of grammar believed to be common to all hu-

mans independent of social determinants, students of communicative competence deal with speakers as members of communities, as incumbents of social roles, and seek to explain their use of language to achieve self-identification and to conduct their activities. While for linguistic theory in the former sense the ability to formalize sentences as grammatically acceptable is the central notion, for sociolinguistics as represented in the book, the central notion is the appropriateness of verbal messages in context of their acceptability in the broader sense.

Several master collections of theoretical and research articles are available to acquaint the teacher of composition with this view of users and uses and to provide immediate access to the breadth and depth of sociolinguistic concerns. *Readings in the Sociology of Language*, edited by Joshua F. Fishman (The Hague: Mouton, 1968) provides an introduction to the general categories through the collected articles of forty-five contributors who present perspectives on the sociology of language (Sebeok, Lounsbury, Ervin and Miller, Hymes, and Halliday), on language in small-group interaction (Lennard and Bernstein, Marshall, Joos, Ervin-Tripp, Bock), on language in social strata and sectors (Bernstein, Labov, Brown and Gilman, Nader, Geertz, Zengel, Weinreich), on language through socio-cultural organization (Epstein, Leopold, Garvin and Mathiot, Ferguson, Weinreich, Conklin, Frake, Basilius, and Gumperz), on language within the scope of multilingualism (Lambert, Gardner, Olton and Tunstall, Herman, Rubin, Stewart, Lieberson, and Mackey), on language maintenance and shift (Jakobson, Deutsch, Taylor, Hofman, Kloss, and Samarin), and on language planning (Haugen, Goodman, Berry, Ray, Guxman). This introductory reader serves to orient the reader to the milieu within which varieties of language may be considered. The following articles are of special value: Dell H. Hymes' "The Ethnography of Speaking" defines speech in cognitive and expressive behavior, seeks a descriptive analysis of speaking, explains "speech event" as composed of seven factors (i.e., sender, receiver, message form, channel, code, topic, and setting), and considers the functions of speech events. Susan M. Ervin-Tripp's "An Analysis of the Interaction of Language, Topic, and Listener" defines setting, participant, and topic and explains their functions in dyadic interactions. Changes of form (formal features) which occur when one or another of these factors dominates are considered. Joshua A. Fishman's "The Sociology of Language" defines the combined field of linguistics and sociology as inquiry into "the co-variation of diversity and of pattern in these two fields." Language is explained as consisting of codes, regional varieties, social class varieties, and stylistic varieties.

In *Directions in Sociolinguistics*, edited by John J. Gumperz and Dell Hymes (New York: Holt, Rinehart and Winston, 1972), an ethnography of communication is presented through nineteen articles which explain (a) the socio-cultural shaping of ways of speaking, (b) procedures for discovering and stating rules of conversation and address, and (c) the origin, persistence, and change of varieties of language. The aim is "to present evidence documenting the existence of a level of rule-governed verbal behavior which goes beyond the linguists' grammar to relate social and linguistic constraints on speech, to illustrate the type of data that must be collected for its analysis and the elicitation methods by which it can be gathered." As in so many of these collections, the contributions reflect work done in many different languages and dialects. Thus, the chapter on ethnographic description and explanation contains a study of the Yakan concept of litigation and a study of Afro-American signifying and marking procedures. The chapter on discovering structure in speech contains a study of sequencing in conversational openings and a study of the social context and semantic features which are illustrated through Russian pronominal usage. The chapter on genesis, maintenance, and change of linguistic codes contains a study of code switching in Norway which demonstrates social meaning in linguistic structures, and a description of the mechanism of linguistic change in the Martha's Vineyard and New York City areas.

Sociolinguistics, edited by William Bright (The Hague: Mouton, 1971) introduces the papers of thirteen participants in the 1964 UCLA Sociolinguistics Conference. The purpose of the collection is to present perspectives on the dimensions of sociolinguistics. Included are statements on folk-linguistics (Hoenigswald), the ethnology of linguistic change (Gumperz), linguistics and language planning (Haugen), urban dialect and social differences (McDavid), the effect of lower middle class hypercorrection on linguistic change (Labov), types of linguistic relativity (Hymes), syntax and social structure (Fischer), self-annulling prestige factors (Samarin), structural implications of pronominal usage (Friedrich), writing systems development for preliterate peoples (Sjoberg), language status (Rona, Kelly), and national sociolinguistic profile formulas (Ferguson).

Explorations in Sociolinguistics, edited by Stanley Lieberson (The Hague: Mouton, 1967) is a collection of thirteen articles which represent various views of the purposes of language and dialect. Through, among others, discussions of the effects of social mobility (Labov), elaborated and restricted codes (Bernstein), social stratification and cognitive orientation (Bright), social status and attitude (Heise), and social uniformation (Hertzler), the collection exposes those components which contribute to prestige or nonprestige forms.

Language in Culture and Society, edited by Dell Hymes (New York: Harper & Row, 1964) arranges the now-classic statements of sixty-nine contributors into a ten-division discussion of (a) the scope of linguistic anthropology; (b) equality, diversity, relativity; (c) world view in grammatical categories; (d) cultural focus and semantic field; (e) role, socialization, and expressive speech; (f) speech play and verbal art; (g) social structure and speech community; (h) processes and problems of change; (i) relationships in time and space; and (j) historical perspectives. Here, too, definitions of the fields of study, comments on methodologies, language and dialect studies, mode-of-address studies, levels of usage studies, standard language and vernacular language studies are presented and illustrated through a variety of languages and dialects.

As indicated, the above-listed collections introduce the reader to broad aspects of communicative competence and at the same time demonstrate cross-cultural investigative procedures. An important collection which narrows its procedures and illustrations to present an intra-cultural approach is *Rappin' and Stylin' Out: Communication in Urban Black America*, edited by Thomas Kochman (Urbana: U. of Illinois Press, 1972). This reader presents a study of communication in the urban Black situation through the views of twenty-seven contributors. The spectrum of Black communication from nonverbal and verbal expression to vocabulary and culture and from expressive uses of language to expressive role behavior is reviewed. Visual and verbal illustrations are abundant. Through his collection Kochman attempts "to identify some of the communicative and behavioral norms of urban black Americans and (wherever possible) their source." He has "deliberately and consistently chosen to examine those contexts where the vernacular culture has been most pervasive and articulated and where mainstream cultural norms are likely to have penetrated *least*." This ethnic portrait presents descriptions of street, church, clubhouse, shoeshine stand, park, pool hall, and cafe behavior. Its contributors employ a variety of methodologies to consider nonverbal communication, vocabulary and culture, expressive language, and expressive roles. The development of more intra-cultural collections of this type can only help teachers of composition in their efforts to understand the factors responsible for communicative competence and thus enable them to employ the concept of varieties differentiation in their work with dialect and composition.

304

THIS BOOK WAS DESIGNED BY
JUDITH M. OELFKE
SET IN TEN-POINT CALEDONIA
BY FORT WORTH LINOTYPING COMPANY
AND PRINTED ON WARREN'S OLDE STYLE WOVE
BY MOTHERAL PRINTING COMPANY